Oracle Parallel Processing

Oracle Parallel Processing

Tushar Mahapatra and Sanjay Mishra

O'REILLY®

Beijing · Cambridge · Farnham · Köln · Paris · Sebastopol · Taipei · Tokyo

Oracle Parallel Processing
by Tushar Mahapatra and Sanjay Mishra

Copyright © 2000 O'Reilly & Associates, Inc. All rights reserved.
Printed in the United States of America.

Published by O'Reilly & Associates, Inc., 101 Morris Street, Sebastopol, CA 95472.

Editors: Jonathan Gennick and Deborah Russell

Production Editor: Jeffrey Holcomb

Cover Designer: Edie Freedman

Printing History:

      August 2000:   First Edition.

Nutshell Handbook, the Nutshell Handbook logo, and the O'Reilly logo are registered trademarks of O'Reilly & Associates, Inc. The association between the image of a wasp and a wasp nest and the topic of Oracle parallel processing is a trademark of O'Reilly & Associates, Inc. Oracle® and all Oracle-based trademarks and logos are trademarks or registered trademarks of Oracle Corporation, Inc. in the United States and other countries. O'Reilly & Associates, Inc. is independent of Oracle Corporation.

Many of the designations used by manufacturers and sellers to distinguish their products are claimed as trademarks. Where those designations appear in this book, and O'Reilly & Associates, Inc. was aware of a trademark claim, the designations have been printed in caps or initial caps. While every precaution has been taken in the preparation of this book, the publisher assumes no responsibility for errors or omissions, or for damages resulting from the use of the information contained herein.

CIP data can be found at *http://www.oreilly.com/catalóg/oraclepp*.

ISBN: 1-56592-701-X
[M]

I dedicate this book to my parents.

—Tushar Mahapatra

I dedicate this book to my mother.

—Sanjay Mishra

Table of Contents

Preface

What is parallel processing? What does it have to do with Oracle? And how can you get the most out of Oracle's parallel processing features? These are the questions this book attempts to answer. Oracle's strong support for parallel processing sets it apart from other database systems on the market today. If you're managing a large database, a database with a large number of concurrent users, or a database with high-availability requirements, you probably are already using at least some of Oracle's parallel features. If not, you certainly need to investigate them.

Oracle's support for parallel processing can be divided into two broad categories:

Oracle's parallel execution features

Oracle's support for multiple CPU systems allows you to leverage the power of two or more CPUs to complete a single task. The parallel execution features (provided as a standard part of the database) provide both speedup and scalability. When you use parallel execution features, individual tasks are completed faster than they would be otherwise, and you can increase throughput capacity simply by adding more CPUs and memory to your system.

Oracle Parallel Server (OPS)

While the parallel execution features allow you to leverage the power of many CPUs in a single system, Oracle Parallel Server (an extra-cost option) allows you to leverage the power of many systems against a single database. You can even combine the two features, taking advantage of the combined processing power of many CPUs in many systems, to handle large numbers of users or to complete large and complex jobs. Not only can you add more CPUs to individual systems in order to support growth, you also can add entire new systems. Oracle Parallel Server provides the highest scalability for data warehousing applications. Oracle Parallel Server also supports high availability. With multiple systems accessing a single database, if one system goes down, users can be switched to another, where they can continue to work.

The bottom line is that if you are an Oracle database administrator managing a database in which throughput, scalability, or high availability is important, you need to know the material in this book so you'll be able to use Oracle's parallel processing features to their best advantage.

Why We Wrote This Book

We specialize in managing Oracle Parallel Server databases, and we've experienced firsthand all the benefits that Oracle's parallel processing features have to offer. We've also experienced a great deal of the pain that sometimes goes with these features. As we looked around the marketplace, we realized that there was no good, single source of information for DBAs who are just getting started with Oracle Parallel Server.

Oracle's parallel server and parallel execution features are powerful and offer many benefits, but they carry with them a number of unique database administration challenges. The database creation process for OPS, for example, is somewhat different from that of a typical, non-OPS database. There are tuning issues that are unique to OPS, as well as some that are unique to environments using parallel execution features. We wrote this book to provide a single source of information that would help DBAs who are already experienced with Oracle make the transition to a parallel-processing environment.

Audience for This Book

This book is not an introduction to Oracle. To get the most out of this book, you already should be familiar with Oracle database administration. You should know how to create a database and how to create schema objects such as tables and views. You also need to have some understanding of SQL in order to fully appreciate Oracle's parallel SQL features.

Tuning and space management are critical issues as well. You don't need to be an expert tuner, but some familiarity with the V$ dynamic performance views will help you get the most out of the tuning chapters in this book. Similarly, it will help if you understand the basic concepts of space management: extents, segments, and tablespaces.

We don't want to scare you off. You don't have to be the DBA who walks on water in order to understand this book. If you have no Oracle experience at all, you still should be able to glean something from this book. To get the most benefit, though, you do need some prior knowledge. If you're comfortable creating a database and if you've managed one for any length of time, then you should enjoy this book.

Which Platform and Version?

This book primarily focuses on the parallel features available in Oracle8 and Oracle8*i*. We've noted specifically which features are available only for Oracle8*i*. In general, we've developed the examples on Unix platforms, but virtually all of the material is applicable to other platforms as well.

Note also that installation steps are platform- and release-specific, so detailed installation information is not included in this book. Consult the Oracle documentation for your own platform and release for this information.

Structure of This Book

In this book, we've tried to collect in one place the essential knowledge you'll need to leverage Oracle's parallel processing features. We've also tried to incorporate as much of our actual experience as possible. You will find chapters that clearly explain Oracle's different parallel processing features, chapters on tuning, and an appendix containing real-life case studies that show you how Oracle's parallel processing features are really used in different environments.

The book is divided into three parts:

Part I, *Overview*, contains introductory information about parallel processing and why it's important in an Oracle environment. It consists of the following chapters:

- Chapter 1, *Introduction*, introduces the concept of parallel processing, explains its potential performance advantages, and describes the Oracle parallel technologies.

- Chapter 2, *Architectures for Parallel Processing*, describes the main parallel architectures: Symmetric Multiprocessing (SMP), Massively Parallel Processing (MPP), clusters, and Non Uniform Memory Architectures (NUMA).

Part II, *Oracle Parallel Execution*, focuses on Oracle's parallel execution features. This part will help you exploit the power of a multiple-CPU system to provide both speedup and scalability. It consists of the following chapters:

- Chapter 3, *Parallel Execution Concepts*, presents an overview of Oracle's various parallel execution features (parallel query, parallel DML and DDL, parallel data loading, parallel recovery, and parallel replication propagation).

- Chapter 4, *Using Parallel Execution*, describes specifically how to invoke and use the Oracle parallel execution features introduced in Chapter 3.

- Chapter 5, *Monitoring and Tuning Parallel Execution*, explains how you can get the best performance out of Oracle's parallel execution features.

Part III, *Oracle Parallel Server*, describes the Oracle Parallel Server (OPS) product and describes how to create and manage OPS databases. It consists of the following chapters:

- Chapter 6, *Oracle Parallel Server Architecture*, describes the overall architecture of the product and how OPS instances coordinate activities against a single database.

- Chapter 7, *Administering an OPS Database*, explains what you need to know about creating and managing an OPS database.

- Chapter 8, *Locking Mechanisms in OPS*, describes the locking mechanisms that underlie Oracle Parallel Server operations.

- Chapter 9, *Storage Management in OPS*, explains how to use free lists and other memory structures to optimize performance in OPS.

- Chapter 10, *Monitoring and Tuning OPS*, discusses how you can get the best performance out of OPS.

- Chapter 11, *Partitioning for OPS*, describes application, data, and transaction partitioning techniques for OPS.

- Chapter 12, *Application Failover*, discusses how you can use Oracle Parallel Server to support high availability.

- Chapter 13, *Parallel Execution in OPS*, describes how you can combine both sets of Oracle's parallel features by using parallel execution in OPS environments.

Appendix: Case Studies presents three different examples of how parallel execution and OPS are used in real-life environments.

Conventions Used in This Book

The following conventions are used in this book:

Italic
> Used for filenames, directory names, and URLs, and for the first mention of new terms under discussion.

Constant width
> Used for code examples.

Constant width bold
> Indicates user input in examples showing an interaction (e.g., a SQL*Plus session).

Constant width italic
> In some code examples, indicates an element (e.g., a filename) that you supply.

UPPERCASE

In code examples, indicates SQL keywords.

lowercase

In code examples, indicates user-defined items such as variables.

[ ]   In syntax descriptions, square brackets enclose optional items.

{ }   In syntax descriptions, curly brackets enclose a set of items from which you must choose only one.

| In syntax descriptions, a vertical bar separates the items enclosed in curly brackets, as in {NOPARALLEL | PARALLEL}.

Indicates a tip, suggestion, or general note. For example, we'll tell you if you need to use a particular Oracle version or if an operation requires certain privileges.

Indicates a warning or caution. For example, we'll tell you if Oracle does not behave as you'd expect or if a particular operation has a negative impact on performance.

Comments and Questions

We have tested and verified the information in this book to the best of our ability, but you may find that features have changed (or even that we have made mistakes!). Please let us know about any errors you find, as well as your suggestions for future editions, by writing to:

O'Reilly & Associates, Inc.
101 Morris Street
Sebastopol, CA 95472
(800) 998-9938 (in the United States or Canada)
(707) 829-0515 (international or local)
(707) 829-0104 (fax)

You also can send messages electronically. To be put on the mailing list or request a catalog, send email to:

info@oreilly.com

To ask technical questions or comment on the book, send email to:

bookquestions@oreilly.com

We have a web site for this book, where we'll list examples and errata, at:

> *http://www.oreilly.com/catalog/oraclepp*

For more information about this book and others, see the O'Reilly web site:

> *http://www.oreilly.com*

Acknowledgments

A great number of people have come together to make this book a reality. Our thanks go out to Debby Russell, editor of the O'Reilly Oracle Series, for sharing our vision and agreeing to sign this book. Many others at O'Reilly & Associates also had a hand in this book. Jeff Holcomb was the production editor for the book. Edie Freedman did the cover design. Robert Romano and Rhon Porter took our rough figure drawings and turned them into the art that you now see in this book.

We are grateful to our developmental editor, Jonathan Gennick, for his guidance and encouragement. He provided suggestions at every level of detail and corrected flaws in our writing. He sharpened the text considerably, making this book more readable. We thank the technical reviewers: Ross Mohan, Scott Heisey, Durinda Jones, Christopher Gait, Dave Morgan, Charles Dye, and Narasimha Sarma Brahmanapalli for their feedback, which helped to improve this book.

Special thanks are due to Ken Jacobs, Angelo Prucino, Jonathan Creighton, George Lumpkin, and Alok Srivastav, all of Oracle Corporation. These people generously went out of their way to perform a last-minute technical review of this work and helped us resolve several lingering issues in the text. We would also like to thank Roger Bamford of Oracle Corporation for giving permission to reproduce one of the graphs (Figure 8-9) from an Oracle publication.

From Tushar

I thank my colleague BN Sarma for the many technical discussions we have had on OPS and for his enthusiasm in exploring and experimenting with new Oracle features. Special thanks to Vernon Veira for his vision and interest in new technology that enabled us to use OPS. Thanks to Robert Shapiro for inviting me to give a talk on OPS, which sparked the idea to write this book. Thanks to Sanjay, the coauthor of this book, for his cooperation and best efforts. Finally, thanks to my family: my parents for their continued support; my wife Sasmita for her patience and understanding that chores would get done tomorrow; my children Sibjeet and Sweta—warm hugs to them for allowing me to take the weekends away from them for this book project.

From Sanjay

Thanks to Tushar, my coauthor, for originating the idea of writing this book. I thank the many people with whom I have interacted during my professional and academic career who enhanced my understanding of Oracle in particular, and software systems in general.

Finally, I owe a great debt of thanks to my wife, Sudipti, whom I married during the course of writing this book. I could never have written this book without her incredible patience, understanding, and encouragement.

I

Overview

This part of the book contains introductory information about parallel processing and why it's important in an Oracle environment. It consists of the following chapters:

- Chapter 1, *Introduction*, introduces the concept of parallel processing, explains its potential performance advantages, and describes the Oracle parallel technologies.

- Chapter 2, *Architectures for Parallel Processing*, describes the main parallel architectures: Symmetric Multiprocessing (SMP), Massively Parallel Processing (MPP), clusters, and Non Uniform Memory Architectures (NUMA).

1

Introduction

Parallel processing is becoming increasingly important in the world of database computing. These days, databases often grow to enormous sizes and are accessed by larger and larger numbers of users. This growth strains the ability of single-processor and single-computer systems to handle the load. More and more organizations are turning to parallel processing technologies to give them the performance, scalability, and reliability they need. Oracle Corporation is a leader in providing parallel processing technologies in a wide range of products. This chapter provides an overview of parallel processing in general and also describes how parallel processing features are implemented in an Oracle environment.

About Parallel Processing

Parallel processing involves taking a large task, dividing it into several smaller tasks, and then working on each of those smaller tasks simultaneously. The goal of this divide-and-conquer approach is to complete the larger task in less time than it would have taken to do it in one large chunk.

Your local grocery store provides a good, real-life analogy to parallel processing. Your grocer must collect money from customers for the groceries they purchase. He could install just one checkout stand, with one cash register, and force everyone to go through the same line. However, the line would move slowly, people would get fidgety, and some would go elsewhere to shop. To speed up the process, your grocer doubtless uses several checkout stands, each with a cash register of its own. This is parallel processing at work. Instead of checking out one customer at a time, your grocer can now handle several at a time.

In our grocery store analogy, parallel processing required several checkout stands, each with its own cash register. Without trying to push the analogy too far, think of each checkout stand as a computer and each cash register as a processor. In a computing environment, the multiple processors in a parallel processing system may all reside on the same computer, or they may be spread across separate computers. When they are spread across separate computers, each computer is referred to as a *node*.

There are a few basic requirements of parallel computing:

- Computer hardware that is designed to work with multiple processors and that provides a means of communication between those processors

- An operating system that is capable of managing multiple processors

- Application software that is capable of breaking large tasks into multiple smaller tasks that can be performed in parallel

Weather forecasting provides another real-life example of parallel processing at work. Satellites used for weather forecasting collect millions of bytes of data per second on the condition of earth's atmosphere, formation of clouds, wind intensity and direction, temperature, and so on. This huge amount of data has to be processed by complex algorithms to arrive at a proper forecast. Thousands of iterations of computation may be needed to interpret this environmental data. Parallel computers are used to perform these computations in a timely manner so a weather forecast can be generated early enough for it to be useful.

Why Parallel Processing?

Why do you need parallel processing? Why not just buy a faster computer? The answers to these questions lie largely in the laws of physics.

Computers were invented to solve problems faster than a human being could. Since day one, people have wanted computers to do more and to do it faster. Vendors responded with improved circuitry design for the processor, improved instruction sets, and improved algorithms to meet the demand for faster response time. Advances in engineering made it possible to add more logic circuits to processors. Processor circuit designs developed from small-scale to medium-scale integration, and then to large-scale and very large-scale integration. Some of today's processors have billions of transistors in them. The clock cycle of processors has also been reduced over the years. Some of today's processors have a clock cycle on the order of nanoseconds, and CPU frequencies have crossed the one-gigahertz barrier. All of these advances have led to processors that can do more work faster than ever before.

However, there are physical limitations on this trend of constant improvement. The processing speed of processors depends on the transmission speed of information between the electronic components within the processor. This speed, in turn, is limited by the speed of light, which is 300 mm per nanosecond. But to achieve the speed of light, optical communication methods would have to be used within processors. Therefore, the speed of processors cannot be increased beyond a certain point. Another limiting factor is that the density of the transistors within a processor can be pushed only to a certain limit. Beyond that limit, the transistors create electromagnetic interference for one another.

As improvements in clock cycle and circuitry design reached an optimum level, hardware designers looked for other alternatives to increase performance. Parallelism is the result of those efforts. Parallelism enables multiple processors to work simultaneously on several parts of a task in order to complete it faster than could be done otherwise.

Do You Need Parallel Processing?

Parallel processing not only increases processing power, it also offers several other advantages when it's implemented properly. These advantages are:

- Higher throughput
- More fault tolerance
- Better price/performance

There are hundreds of applications today that benefit from these advantages.

But parallelism is not the answer for everything. There are some added costs associated with parallelism. Synchronization between parts of a program executed by different processors is an overhead of parallelism that needs to be managed and kept at a minimum. Also, administering a parallel computing environment is more complicated than administering a serial environment.

Applications that already run satisfactorily in a serial environment may not benefit from a switch to a parallel processing environment. In addition, not all problems are amenable to parallel solutions. Unless your application is capable of decomposing large tasks into multiple smaller, parallelizable tasks, parallel processing will be of no benefit.

Parallel processing is useful for only those applications that can break larger tasks into smaller parallel tasks and that can manage the synchronization between those tasks. In addition, there must be a performance gain large enough to justify the overhead of parallelism.

Parallel Hardware Architectures

The subject of parallel computing has attracted attention from scientists and engineers, as well as from commercial vendors. Over the years, several commercially successful parallel hardware platforms have been developed. The most common of these are listed here, and are described in greater detail in Chapter 2, *Architectures for Parallel Processing*.

Symmetric Multiprocessing systems

Symmetric Multiprocessing (SMP) systems have multiple CPUs. The number usually varies from 2 to 64. All of the CPUs in an SMP machine share the same memory, the system bus, and the I/O system. A single copy of the operating system controls all of the CPUs.

Massively Parallel Processing systems

Massively Parallel Processing (MPP) systems consist of several nodes connected together. Each node has its own CPU, memory, bus, disks, and I/O system. Each node runs its own copy of the operating system. The number of nodes in an MPP system can vary from two all the way to several thousand.

Clustered systems

A clustered system consists of several nodes loosely coupled using local area network (LAN) interconnection technology. Each of these nodes can be a single-processor machine or SMP machine. In a cluster, system software balances the workload among the nodes and provides for high availability.

Non Uniform Memory Access systems

Non Uniform Memory Access (NUMA) systems consist of several SMP systems that are interconnected in order to form a larger system. All of the memory in all of the SMP systems are connected together to form a single large memory space. NUMA systems run one copy of the operating system across all nodes.

Parallel Processing for Databases

Three issues are driving the increasing use of parallel processing in database environments:

The need for increased speed or performance

Database sizes are increasing, queries are becoming more complex—especially in data warehouse systems—and the database software must somehow cope with the increasing demands that result from this complexity.

The need for scalability

This requirement goes hand-in-hand with performance. Databases often grow rapidly, and companies need a way to easily and cost-effectively scale their systems to match that growth.

The need for high availability

High availability refers to the need to keep a database up and running with minimal or no downtime. With the increasing use of the Internet, companies need to accommodate users at all hours of the day and night.

Speedup

Database sizes have been increasing steadily, and it's now quite common to find data warehouses holding several hundred gigabytes of data. Some databases, referred to as Very Large Databases (VLDBs), even hold several terabytes of data. Complex queries are run on these data warehouses to gather business intelligence and to aid in decision making. Such queries require a lot of processing time to execute. By executing these queries in parallel, you can reduce the elapsed time while still providing the required processor time.

Speedup is defined as the ratio between the runtime with one processor and the runtime using multiple processors. It measures the performance improvement gained using multiple processors instead of a single processor and is calculated using the following formula:

```
Speedup = Time₁ / Timeₘ
```

$Time_1$ is the time it takes to execute a task using only one processor, while $Time_m$ is the time it takes to execute that same task using *m* processors.

Speedup example

Figure 1-1 shows a query that takes four minutes to complete using one processor, but that takes only one minute to complete using four processors.

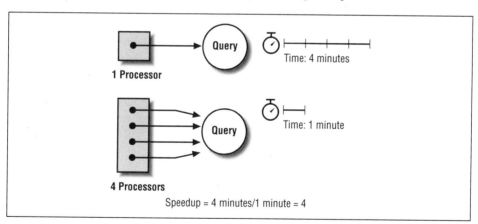

Figure 1-1. Parallel processing speedup

Plugging the values from Figure 1-1 into the speedup formula yields the following results:

```
Speedup = 4 / 1
Speedup = 4.0
```

In this case, the speedup is 4. Multiplying the number of processors by 4 caused the query to finish in one-fourth the time. Unfortunately, such an ideal result is seldom achieved in real life.

Speedup curve

In an ideal world, the parallel processing speedup would track with the number of processors used for any given task. In other words, the ideal speedup curve is a 45-degree line like the one you see in Figure 1-2.

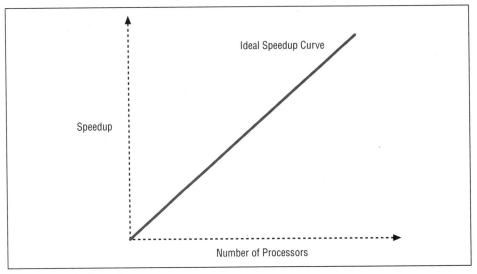

Figure 1-2. Ideal speedup curve

The ideal speedup curve is rarely reached because parallelism entails a certain amount of overhead. The inherent parallelism of the application also plays an important role in the amount of speedup you can achieve. Some tasks are easily divided into parts that can be processed in parallel. The join of two large tables, for example, can be done in parallel. Other tasks, however, cannot be divided. A nonpartitioned index scan is one such example. If an application has little or no inherent parallelism, then little or no speedup will be achieved.

Efficiency is the speedup divided by the number of processors used. In our example, the number of processors is 4, and the speedup achieved is also 4. The efficiency then is 100%, which represents an ideal case.

Scalability

Scalability is the ability to maintain performance levels as the workload increases by incrementally adding more system capacity (adding more processors and disks). On a single-processor system, it is very difficult to achieve scalability beyond a certain point. Parallel systems provide better scalability.

Parallel systems improve scalability

In many applications, the number of database users and the transaction volume are both likely to increase over time. The demand for added processing power to handle the increased load, without the loss of response time, can be met by using parallel systems. For example, to handle a higher load, an SMP system with four processors can be augmented to eight processors with additional memory and disk capacity.

In situations in which several thousand users are expected to use a database, the processing and memory requirements may be beyond the capacity of a single SMP system. In such a situation, you'll want to consider using parallel database systems. These allow you to have several nodes, each with its own copy of the database server software and memory structures, working together on a single, shared database. Such parallel systems can be clusters or MPP systems. As the user population grows, the number of nodes in the cluster or MPP system may be increased as needed to handle the additional load.

Scaleup

Scaleup is the ability of an application to retain response time as the job size or the transaction volume increases by adding additional processors and disks. The term scalability often is used in reference to scaleup.

In database applications, scaleup can be either batch or transactional. With *batch scaleup*, larger batch jobs can be supported without a loss of response time. With *transaction scaleup*, larger numbers of transactions can be supported without loss of response time. In both cases, response time is maintained by the addition of more processors. For example, a 4-processor system can provide the same response time with a workload of 400 transactions per minute as the response time of a single-processor system that supports a workload of 100 transactions per minute.

There is a key difference between scaleup and speedup: when calculating speedup, the problem size is kept fixed, whereas scaleup is calculated by increasing the problem size or transaction volume. Scaleup is measured in terms of how much the transaction volume can be increased by adding more processors while still maintaining a constant response time. Scaleup is calculated using the following formula:

```
Scaleup = Volume_m / Volume_1
```

$Volume_m$ is the transaction volume executed in a given amount of time using *m* processors, while $Volume_1$ is the transaction volume executed in the same time using one processor. For our previous example:

```
Scaleup = 400 / 100
Scaleup = 4
```

this scaleup of 4 is achieved with 4 processors. This is an example of ideal (linear) scaleup. Figure 1-3 shows a graph of an ideal transaction scaleup. Notice that the response time remains constant by increasing the number of processors as the transaction volume is increased.

The curve, or flat line, really, in Figure 1-3 represents an ideal. In reality, after a certain point, the response time increases for higher transaction volumes even if additional processors are added.

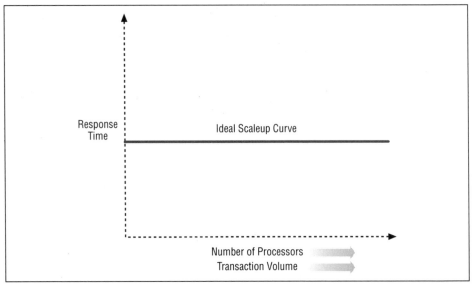

Figure 1-3. Ideal scaleup curve

High Availability

Databases are used in the mission-critical applications in organizations such as stock exchanges, banks, and airlines. Many database applications are expected to be available 24 hours a day, 7 days a week, all year round. The availability of such databases (along with other system components) is crucial to the success of these organizations. With an e-commerce application, for example, customers may log in any time of the day or night to request products and services. Database downtime causes loss of revenue and customer dissatisfaction. As the negative impact of database downtime has increased for many applications, high availability requirements have become an important factor in the design of database software.

Running parallel databases on a multinode parallel system is one way to provide high availability. Other high availability options include maintaining standby databases and replicated databases. With a parallel database, when one node goes down, it affects only the subset of users connected to the failed node; moreover, users of the failed node still can access the database after switching to one of the surviving nodes.

Price/Performance

Economics is another driver toward parallel computing. It costs money to make processors faster. After a certain limit, increasing the processing power on a single CPU system becomes technically very difficult. Once that limit has been reached, SMP systems often provide better performance for the price. Likewise, when the scalability limit of SMP systems is reached, clusters or MPP systems may provide better price/performance ratios.

Types of Parallelism in Databases

Database applications can exploit two types of parallelism in a parallel computing environment: *inter-query parallelism* and *intra-query parallelism*. While inter-query parallelism has been around for many years, database vendors recently have started to implement intra-query parallelism as well.

Inter-query parallelism

Inter-query parallelism is the ability to use multiple processors to execute several independent queries simultaneously. Figure 1-4 illustrates inter-query parallelism, showing how three independent queries can be performed simultaneously by three processors. Inter-query parallelism does not provide speedup, because each query is still executed by only one processor.

In online transaction processing (OLTP) applications, each query is independent and takes a relatively short time to execute. As the number of OLTP users increases, more queries are generated. Without inter-query parallelism, all queries will be performed by a single processor in a time-shared manner. This slows down response time. With inter-query parallelism, queries generated by OLTP users can be distributed over multiple processors. Since the queries are performed simultaneously by multiple processors, response time remains satisfactory.

Intra-query parallelism

Intra-query parallelism is the ability to break a single query into subtasks and to execute those subtasks in parallel using a different processor for each. The result is a decrease in the overall elapsed time needed to execute a single query. Intra-query parallelism is very beneficial in decision support system (DSS) applications, which often have complex, long-running queries. As DSS systems have become more widely used, database vendors have been increasing their support for intra-query parallelism.

Figure 1-5 shows how one large query may be decomposed into two subtasks, which then are executed simultaneously using two processors. The results of the subtasks then are merged to generate a result for the original query. Intra-query

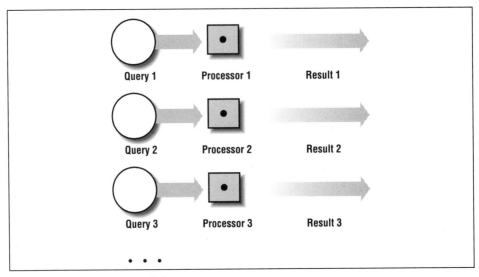

Figure 1-4. Inter-query parallelism

parallelism is useful not only with queries, but also with other tasks such as data loading, index creation, and so on. Chapter 3, *Parallel Execution Concepts*, and Chapter 4, *Using Parallel Execution*, provide detailed information on Oracle's support of intra-query parallelism.

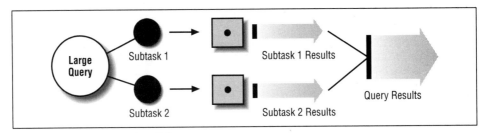

Figure 1-5. Intra-query parallelism

Parallel Processing in Oracle

Most modern commercial DBMS products have implemented parallel features, and Oracle is no exception. With every release, Oracle has consistently improved its support for parallel processing. Oracle's support for parallel processing can be divided into the following two specific feature sets:

Parallel execution
  Refers to intra-query parallelism

Parallel server
  Refers to the use of multiple instances to open a single, shared database

Terminology

As you delve into Oracle's parallel feature set, you'll encounter several very similar terms that all begin with the word "parallel." Read through the following definitions; they will help you understand these terms before you read further:

Oracle Parallel Server

Refers to the Oracle option allowing you to share one database among multiple instances. Typically, these instances will be running on separate nodes of a clustered system.

Parallel Server

The same as Oracle Parallel Server.

Parallel execution

Refers to Oracle's ability to apply multiple CPUs to the task of executing a single SQL statement in order to complete execution faster than would be possible using only a single CPU.

Parallel SQL

Means the same thing as parallel execution.

Parallel Query

Refers to Oracle's ability to execute SELECT statements in parallel, using multiple CPUs. When parallel features first were introduced into Oracle years ago, the only support was for parallel SELECT statements, and at that point the feature was known as Parallel Query and was available through the Parallel Query Option (PQO). Now, Parallel Query is only a subset of Oracle's parallel execution features.

Parallel DML

Refers to Oracle's ability to execute Data Manipulation Language (DML) statements in parallel. Parallel DML is a subset of Oracle's parallel execution feature set.

Parallel DDL

Refers to Oracle's ability to execute some Data Definition Language (DDL) statements in parallel. Parallel DDL is a subset of Oracle's parallel execution feature set.

Parallel Execution

Oracle's parallel execution features enable Oracle to divide a task among multiple processes in order to complete the task faster. This allows Oracle to take advantage of multiple CPUs on a machine. The parallel processes acting on behalf of a single task are called *parallel slave processes*. Parallel execution features first were introduced in Oracle Version 7.1 in the form of the Parallel Query Option, which supported only parallel SELECT statements. Since then many new functions have been added. In Oracle7, support for parallel execution was a separately installed option. However, in Oracle8 and Oracle8*i*, it is embedded into the Oracle RDBMS product.

Let's look at a simple example that illustrates how parallel execution works in Oracle. The following SQL statement counts the number of orders in the orders table:

```
SQL> SELECT COUNT(*) FROM orders;
```

When you execute this statement serially—that is, without using any parallel execution features—a single process scans the orders table and counts the number of rows. However, if you had a four-processor machine and used Oracle's parallel execution features, the orders table would be split into four parts. A process would be started on each CPU, and the four parts of the table would be scanned simultaneously. The results of each of the four processes then would be merged to arrive at the total count. Figure 1-6 illustrates this situation.

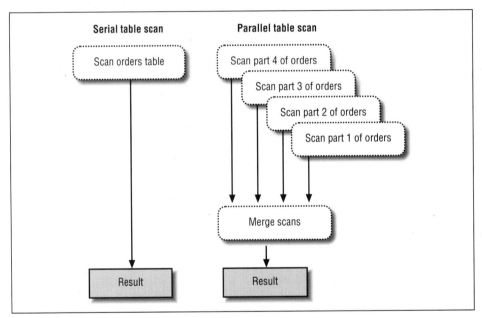

Figure 1-6. Serial and parallel scans of a table

Oracle's parallel execution support extends far beyond simply executing SELECT statements in parallel. The full range of features includes all of the following:

Parallel Query

> Large queries (SELECT statements) can be split into smaller tasks and executed in parallel by multiple slave processes in order to reduce the overall elapsed time. The task of scanning a large table, for example, can be

performed in parallel by multiple slave processes. Each process scans a part of the table, and the results are merged together at the end. Oracle's parallel query feature can significantly improve the performance of large queries and is very useful in decision support applications, as well as in other environments with large reporting requirements.

Parallel DML

In addition to SELECT statements, Oracle can execute DML operations such as INSERT, UPDATE, and DELETE in parallel. There are some restrictions on this capability, however. UPDATE and DELETE operations can be parallelized only on partitioned tables. INSERT INTO . . . SELECT . . . FROM statements can be parallelized for nonpartitioned as well as partitioned tables. Parallel DML is particularly advantageous in data warehouse environments that maintain summary and historical tables. The time needed to rebuild or otherwise maintain these tables is reduced because the work can be done in parallel. Parallel DML also is useful in OLTP systems to improve the performance of long-running batch jobs.

Parallel DDL

Oracle now has the ability to parallelize table and index creation. Statements such as the following can be parallelized:

```
CREATE TABLE...AS SELECT...FROM
CREATE INDEX
ALTER INDEX REBUILD
```

Data warehouse applications frequently require summary and temporary tables to be built, and the parallel object creation feature can be very useful in performing such tasks. OLTP applications can use this feature to rebuild indexes at regular intervals in order to keep those indexes efficient.

Parallel data loading

Bulk data loading can be parallelized by splitting the input data into multiple files and running multiple SQL*Loader sessions simultaneously to load data into a table. Loading large amounts of data in bulk is a necessary requirement of all data warehouse applications, and Oracle's parallel loading feature can greatly reduce the time needed to load that data.

Parallel recovery

Oracle's parallel recovery feature can reduce the time needed for instance and media recovery. With parallel recovery, multiple parallel slave processes will be used to perform recovery operations. The system monitor (SMON) background process reads the redo log files, and the parallel slave processes apply the changes to the datafiles. Recovery of a large database takes a significant amount of time, and parallel recovery can be used to reduce that time.

Parallel replication propagation

    If you are using replication to maintain copies of database objects in multiple databases, you can use parallel propagation to update those copies efficiently. Changes made in one database can be propagated to another database using multiple slave processes to speed up the propagation.

Oracle Parallel Server

Oracle Parallel Server (OPS) enables one database to be mounted and opened concurrently by multiple instances. Each OPS instance is like any standalone Oracle instance and runs on a separate node having its own CPU and memory. The database resides on a disk subsystem shared by all nodes. OPS takes parallelism to a higher plane by allowing you to spread work not only over multiple CPUs, but also over multiple nodes. OPS offers many more advantages that we'll explain later in this section.

Figure 1-7 illustrates an OPS database comprised of two nodes. Each node runs one Oracle instance. Each instance has its own set of background processes and its own System Global Area (SGA). Both of the instances mount and open a database residing on a shared disk subsystem.

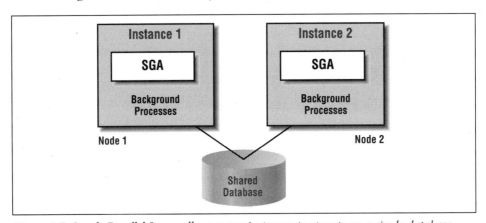

Figure 1-7. Oracle Parallel Server allows many instances to operate on a single database

Oracle Parallel Server is a separately installable option available with the Oracle RDBMS software. If you are planning to run a parallel server database, you need to install this option, along with the Oracle RDBMS software, on a system with a shared disk architecture. In addition, even after installation, you need to enable the parallel server option. Chapter 6, *Oracle Parallel Server Architecture*, and Chapter 7, *Administering an OPS Database*, cover this subject in detail.

Because a parallel server system is a multi-instance configuration, such a system provides some distinct advantages over a single-instance (often referred to as a standalone-instance) system. These advantages include:

- High availability
- Better scalability
- Load balancing

When one instance goes down, other instances continue functioning. This increases availability, because the failure of one instance does not result in the database's becoming unavailable to users. Users connected to other instances continue working without disruption. Users connected to the instance that failed can reconnect to any of the surviving instances.

If you get more users on an OPS system than can be handled by the existing nodes, you can add another node easily and start an additional instance on that node. Doing so results in better scalability than you typically would get with a single-instance system. Oracle also has features that allow you to balance the workload among the instances of an OPS database, enabling you to optimize the load on each node.

Managing an OPS database is a much more complex task than managing a stand-alone, single-instance database. Not only do you have the complexity of dealing with multiple instances, you also have several performance issues that come about as a result. Part III, *Oracle Parallel Server*, discusses the unique aspects of managing Oracle Parallel Server.

 Parallel execution and the Oracle Parallel Server Option are two separate Oracle features that can work independently as well as together. Parallel execution features can be utilized on databases with or without the Oracle Parallel Server Option. Without OPS, the parallel slave processes on behalf of a task run on only one instance, whereas with OPS the parallel slave processes on behalf of a task run on one or more instances.

Overhead for Oracle Parallel Processing

As you might imagine, the benefits of parallel execution and Oracle Parallel Server do not come without a price. The next two sections discuss the various overhead issues that apply to parallel execution and Oracle Parallel Server.

Parallel Execution Overhead

Parallel execution entails a cost in terms of the processing overhead necessary to break up a task into pieces, manage the execution of each of those pieces, and combine the results when the execution is complete. Figure 1-8 illustrates some of the steps involved in parallel execution.

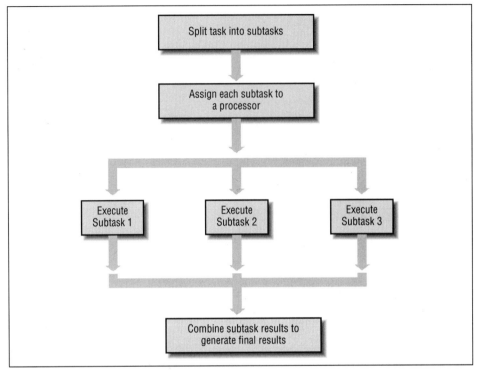

Figure 1-8. Steps in parallel execution

Parallel execution overhead can be divided into three areas: startup cost, interference, and skew.

Startup cost

Startup cost refers to the time it takes to start parallel execution of a query or a DML statement. It takes time and resources to divide one large task into smaller subtasks that can be run in parallel. Time also is required to create the processes needed to execute those subtasks and to assign each subtask to one of these processes. For a large query, this startup time may not be significant in terms of the overall time required to execute the query. For a small query, however, the startup time may end up being a significant portion of the total time.

Interference

Interference refers to the slowdown that one process imposes on other processes when accessing shared resources. While the slowdown resulting from one process is small, with a large number of processors the impact can be substantial.

Skew

Skew refers to the variance in execution time of parallel subtasks. As the number of parallel subtasks increases (perhaps as a result of using more processors), the amount of work performed by each subtask decreases. The result is a reduction in processing time required for each of those subtasks and also for the overall task. There are always variations, however, in the size of these subtasks. In some situations these variations may lead to large differences in execution time between the various subtasks. The net effect, when this happens, is that the processing time of the overall task becomes equivalent to that of the longest subtask.

Let's suppose you have a query that takes ten minutes to execute without parallel processing. Let's further suppose when parallel processing is used that the query is broken down into ten subtasks and that the average processing time of each subtask is one minute. In this perfect situation, the overall query is also completed in one minute, resulting in a speedup of ten. However, if one subtask takes two minutes, the response of the overall query becomes two minutes. The speedup achieved is then only five. The skew, or the variation in execution time between subtasks, has reduced the efficiency of this particular parallel operation.

Oracle Parallel Server Overhead

When Oracle Parallel Server is used, multiple instances need to synchronize access to the objects in the shared database. Synchronization is achieved by passing messages back and forth between the OPS nodes. A Lock Manager called Integrated Distributed Lock Manager (IDLM) facilitates this synchronization. The amount of synchronization required depends on the data access requirements of the particular applications running on each of the OPS nodes. If multiple OPS nodes are trying to access the same object, then there will be a lot of conflict. This increases the need for synchronization, resulting in a high amount of overhead. An OPS database needs to be designed and tuned to minimize this overhead. Otherwise, the required synchronization overhead may reduce, or even negate, the benefits of using OPS in the first place.

Oracle's parallel execution features also may be used, and often are used, in an OPS environment. If you do use Oracle's parallel execution features in an OPS environment, then all the issues discussed in the previous section on parallel execution overhead also apply.

Requirements for Oracle's Parallel Features

In order to use Oracle's parallel processing features for your database applications, you must:

- Have both suitable hardware and operating system software that supports parallel processing

- Configure Oracle Server appropriately

- Modify your database applications to get the benefit of parallel processing

Table 1-1 briefly summarizes the requirements for using Oracle's parallel execution features and for using Oracle Parallel Server.

Table 1-1. Requirements for Using Oracle's Parallel Features

Type of Requirement	Parallel Execution	Oracle Parallel Server
Hardware	Multiple processors (SMP, MPP, or NUMA).	Multiple nodes (cluster, MPP, or NUMA cluster) shared disk architecture.
Operating system software	Operating system must support multiple processors.	Operating system must support resource management and communication across nodes. The operating system also must support a disk-sharing configuration such as the use of raw devices on Unix and NT platforms.
Oracle DBMS	Configure initialization parameters. If using Oracle7, install the Oracle Parallel Query Option.	Purchase and install the Oracle Parallel Server Option. Configure initialization parameters.
Application	Minor changes to SQL statements.	Application partitioning.

The following sections discuss some of the Table 1-1 requirements in greater detail.

Parallel Execution Requirements

Requirements for implementing parallel execution in Oracle are relatively straightforward. You need a computer with multiple processors, and you need to make relatively minor changes to Oracle initialization parameters and to your database application for parallel execution.

Hardware requirements

Parallel execution is not beneficial with a single-processor machine. In order to take advantage of Oracle's parallel execution features, you need to be running in an environment that supports multiple CPUs. This could be an SMP system, an MPP system, or a clustered system. In MPP systems and clusters, parallel tasks are run on different nodes. Sometimes, each node of the clusters or MPP systems may be another SMP system.

Software requirements

Not only does your hardware need to support multiple CPUs, but your operating system also needs to be capable of managing multiple processors and be able to share common resources (memory, I/O, and system bus) among multiple processors. For example, several operating systems such as various flavors of Unix (AIX, Sun Solaris, HPUX, etc.), Windows NT, and VAX/VMS support multiprocessing.

Oracle DBMS requirements

In Oracle7, the parallel execution features were a separately installed option known as the Oracle Parallel Query Option. In Oracle8, these features are now part of the core database product. To enable them, all you need to do is to properly set some initialization parameters.

Application requirements

Setting up parallel execution in database applications is simple compared to scientific and other applications. In scientific applications, special algorithms are required to take advantage of parallel processing. Parallel compiling also is needed to compile those algorithms.

In contrast, once you've enabled the parallel execution features in Oracle, only minimal application modifications are necessary to take advantage of them. The number of parallel processes used to execute a query is referred to as the *degree of parallelism*. Minor changes may be required to the SQL statements in your application in order to specify the degree of parallelism to be used for each. The rest of the work required for parallel execution is handled transparently by the database server software. Oracle Server automatically takes care of dividing the task into smaller units, assigning work to multiple slave processes, and combining the results of individual slave processes to make the final result.

Oracle Parallel Server Requirements

Setting up Oracle Parallel Server is somewhat more complex than setting up parallel execution in an SMP environment. The installation process for Oracle Parallel Server is platform-specific, so be sure to check your platform-specific documentation before attempting an OPS install. Once you have the software installed, read Chapter 6 for a detailed explanation of the OPS architecture, and read Chapter 7 for detailed information on the steps involved in creating and managing an OPS database.

Hardware requirements

An Oracle Parallel Server runs on shared disk architectures where multiple nodes share common databases that are accessible from all nodes. Oracle Parallel Server can run on clusters and MPP systems but cannot be used on an SMP system, because SMP systems do not have more than one node.

System software requirements

To meet the system software requirements for parallel server execution, you must have a copy of the operating system on each node, and you must have system software to manage resources and communication among nodes. This management component often is referred to as a *cluster manager.* The system software also should be capable of making disks sharable among all the nodes. For example, on IBM RISC/6000 clusters, this component is referred to as HACMP (High Availability Clusters Multiprocessing).

Oracle DBMS requirements

Oracle Parallel Server is a separate option that has to be purchased and installed on all the nodes. Setting up and configuring the OPS option is more involved than setting up and configuring a standalone Oracle instance. Several additional initialization parameters have to be configured for OPS. Also, in order to synchronize database activity across multiple database instances, you will need to configure a new kind of database lock, referred to as an *instances lock.* Installation and configuration of OPS is quite involved, and you will find that it requires additional planning and careful analysis.

You can use the following query to check to see if the Oracle Parallel Server Option has been installed in your database. If the OPS option is installed, the VALUE column will return TRUES; otherwise, the VALUE column will return FALSE:

```
SQL> SELECT * FROM V$OPTION WHERE PARAMETER = 'Parallel Server';

PARAMETER                                    VALUE
------------------------------------------   --------
Parallel Server                              TRUE
```

Application requirements

In Oracle Parallel Server, database applications run on more than one instance but access the same physical database. As we have mentioned before, OPS overhead increases if database applications running on multiple instances access the same set of database tables. Thus, in designing a database application for OPS, you need to give additional consideration to the application design to ensure that applications running on multiple database instances access different set of database tables. This process, referred to as *application partitioning*, has a huge impact on the performance of an OPS database.

2

Architectures for Parallel Processing

In the never-ending quest for increased performance, vendors over the years have developed several different hardware and software architectures to use as a basis for parallel processing. In this chapter, we present the different hardware architectures used for parallel processing in databases. This chapter discusses the basic characteristics of these hardware architectures and contrasts their relative strengths and weakness. In addition, this chapter also discusses the three types of software architectures commonly used by DBMS vendors to implement parallel processing in their database software; this discussion provides you with a framework for understanding the software architecture choices made by Oracle when implementing parallel processing under the different hardware architectures. Finally, this chapter describes the availability of Oracle's parallel processing features on each type of hardware architecture.

Hardware Architectures

Parallel processing refers to the use of multiple processors to reduce the time needed to complete a given task. Instead of one processor's executing an entire task, several processors each work on a separate piece of the task. Obviously, parallel processing requires computer hardware that can support more than a single processor. Several architectural approaches to multiple processor systems have been developed over the years. The following four are in commercial use today:

- Symmetric Multiprocessing (SMP)

- Clustered

- Massively Parallel Processing (MPP)

- Non Uniform Memory Access (NUMA)

The next four sections describe each of these architectures.

Symmetric Multiprocessing (SMP) Systems

In a Symmetric Multiprocessing (SMP) architecture, multiple processors (CPUs) within a single computer share the same system memory and I/O resources. (See Figure 2-1 for an illustration.) The sharing is accomplished through the use of a high-speed system bus. One copy of the operating system runs on the computer and controls all of the processors. This operating system must be designed to support multiple processors, and it must have a scheduling algorithm that utilizes all the processors in the system evenly. The SMP architecture also is referred to as a *tightly coupled* or *shared memory architecture*.

 Please assume that all of the figures presented in this chapter are conceptual. The figures show notable features of the architectures being discussed and illustrate differences between them. Although the concepts remain the same, the detailed hardware implementations will vary significantly among various vendors.

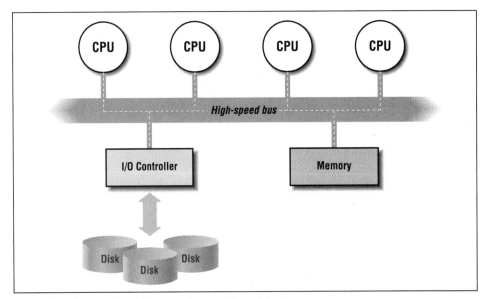

Figure 2-1. Symmetric Multiprocessing (SMP) architecture

Each processor in an SMP system can execute programs independently, with each processor accessing a separate area of memory. A single-processor system running in a *time-sharing* mode really can work on only one job at a time. It accomplishes the *illusion* of doing several things at once by rapidly cycling through all the different jobs that are running. An SMP system, on the other hand, really can work on several jobs simultaneously, because separate processors are dedicated to each job. (This is equivalent to the inter-query parallelism that you read about in Chapter 1, *Introduction.*) Because processor job assignment is entirely transparent to applications, database applications can reap the benefits of increased through-put from SMP systems without requiring that any changes be made to the RDBMS software. In addition, the many processors in an SMP system can be made to work cooperatively together on a single large program in order to complete it faster than any single processor could. (This is the equivalent of intra-query parallelism, which you also read about in Chapter 1.) Intra-query parallelism, however, does require specific support from the RDBMS software and from database applications.

Advantages of SMP systems

SMP architectures have a long history, and most major hardware vendors provide SMP-based systems. SMP architectures bring several advantages to the table:

- SMP provides a smooth way to increase the performance of a system; you simply add more processors. You also may add additional memory and disk capacity if required.

- Software designed for uniprocessor systems will work on an SMP system without any modification.

- SMP systems represent a cost-effective way to achieve scalability in cases in which a uniprocessor system cannot meet performance requirements. SMP is an ideal platform so long as your scalability requirements are within the current limits of SMP hardware and software technologies.

- SMP architecture is mature and widely used.

- Because only one copy of the operating system runs on an SMP system, the administrative overhead of managing an SMP system is similar to that of managing a uniprocessor system.

Disadvantages of SMP systems

Along with all their good points, SMP architectures carry with them two significant disadvantages:

- The SMP architecture does not scale well to a large number of processors.

- The SMP architecture does not provide high availability.

The number of processors that can be added to an SMP system is limited, because all processors share the same memory. Add too many processors, and you end up with memory and system-bus bottlenecks. The maximum number of processors that can be configured on an SMP system varies from one vendor and operating system to the next. Windows NT supports from two to a maximum of only four processors. Unix-based SMP systems, on the other hand, often support anywhere from 2 to a maximum of 64 processors.

Because only one copy of the operating system runs on an SMP system, the operating system represents a single point of failure. In addition, certain hardware failures also can bring down the system. Consequently, SMP systems by themselves aren't a good choice when high availability is important.

Clustered Systems

In clustered architectures, a small set of nodes (between 2 and 64 based on specific vendor implementation) are interconnected and share storage devices. Each node is an independent system with its own processor and memory, running its own copy of the operating system. Figure 2-2 illustrates a two-node cluster. Each node in the cluster can be a single-processor system or an SMP system. In Figure 2-2, each node is an SMP system having two processors. Cluster architecture also is referred to as a *loosely coupled architecture*, because it allows different processor and memory configurations in each node.

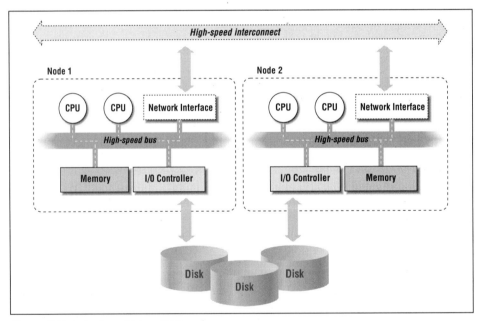

Figure 2-2. A cluster with two SMP nodes

Advantages of clustered systems

Clustered systems have advantages over both SMP systems and other parallel architectures:

- Clusters provide greater performance and scalability than can be possible with any single SMP system. The scalability of a clustered system can be increased in two ways: by increasing the number of processors within each node and/or by increasing the number of nodes in the cluster.

- Clustering provides a relatively inexpensive way to achieve scalability by leveraging commonly used processor architectures and standard networking technologies.

- Clusters can provide high availability (HA). Often the networking between nodes is done with dual connections to provide redundancy. If one node of the cluster fails, other nodes in the cluster will continue to operate, and users connected to the node that failed can be redistributed to the surviving nodes.

Disadvantages of clustered systems

Clustered systems also have some disadvantages:

- Additional system software is required to manage and monitor clustered systems. For example, to manage IBM RS/6000 clusters running the AIX operating system, you also need IBM's HACMP (High Availability Clusters Multiprocessing) software.

- Managing a clustered system is a much more complex task than managing a single-node SMP system. The complexity increases as the number of nodes in the cluster increases.

- Compared to an SMP system, a clustered system requires more programming effort to coordinate processing on the different nodes, as well as to balance the processing workload across those nodes.

Massively Parallel Processing (MPP) Systems

In a Massively Parallel Processing (MPP) architecture, several nodes are connected via a proprietary high-speed network. Each node has its own CPU and memory. Figure 2-3 shows an MPP system with four nodes. Because each node has its own memory, MPP systems are referred to as *distributed memory* systems. Each node runs its own copy of the operating system, and inter-node communication is done through message passing. The number of nodes that can be configured in an MPP architecture varies from as few as two to as many as several hundred. As with clustered systems, the individual nodes in an MPP system can be uniprocessor nodes, or they can be SMP nodes. MPP systems were developed originally for highly parallelizable scientific computations but are increasingly being used for data warehousing applications.

MPP systems and clusters have many similarities from an architectural point of view. Both use a distributed memory architecture, and in both cases each node runs its own copy of the operating system. Both architectures use message passing for communication between nodes and require additional application programming effort to exploit parallelism. The main difference between MPP and cluster

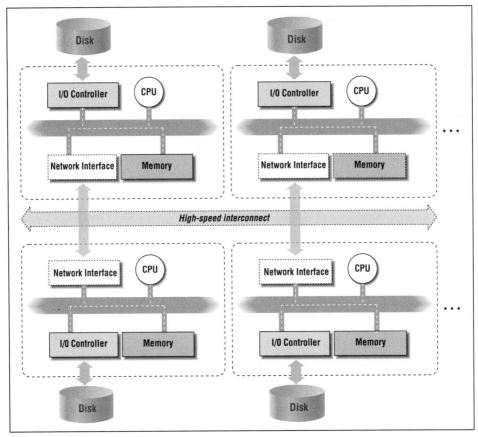

Figure 2-3. Massively Parallel Processing (MPP) architecture

architectures is that the number of nodes that can be configured with MPP is quite large compared to the number of nodes that can be configured in a cluster. In addition, the characteristics of the interconnect differ between MPP and cluster architectures.

Advantages of MPP systems

The main advantage of MPP systems is that they do not experience the memory bottlenecks that limit the scalability of SMP systems because each node in an MPP system has its own memory. While the individual nodes of an MPP system may themselves be SMP systems, they typically have only a very few processors, keeping them well below the limits of SMP scalability.

MPP systems are suitable for large data warehousing applications, and a large MPP configuration easily can support several thousand users and 10,000 or more transactions per minute.

Disadvantages of MPP systems

MPP systems have two major disadvantages:

- Because the memory for each node in an MPP system is separate from the others, special features must be built into the operating system to enable communication between the nodes. In MPP systems, when one node needs data held by another, messages are exchanged between the nodes in order to transfer that data.

- MPP systems are more difficult to manage than SMP systems, because each node in an MPP system runs its own copy of the operating system and its own copy of the database software. Thus, the MPP architecture is best used when you have reached the current limits of SMP or cluster scalability.

Non Uniform Memory Access (NUMA) Systems

In a Non Uniform Memory Access (NUMA) architecture, multiple SMP systems are interconnected to form a single large system. This is illustrated in Figure 2-4, which shows a NUMA system comprised of two such SMP systems. The SMP systems that you see in the figure really are not complete systems, because each does not run its own copy of the operating system. For this reason, the SMP systems in a NUMA architecture are not referred to as nodes, but as *groups*. Each SMP group in this figure consists of two CPUs, and each group has its own dedicated memory and I/O controller. The two groups are connected using a high-speed interconnect. Note that this figure looks very similar to Figure 2-2, which depicts a cluster architecture. Unlike a cluster, however, NUMA functions as a large, single SMP system. In a NUMA system, all the memory from all the SMP groups is treated as a large, single, contiguous memory space. In addition, only one copy of the operating system runs across all the nodes. One way to think of a NUMA system is as a cluster within one computer.

In Figure 2-4, the network interface box connects each SMP group to the high-speed interconnect. It also has the added functionality of creating a single, large, continuous view of the memory contained in those SMP groups. To the processors, all memory appears the same. The only difference is in access time. When a processor accesses local memory (memory in its own SMP group), the access is fast. When a process accesses nonlocal memory (memory from another SMP group), that access has to go across the interconnect and as a result is much slower. This is where the NUMA architecture gets its name, because the memory access time is not uniform.

Recall that SMP systems are based on a shared memory architecture. MPP and clustered systems represent distributed memory architectures, because memory is

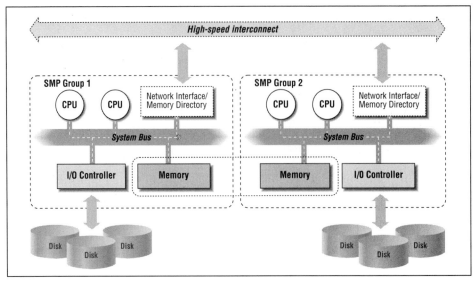

Figure 2-4. Non Uniform Memory Access (NUMA) architecture

distributed across nodes. NUMA systems represent a hybrid architecture referred to as a *distributed shared memory* architecture. NUMA attempts to combine the best of both distributed and shared architectures. NUMA systems have the simplicity of SMP systems, because they operate as a single, large system. You don't have the complexity of message passing that you get with an MPP system. In addition, as your processing needs increase, you can grow a NUMA system by adding more SMP groups, without the scalability limitations inherent in a stand-alone SMP architecture.

Several vendors, such as IBM (NUMA-Q), Data General (AV-2000), SGI (Origin 2000), and NCR have adopted NUMA technology and have implemented variations on NUMA architecture, including NUMA clusters. NUMA is a recently developed architecture, and it remains to be seen if the architecture will live up to its promise and become as commonly used as SMP systems are today.

Advantages of NUMA systems

The NUMA architecture was developed to address the scalability limits of SMP systems and has the following advantages:

- It provides the scalability of a loosely coupled architecture such as MPP.

- Software applications do not have to change to accommodate the architecture.

Disadvantages of NUMA systems

NUMA systems do have some disadvantages:

- While local-memory access is fast, nonlocal memory access is not. A high percentage of nonlocal memory accesses can slow down the system.

- Performance depends not only on the high-speed interconnect, but also on the proper tuning of the operating system. To fully exploit the NUMA architecture, databases and applications need to be NUMA-aware.

- As with SMP systems, a single copy of the operating system makes for a single point of failure.

High-Speed Interconnect

In Figures 2-2 through 2-4, we've referred to the connection networks used in cluster, MPP, and NUMA architectures as *high-speed interconnects*. Performance of this interconnect is an important consideration in parallel architectures. Interconnect performance is measured in two dimensions: bandwidth and latency. *Bandwidth* is the rate at which data can be moved between nodes and is measured in megabytes (MB) per second. *Latency* is defined as the time spent in setting up access to a remote node so that communications can occur. Interconnects should have low latency in order to maximize the number of messages that can be set up and placed on the interconnect in a given period of time. As the number of nodes in a configuration increases, more data and messages are passed around between nodes. It's important that the interconnect have a high enough bandwidth and a low enough latency to support this message traffic.

Cluster interconnects often are implemented using standard LAN-based technology such as Ethernet or Fiber Distributed Data Interchange (FDDI). When a cluster is configured with a large number of nodes, the limitations of the network can degrade performance. The bandwidth and latency of the cluster interconnect is the key to improving the scalability of a cluster.

Figure 2-5 shows a sample network configuration in a two-node cluster. Nodes in the cluster are connected to the network with both primary and standby interface cards. When the primary interface fails, the operating system switches the IP address assigned to the primary interface to the standby interface, and the system continues to operate. In addition to redundant network interface cards, a secondary LAN also is provided. In the event that the primary LAN fails, the secondary LAN will take over, and the cluster will continue to operate.

The interconnect in IBM RS/6000 (an MPP architecture) is referred to as a *high-performance switch* (HPS). The switch architecture is such that as the number of nodes is increased in an MPP system, switching components are added to maintain node-to-node bandwidth. Because of this feature, HPS scales well and can support a large number of nodes. RS/6000 SP systems have latency on the order of a microsecond, and peak node-to-node bandwidth of 100 MB per second.

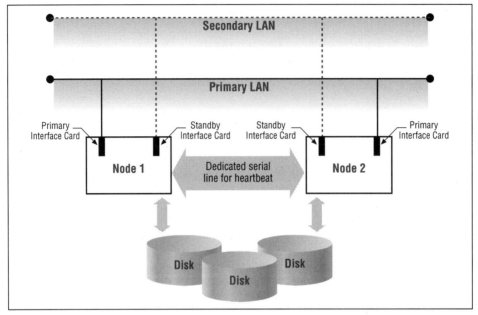

Figure 2-5. Redundant network components in a two-node cluster

IBM uses a low-latency connection network called IQ-link for their NUMA-Q systems. IQ-link is based on a recently developed technology called a *scalable coherent interconnect* (SCI) and provides a bandwidth of 1 GB per second. When data is not available in local memory, SCI transmits the data request to the remote node. The remote node then sends the requested data back to the node that requested it. This interconnect creates a large, single, coherent view of all the memory from the individual SMP groups that make up the NUMA system.

Software Architectures of Parallel Database Systems

In implementing parallelism in their database software, database vendors use one of three software architectures, commonly referred to as:

- Shared everything
- Shared disk
- Shared nothing

The sharing refers to the sharing of disk and memory by multiple processors.

Implementing each of these software architectures requires an appropriate underlying parallel hardware architecture. Some software architectures are a better match than others for a given hardware architecture. For example, a shared everything software architecture is a natural match for SMP hardware, because all processors in an SMP system share the same memory and disk. Other combinations are not so good. Implementing a shared everything software architecture on an MPP platform, for example, is not a good choice, because MPP hardware is based on a distributed memory architecture. The software implementation of a shared memory abstraction on top of the distributed memory of the individual nodes in an MPP system would be difficult, and performance would be poor.

The three figures in this section, Figures 2-6 through 2-8, highlight the differences among the three database software architectures with respect to the sharing of memory and disks. They do not imply any particular underlying hardware architecture. It is possible to implement more than one software architecture on a given type of hardware architecture. For example, on IBM RS/6000 SP, which is an MPP system, Oracle Parallel Server runs with a shared disk software architecture. DB2/6000 Parallel Edition, on the other hand, runs on the same IBM RS/6000 SP system with a shared nothing software architecture.

Shared Everything

In a shared everything database architecture, all processors share the same memory and disks. Figure 2-6 illustrates such a system. One copy of the operating system and one copy of the database software run on the system. Shared memory allows for efficient coordination between DBMS processes. In this architecture, it is relatively simple to implement inter-query and intra-query parallelism, because the operating system automatically allocates the queries and subqueries to available CPUs. The shared everything software architecture is widely used on SMP hardware. The NUMA hardware architecture also is suitable for a shared everything software architecture.

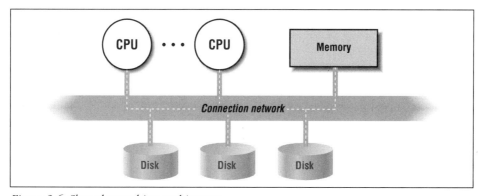

Figure 2-6. Shared everything architecture

All major DBMS vendors provide support for shared everything architectures. Oracle supports parallel execution on the shared everything software architecture.

Shared everything software architectures have the scalability and availability limitations of the underlying hardware architecture. For example, with SMP hardware, memory, and system bottlenecks limit the number of processors that can be used in a shared everything architecture. In addition, there are two single points of failure because only one copy of the operating system and only one copy of the database software run in a shared everything architecture.

Shared Disk

In a shared disk database architecture, each node has its own CPU and memory. Storage devices (disks) are connected using a high-speed network and are shared by all nodes. Each node has access to any disk. Each node also runs its own copy of the operating system and database software. Logically and physically there is just one database, distributed among all the disks, which is accessed by all the nodes. Figure 2-7 illustrates the shared disk architecture.

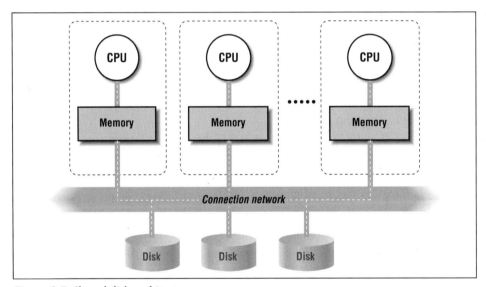

Figure 2-7. Shared disk architecture

The shared disk approach eliminates the performance bottleneck of shared memory systems as it is implemented on distributed memory hardware. To increase performance or to support a greater number of users, you can add additional nodes and disks. Because you are adding nodes, you don't encounter the memory bottlenecks to which SMP systems are prone. Both shared disk and shared nothing systems have this scalability advantage over shared everything systems and, consequently, often are used to host very large databases. Oracle Parallel Server is based on the shared disk approach and is available on clusters (including NUMA clusters) and MPP systems.

On some platforms, such as the HP Enterprise Server, the hardware vendor supports shared disks at the hardware level by connecting nodes directly to the disks. With the HP Enterprise Server, there is no need for a software layer to simulate shared disks. On other platforms that do not provide hardware support for a shared disk architecture, a software layer simulates it. For example, IBM RS/6000 SP is a hardware platform based on MPP architecture, and each node in RS/6000 SP has its own disk. However, using a software layer called Virtual Shared Disk (VSD), any node can transparently access any disk physically located on any other node. The Virtual Shared Disk layer traps all requests for disk access. If the access is to a shared disk that is locally connected, then the VSD layer passes the request to the Logical Volume Manager (LVM) of the local node. The LVM is the operating system module that manages storage in an IBM RS/6000 SP system. When the access is to a shared disk that is connected to a remote node, the VSD layer sends the request to the LVM of the remote node via the high-speed interconnect. The remote node then accesses the disk and returns the requested data back through the interconnect to the originating node.

Shared Nothing

In a shared nothing database architecture, each node is independent and has its own memory and disk. Each node runs its own copy of the operating system and its own copy of the DBMS software. A high-speed network is used to connect the nodes together. As illustrated in Figure 2-8, processors in a shared nothing architecture do not share memory and disks with other nodes. Shared nothing architectures are possible on cluster and MPP systems.

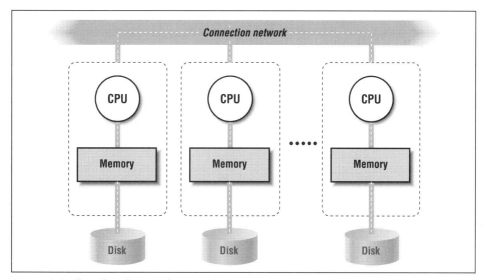

Figure 2-8. Shared nothing architecture

Databases in a shared nothing architecture are partitioned, or divided, among nodes. In this sense, the term *partition* refers to part of a database, and not to partitions of a table or an index in the sense that Oracle uses the term. Each node has direct access to only that part of the database, referred to as the *local partition*, that is stored on its local disk. Nodes do not have direct access to data in nonlocal partitions.

In a shared nothing environment, database queries that access only data from the local partition execute much faster than queries that require data from a nonlocal node. When data is required from a nonlocal partition, the DBMS software transmits a query for that data to the remote node owning the partition in question. That node then executes the query, retrieves the data, and sends the results back to the requesting node. IBM's DB2/6000 Parallel Edition, Informix's Extended Parallel Server, and NCR's Teradata are based on this architecture.

 Oracle's parallel processing implementation is *not* based on the shared nothing architecture.

Oracle's Parallel Processing Architecture

Oracle's parallel features fall into two broad categories: parallel execution and parallel server. Table 2-1 shows which parallel features are available under each combination of hardware and software architecture that Oracle supports. Oracle's parallel processing features are available on all parallel hardware architectures. Table 2-1 provides examples of specific hardware architectures in each type. Oracle runs under many operating systems, including Windows NT, Alpha VMS, and variations of Unix.

Table 2-1. Availability of Oracle's Parallel Processing Features on Different Hardware Architectures

Hardware/Software Architecture	Oracle Parallel Server?	Parallel Execution?	Vendor Platform Examples
SMP/shared everything	No	Yes	IBM RS/6000 Sun Enterprise 4500 SGI Origin 2000 HP 9000 Windows NT
Cluster/shared disk	Yes	Yes	HP 9000 S800 Cluster IBM RS/6000 HACMP Cluster Sun Ultra Enterprise PDB Cluster Pentium-based NT Clusters

Table 2-1. Availability of Oracle's Parallel Processing Features on Different Hardware Architectures (continued)

Hardware/Software Architecture	Oracle Parallel Server?	Parallel Execution?	Vendor Platform Examples
MPP/shared disk	Yes	Yes	IBM RS/6000 SP Siemens MPP RM1000
NUMA/shared everything	No	Yes	IBM NUMA-Q
NUMA cluster/shared disk	Yes	Yes	IBM NUMA-Q Cluster

Oracle Parallel Server (OPS) requires either a clustered system or an MPP system, because it uses a shared disk configuration. OPS is available for several Unix-based clusters and MPP systems. It also is available for Windows NT clusters. In addition, OPS runs on NUMA clusters such as IBM's NUMA-Q. All major vendors, including Sun Microsystems, IBM, and HP, have platforms for which OPS is available.

Oracle's parallel execution features are available on all types of parallel hardware architectures. Parallel execution works on both shared everything and shared disk software architectures. SMP and NUMA systems easily support parallel execution with their multiple processors. On MPP and clustered systems, any nodes that are themselves SMP systems also can take advantage of parallel execution. Chapter 13, *Parallel Execution in OPS*, discusses the details of parallel execution in an OPS environment.

II

Oracle Parallel Execution

This part of the book focuses on Oracle's parallel execution features and will help you exploit the power of a multiple-CPU system to provide both speedup and scalability. It consists of the following chapters:

- Chapter 3, *Parallel Execution Concepts*, presents an overview of Oracle's various parallel execution features (parallel query, parallel DML and DDL, parallel data loading, parallel recovery, and parallel replication propagation).

- Chapter 4, *Using Parallel Execution*, describes specifically how to invoke and use the Oracle parallel execution features introduced in Chapter 3.

- Chapter 5, *Monitoring and Tuning Parallel Execution*, explains how you can get the best performance out of Oracle's parallel execution features.

3

Parallel Execution Concepts

This chapter presents Oracle's parallel execution (sometimes known as parallel SQL) features: parallel query, parallel DML, parallel DDL, and several other types of parallel operations. If implemented effectively, parallel operations can significantly improve the performance of data-intensive jobs. The decision to execute an operation in parallel is made by Oracle at runtime and is mostly transparent to programmers and end users.

Oracle's parallel execution features are different from the features provided by Oracle Parallel Server (OPS). You don't need OPS to perform parallel SQL execution. However, parallel SQL execution can work in conjunction with OPS, and some aspects of parallel execution apply only to Oracle Parallel Server. Throughout this chapter, unless we note otherwise, we are dealing with parallel SQL operations in a standalone instance environment. Part III of this book discusses OPS; in particular, Chapter 13, *Parallel Execution in OPS*, deals with parallel execution in an OPS environment.

What Is Parallel SQL?

When a user connects to an Oracle instance, a process referred to as a *server process*, or *shadow process*, starts on the database server. The purpose of this shadow process is to perform the operations requested by the user process. When the user executes a SQL statement, the corresponding shadow process performs the necessary tasks to get the result. In a serial execution environment, all the tasks are performed by a single process (the shadow process), as shown in Figure 3-1.

Things are different in a parallel execution environment. In a parallel execution environment, the tasks involved in executing a SQL statement are divided among multiple processes, which work together to complete the execution faster. These multiple processes are referred to as *slave processes*. Figure 3-2 illustrates parallel execution.

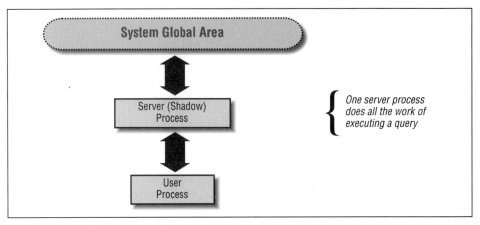

Figure 3-1. Serial statement execution

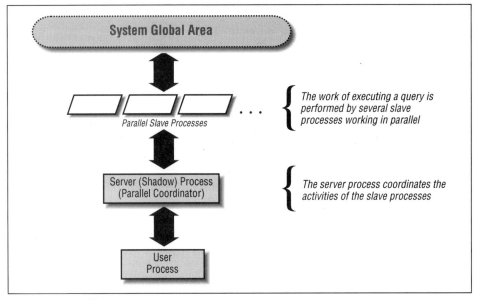

Figure 3-2. Parallel statement execution

Symmetric Multiprocessing (SMP) systems, Massively Parallel Processing (MPP) systems, and clustered systems benefit significantly from executing SQL statements in parallel, because they allow tasks to be spread across the multiple CPUs available in these systems. You can use parallel SQL on single-CPU machines too. However, multiple parallel processes working on behalf of one SQL statement would contend for the same CPU and ultimately might result in poor performance.

Parallel SQL was first introduced in Oracle7 (release 7.1) as the Oracle Parallel Query Option (PQO). PQO is a separately installable option in Oracle7 and helps in parallelizing queries (SELECT statements). With the release of Oracle8, PQO was incorporated into the core RDBMS product and now gets installed along with it. In addition, the parallel execution feature was enhanced to add support for more parallel operations. The full list of Oracle parallel execution features currently includes the following:

Parallel query

The ability to break up the execution of a SELECT statement into multiple tasks and then to execute those tasks in parallel using multiple processors

Parallel data loading

The ability to run multiple SQL*Loader sessions in parallel, which all load data into the same table

Parallel DML

The ability to parallelize INSERT, UPDATE, and DELETE statements

Parallel DDL (object creation)

The ability to parallelize DDL statements such as CREATE TABLE, CREATE INDEX, and ALTER INDEX

Parallel recovery

The ability to use multiple processes to perform instance and media recovery

Parallel replication propagation

The ability to propagate changes from one database to another using multiple processes working together in parallel

In the following sections we'll talk in somewhat more detail about the types of operations that can be parallelized and the benefits that can accrue from parallelization. We'll also include a specific example showing both a statement that benefits from parallelism and a statement that does not.

Operations That Can Be Parallelized

Oracle can parallelize operations that involve processing an entire table or an entire partition. These operations include:

- SQL queries requiring at least one full table scan or queries involving an index range scan spanning multiple partitions

- Operations such as creating or rebuilding an index or rebuilding one or more partitions of an index

- Partition operations such as moving or splitting partitions

- CREATE TABLE AS SELECT operations, if the SELECT involves a full table or partition scan

- INSERT INTO . . . SELECT operations, if the SELECT involves a full table or partition scan

- Update and delete operations on partitioned tables

When Parallel Execution Is Beneficial

Parallel execution of SQL statements is not beneficial in all circumstances. To gain
a benefit from parallelization, one or more of the following must apply:

The host computer has spare CPU and memory capacity
Oracle parallellizes a SQL statement by breaking it down into smaller units,
assigning each unit to a slave process, and executing all of the units in parallel. Each of these slave processes needs CPU and memory resources in order to
run. We recommend not using parallel execution when your system is running
at full CPU or memory utilization. Doing so will cause memory and CPU bottlenecks as a result of competition for these resources by the slave processes.

The data being accessed is spread across multiple disk drives
Multiple parallel slave processes can simultaneously read data from multiple
disks without having to compete with one another. If the data being accessed
resides on a single disk, then all of the parallel slave processes working on this
data will contend for that same disk, and I/O bottlenecks will occur.

Jobs are long running or resource intensive
Executing a SQL statement in parallel involves some overhead. The coordinator process must divide up the work of executing the statement among two or
more slave processes. It then must collect the results from each of those slave
processes and combine them. All of these operations add to the burden of executing the query. For SQL statements that already execute quickly, the overhead involved in parallelizing them will exceed the savings. It's the long-
running and resource-intensive queries that benefit most from being executed
in parallel.

Examples of Parallelism's Impact on Performance

Let's look at some examples that demonstrate the effect of parallel execution on
performance. You will see that while parallel execution is not always beneficial
when small amounts of data are involved, it can improve performance for queries
involving a large amount of data.

The following example shows the DEGREE setting for the customers table, as well
as the elapsed time needed to execute a query to count the number of records in
the table. The DEGREE setting determines the number of parallel slave processes
to be used to execute the query in parallel. The section later in this chapter titled
"The Degree of Parallelism" discusses the DEGREE setting (and how it is set) in
more detail. For example:

```
SQL> SELECT degree
  2  FROM user_tables
  3  WHERE table_name = 'CUSTOMERS';

DEGREE
----------
         1
```

```
SQL> SELECT COUNT(*) FROM customers;
  COUNT(*)
----------
       984
Elapsed: 00:00:00.09
```

The customers table is small and won't be accessed in parallel because DEGREE is set to 1. The COUNT(*) query on this table returned a result in 0.09 seconds.

Now, let's enable parallel query for the customers table and see what difference that makes on execution time. We'll set the table's DEGREE parameter to 4 (via the ALTER TABLE statement), thus requesting the use of four parallel slave processes. Notice the effect on elapsed execution time:

```
SQL> ALTER TABLE customers PARALLEL(DEGREE 4);
Table altered.

SQL> SELECT degree FROM user_tables
       WHERE table_name = 'CUSTOMERS';
    DEGREE
----------
         4

SQL> SELECT COUNT(*) FROM customers;
  COUNT(*)
----------
       984
Elapsed: 00:00:00.18
```

Enabling parallel execution for this small table actually hurts the performance of the query in this example. Using parallel execution and a DEGREE of 4, it takes 0.18 seconds to count the records in the table. That's twice as long as the 0.09 seconds required to count the records when parallel execution was not used. In this case, because the query is so small, the overhead of parallelism is not justified.

Next, let's look at an example in which we query a larger table. This example shows the benefit of parallelism in larger queries. The orders table currently has a DEGREE setting of 1. Note the elapsed time for the COUNT(*) query with serial execution:

```
SQL> SELECT degree FROM user_tables
  2  WHERE table_name = 'ORDERS';
    DEGREE
----------
         1

SQL> SELECT COUNT(*) FROM orders;
  COUNT(*)
----------
   2465726
Elapsed: 00:00:01.32
```

The serial COUNT(*) query takes 1.32 seconds to complete. Now, let's alter the table definition to set DEGREE to 4, thereby requesting that Oracle use four parallel slave processes to execute a query on the table. Note the elapsed time for the parallel COUNT(*) query with DEGREE 4:

```
SQL> ALTER TABLE orders PARALLEL(DEGREE 4);
Table altered.

SQL> SELECT degree FROM user_tables
  2  WHERE table_name = 'ORDERS';
   DEGREE
----------
        4

SQL> SELECT COUNT(*) FROM orders;
  COUNT(*)
----------
   2465726
Elapsed: 00:00:00.74
```

With serial execution, a COUNT(*) query on the orders table returns a result in 1.32 seconds. With parallel execution and with DEGREE set to 4, the same query takes 0.74 seconds. With DEGREE set to 4, 4 parallel processes are used by this query to produce the result. However, it's interesting to notice that the improvement in performance (from 1.32 seconds to 0.74 seconds) is not fourfold. This is because time is spent in splitting the job into four smaller units, assigning each unit of work to a separate process and combining the results. This simple example illustrates the impact of parallelism on performance. However, queries taking only a few seconds to execute may not be ideal candidates for parallel execution in all situations. As discussed in the previous section, long-running queries are the ones that gain maximum advantage from parallel execution.

How Parallel Execution Works

Parallel execution of SQL statements is mostly transparent to end users. Oracle divides the task of executing a SQL statement into multiple smaller units, each of which is executed by a separate process. When parallel execution is used, the user's shadow process takes on the role of the *parallel coordinator*. The parallel coordinator is also referred to as parallel execution coordinator or query coordinator. The parallel coordinator does the following:

1. Dynamically divides the work into smaller units that can be parallelized.

2. Acquires a sufficient number of parallel processes to execute the individual smaller units. These parallel processes are called *parallel slave processes*. They also are sometimes referred to as *parallel execution server processes, parallel server processes, parallel query slaves*, or simply *slave processes*. The most

common of the terms, parallel slave processes and slave processes, are used throughout this book.

3. Assigns each unit of work to a slave process.

4. Collects and combines the results from the slave processes, and returns those results to the user process.

5. Releases the slave processes after the work is done.

The Pool of Parallel Slave Processes

Oracle maintains a pool of parallel slave processes for each instance. The parallel coordinator for a SQL statement assigns parallel tasks to slave processes from this pool. These parallel slave processes remain assigned to a task until its execution is complete. After that, these processes return to the pool and can be assigned tasks from some other parallel operation. A parallel slave process serves only one SQL statement at a time.

The following parameters control the number of parallel slave processes in the pool:

PARALLEL_MIN_SERVERS

Specifies the minimum number of parallel slave processes for an instance. When an instance starts up, it creates the specified number of parallel slave processes. The default value for this parameter is 0, meaning that no slave processes would be created at startup.

PARALLEL_MAX_SERVERS

Specifies the maximum number of parallel slave processes that an instance is allowed to have at one time. The default value for PARALLEL_MAX_SERVERS is platform-specific.

PARALLEL_SERVER_IDLE_TIME

Sets a limit on the amount of time that a slave process can remain idle before it is terminated. This is specified in minutes. Oracle terminates any parallel slave processes that remain idle for the period of time specified by this parameter. The default value for PARALLEL_SERVER_IDLE_TIME is platform-specific.

Oracle manages parallel slave processes within the limits specified by these three parameters. The number of slave processes in the pool will always be at least that specified by PARALLEL_MIN_SERVERS. More slave processes will be created as necessary, until the maximum specified by PARALLEL_MAX_SERVERS is reached. Excess slave processes will die off as their lifetime exceeds that specified by PARALLEL_SERVER_IDLE_TIME. However, regardless of the idle time setting, the number of slave processes will not be allowed to drop below PARALLEL_MIN_ SERVERS.

The default value for PARALLEL_SERVER_IDLE_TIME is platform-specific, and this default value is adequate for most applications. In Oracle8*i*, this parameter has been made obsolete and the platform-specific default value is maintained internally by Oracle. Oracle terminates idle parallel slave processes based on this internally set threshold time.

It takes time and resources to create parallel slave processes. Since parallel slave processes can serve only one statement at a time, you should set PARALLEL_MIN_SERVERS to a relatively high value if you need to run lots of parallel statements concurrently. That way, performance won't suffer from the need to constantly create slave processes.

You also need to consider how to set PARALLEL_MAX_SERVERS. Each parallel slave process consumes memory. Setting PARALLEL_MAX_SERVERS too high may lead to memory shortages during peak usage times. On the other hand, if PARALLEL_MAX_SERVERS is set too low, some operations may not get a sufficient number of parallel slave processes.

The Degree of Parallelism

The number of parallel slave processes associated with an operation is called its *degree of parallelism*. Don't confuse this term with the DEGREE keyword. They aren't exactly the same thing. In Oracle, the degree of parallelism consists of two components—the number of instances to use and the number of slave processes to use on each instance. In Oracle's SQL syntax, the keywords INSTANCES and DEGREE are always used to specify values for these two components as follows:

INSTANCES
    Specifies the number of instances to use

DEGREE
    Specifies the number of slave processes to use on each instance

INSTANCES applies only to the Oracle Parallel Server configuration. Unless you are using OPS, the value of INSTANCES should be set to 1; any other value is meaningless. Parallel SQL execution in an OPS environment is discussed in Chapter 13.

The degree of parallelism used for a SQL statement can be specified at three different levels:

Statement level
    Using hints or the PARALLEL clause

Object level

Found in the definition of the table, index, or other object

Instance level

Using default values for the instance

Oracle determines the degree of parallelism to use for a SQL statement by checking each item in this list in the order shown. Oracle first checks for a degree of parallelism specification at the statement level. If it can't find one, it then checks the table or index definition. If the table or index definition does not explicitly specify values for DEGREE and INSTANCES, Oracle uses the default values established for the instance.

The values you specify for DEGREE and INSTANCES can be either integers or the keyword DEFAULT. The keyword DEFAULT tells Oracle to use the default value for the instance.

Specifying the degree of parallelism at the statement level

You can specify the degree of parallelism at the statement level by using hints or by using a PARALLEL clause. PARALLEL and PARALLEL_INDEX hints are used to specify the degree of parallelism used for queries and DML statements. However, DDL statements that support parallel execution provide an explicit PARALLEL clause in their syntax.

In the following example, the PARALLEL hint specifies the degree of parallelism in a SELECT statement. The hint asks Oracle to scan the orders table in parallel using four parallel slave processes, all running on one instance. The hint will override any DEGREE and INSTANCES settings in the table definition and also will override the default degree of parallelism for the instance:

```
SELECT /*+ PARALLEL(orders,4,1) */
COUNT(*)
FROM orders;
```

Chapter 4, *Using Parallel Execution*, discusses hints and the PARALLEL clause in more detail.

Specifying the degree of parallelism at the object definition level

You can specify the degree of parallelism to use for a table or an index when you create it. You do that by using the PARALLEL clause of the CREATE TABLE and CREATE INDEX statements. For example:

```
CREATE TABLE customers
    .
    .
    .
PARALLEL (DEGREE 4 INSTANCES 2);
```

You also can specify a PARALLEL clause when you alter a table or an index. The following ALTER command changes the order_items table to have a default DEGREE value of 6 and a default INSTANCES value of 1:

```
ALTER TABLE order_items PARALLEL (DEGREE 6 INSTANCES 1);
```

When you specify DEGREE and INSTANCES values at the table or index level, those values are used for all SQL statements involving the table or index unless overridden by a hint.

Specifying the degree of parallelism at the instance level

Each instance has associated with it a set of default values for DEGREE and INSTANCES. The default DEGREE value is either the number of CPUs available or the number of disks upon which a table or index is stored, whichever is less. The default INSTANCES value is controlled by the PARALLEL_DEFAULT_MAX_ INSTANCES initialization parameter.

> The PARALLEL_DEFAULT_MAX_INSTANCES parameter is obsolete in Oracle8*i*. Oracle decides the default INSTANCES value based on PARALLEL_INSTANCE_GROUP. PARALLEL_INSTANCE_GROUP is discussed in Chapter 13.

Oracle will use the instance-level defaults whenever the keyword DEFAULT is used in a hint or in a table or index definition. Oracle also will use the instance-level defaults when there are no hints and when no degree of parallelism has been specified at the table or index level.

The actual degree of parallelism

In previous sections, we discussed how you can specify the degree of parallelism. Oracle, however, doesn't always honor the degree of parallelism that you request. While the parallel coordinator requests the specified number of parallel slave processes, the actual number of parallel processes used for an operation depends upon the availability of these slave processes. The PARALLEL_MAX_SERVERS parameter sets an upper limit on the number of parallel slave processes that an instance can have. Since you can't create new parallel slave processes once that limit is reached, it's possible that not enough of these parallel slave processes will be available to supply the number requested by a given statement. If a statement doesn't get the requested number of parallel slave processes, one of the following will happen:

- If no parallel slave processes are available, the statement will run serially.

- If fewer than the requested number of slave processes are available, then Oracle will either return an error or execute the statement with fewer than the requested number of slave processes.

The PARALLEL_MIN_PERCENT parameter is the key to making the decision about whether to run a statement with fewer than the requested number of slave processes. PARALLEL_MIN_PERCENT specifies a minimum percentage of parallel slave processes that must be available in order for a statement to run with a reduced degree of parallelism. As long as the number of available slave processes exceeds this percentage, the statement will execute. Otherwise, the statement will fail and Oracle will return an error.

Parallel Execution in an MTS Environment

In a dedicated server architecture, a dedicated server process works on behalf of a user process. Under parallel execution, this shadow process takes the role of parallel coordinator. In a multithreaded server (MTS) architecture, a shared server process works on behalf of the user process. This shared server process then acts as the parallel coordinator during parallel execution, as illustrated in Figure 3-3. All other aspects of parallel execution are the same under MTS as in a dedicated server architecture.

Intra-Operation and Inter-Operation Parallelism

A SQL statement may consist of more than one operation that can be parallelized. For example, if a statement doing a full table scan has an ORDER BY clause, there will be two parallel operations: the scan operation and the sort operation. Oracle not only allows an operation to be executed by multiple parallel processes, it also allows multiple operations from one SQL statement to be executed simultaneously. Execution of a single SQL operation using multiple parallel processes is referred to as *intra-operational parallelism*. Execution of multiple operations from one SQL statement simultaneously is referred to as *inter-operational parallelism*. Examples of SQL statements in which inter-operation parallelism occurs include those involving ORDER BY, GROUP BY, hash joins, and sort-merge joins.

Let's look at an example that illustrates both inter-operational and intra-operational parallelism. The following statement contains an ORDER BY clause and has two operations that can be parallelized: the sort and the table scan. For example:

```
SELECT * FROM customers ORDER BY cust_name;
```

Assuming that the degree of parallelism is set to 4, Figure 3-4 depicts the inter-operational and intra-operational parallelism for this example. Four parallel slave

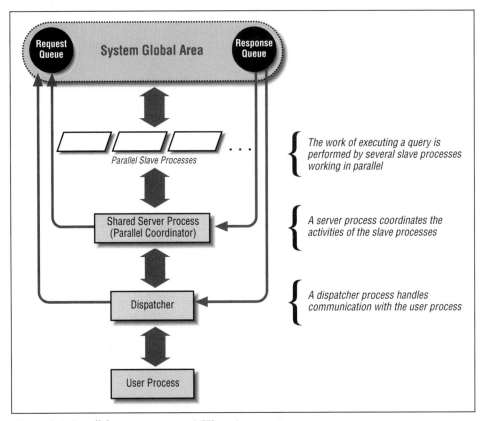

Figure 3-3. Parallel execution in an MTS environment

processes are used for scanning the table, and four more are used to perform the sort. These two sets of parallel slave processes form a producer-consumer relationship. The parallel slave processes scanning the table act as producers, and the parallel slave processes sorting the rows act as consumers.

As soon as the producers start producing rows from the table scan, the consumers can start sorting those rows. Thus, the scanning and sorting operations can execute in parallel. The parallelization of the individual scan and sort operations using multiple slave processes is a case of intra-operational parallelism. However, performing multiple operations, such as scanning and sorting, in parallel is a case of inter-operational parallelism.

Note that the output of the producers gets redistributed among all the consumers. As Figure 3-4 illustrates, the output of all of the slave processes involved in the scan operation is fed collectively as input into the slave processes performing the sort. Oracle divides the sort operation into four ranges and assigns one range to each parallel slave process. Each slave process then takes the input that falls within its range and sorts it.

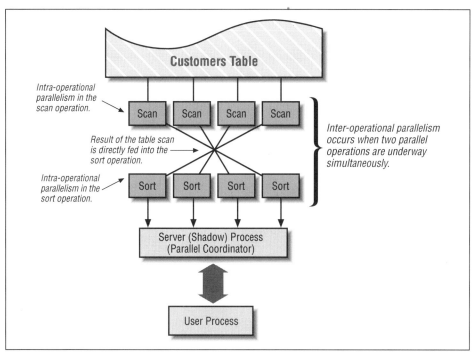

Figure 3-4. Intra-operational and inter-operational parallelism

 Don't confuse the inter-query and intra-query parallelism discussed in Chapter 1, *Introduction,* with the inter-operational and intra-operational parallelism discussed here. Oracle's parallel execution is an implementation of intra-query parallelism.

When inter-operational parallelism is occurring, Oracle uses two sets of parallel slave processes to execute a SQL statement. Regardless parallel operations in the statement. The number of parallel processes, therefore, will be twice the specified degree of parallelism. If a SQL statement has three possible parallel operations, the parallel slave processes will execute the first two parallel operations using the two sets of slave processes. After the first operation is complete, the first set of slave processes will execute the third parallel operation.

4

In this chapter:
- *Parallel Query*
- *Parallel DML*
- *Parallel DDL*
- *Parallel Data Loading*
- *Parallel Recovery*
- *Parallel Replication Propagation*

Using Parallel Execution

In Chapter 3, *Parallel Execution Concepts*, we introduced Oracle's parallel execution features and talked about the concepts behind how they work. These features include:

- Parallel query

- Parallel DML

- Parallel DDL

- Parallel data loading

- Parallel recovery

- Parallel replication propagation

In this chapter, we'll describe how to use each of these features and show you how to take advantage of them. Most of these features come with a list of restrictions and caveats that may affect your ability to use them in a given situation. We'll describe those as well.

Throughout this chapter, we assume that you're familiar with the basic Oracle features being discussed. This isn't, for example, a tutorial on recovery or replication. The focus is always on the parallel features that can be applied to the task at hand. If you're familiar with DML and DDL, for example, you won't have any problem following the discussion of how to parallelize those types of statements. The same is true for the other types of operations covered in this chapter.

Parallel Query

Parallel query is the most commonly used of Oracle's parallel execution features. It was the first parallel execution feature to be developed by Oracle and was introduced in Oracle7 (release 7.1) as the Oracle Parallel Query Option (PQO). Parallel execution can significantly reduce the elapsed time for large queries, but it doesn't apply to every query. To parallelize a SELECT statement, the following conditions must be met:

- At least one of the tables is accessed through a full table scan, or an index is accessed through a range scan involving multiple partitions.

- If the execution involves a full table scan, the statement must contain a PARALLEL hint specifying the corresponding table, or the corresponding table must have a parallel declaration in its definition.

- If the execution involves an index range scan spanning multiple partitions, the statement must contain a PARALLEL_INDEX hint specifying the corresponding index, or the corresponding index must have a parallel declaration in its definition.

The following two sections explain how the degree of parallelism is chosen for a SELECT statement and discuss restrictions on the use of the parallel query feature.

Setting the Degree of Parallelism

Once Oracle decides to execute a SELECT statement in parallel, the degree of parallelism is determined by following precedence rules:

1. Oracle retrieves the DEGREE and INSTANCES specifications from the definition of all tables and indexes involved in the query and chooses the highest values found for those settings.

2. Oracle checks the statement for a parallel hint. If such a hint is found, the hint overrides the degree of parallelism obtained as a result of the previous step.

You can use the PARALLEL and PARALLEL_INDEX hints to specify the degree of parallelism for a SELECT statement. You can use the NOPARALLEL and NOPARALLEL_INDEX hints to ensure that parallel execution is not performed for the SELECT.

The PARALLEL hint controls the degree of parallelism applied to tables accessed by a query and takes this form:

```
/*+ PARALLEL (table_name[, degree[, instances]]) */
```

where:

table_name
> Is the name of the table on which to parallelize operations

degree
> Specifies the number of parallel slave processes that each instance should use when performing operations on this table

instances
> Is the number of instances to be used for parallel operations on the table

The scope of the PARALLEL hint is the SELECT statement in which it appears. Subsequent SQL statements are not affected.

The PARALLEL_INDEX hint does for indexes what the PARALLEL hint does for tables. It can be used with SELECT statements to enable parallelized index range scans for partitioned indexes. The hint takes this form:

```
/*+ PARALLEL_INDEX (table_name[, index_name
                    [, degree[, instances]]]) */
```

where:

table_name
> Is the name of the table on which to parallelize operations

index_name
> Is the name of the partitioned index on which to parallelize an index range scan

degree
> Specifies the number of parallel slave processes that each instance should use when performing operations on this index

instances
> Is the number of instances to be used for parallel operations on the index

The scope of the PARALLEL_INDEX hint is the SQL statement in which it appears. It also applies only to partitioned indexes and only when range scans are being performed on those indexes.

The values for *degree* and *instances* can be either integers or the keyword DEFAULT. DEFAULT tells Oracle to use the default value for the instance.

Let's look at some examples that demonstrate how hints are used to specify the degree of parallelism. The following example shows a hint that tells Oracle to scan the orders table in parallel using four parallel slave processes on one instance only. The hint will override any DEGREE and INSTANCES specifications in the table definition and also will override the default degree of parallelism for the instance:

```
SELECT /*+ PARALLEL(orders,4,1) */
       COUNT(*)
FROM orders;
```

The next example uses a PARALLEL_INDEX hint that calls for a parallel index range scan of the partitioned index named orders_uk. This parallel range scan will be performed with four parallel slave processes, with two instances each running two parallel slave processes:

```
SELECT /*+ PARALLEL_INDEX(orders,orders_uk,2,2) */
       COUNT(*)
FROM orders;
```

Here's an example that specifies only a *degree* value in the hint. Since no value is specified for *instances*, the default value from the table definition will be used. If the table definition does not have an INSTANCES specification or if the value is DEFAULT, then *instances* will pick up the instance-level default value. (See the section "The Degree of Parallelism" in Chapter 3 for a discussion of statement-level, table-level, and instance-level default values.) For example:

```
SELECT /*+ PARALLEL(orders,4) */
       COUNT(*)
FROM orders;
```

In the following example, the PARALLEL hint tells Oracle to scan the orders table in parallel. Since no *degree* and *instances* values are specified, Oracle will pick up those values from the table's definition. If they weren't defined at the table level, Oracle will use the instance-level default values:

```
SELECT /*+ PARALLEL(orders) */
       COUNT(*)
FROM orders;
```

In the following example, the hint tells Oracle to scan the orders table in parallel using the default number of instances and using six slave processes on each instance. When you specify DEFAULT for either *degree* or *instances* in a hint, Oracle ignores the values in the table definition and uses the instance-level values. Since DEFAULT is specified in the example for *instances*, Oracle will use the instance-level value here:

```
SELECT /*+ PARALLEL(orders, 6, DEFAULT) */ COUNT(*)
FROM orders;
```

You can turn off parallel operations for a statement using the NOPARALLEL hint. The NOPARALLEL hint takes this form:

```
/*+ NOPARALLEL (table_name) */
```

where *table_name* is the name of the table.

The following example includes the NOPARALLEL hint, ensuring that the customers table will not be accessed in parallel:

```
SELECT /*+ NOPARALLEL(customers) */ customer_id, location, name
FROM customers;
```

If an index has a parallel specification in its definition, and you want to avoid a parallel index scan operation, you can use a NOPARALLEL_INDEX hint to achieve this goal. The NOPARALLEL_INDEX hint takes this form:

```
/*+ NOPARALLEL_INDEX (table_name[,index_name]) */
```

where:

table_name
> Is the name of the table

index_name
> Is the name of the index

Restrictions on Parallel Query

Oracle can parallelize individual SELECT statements, and it can parallelize subqueries that appear in SELECT statements, other DML statements, or DDL statements. Parallelizing a SELECT statement has the following restrictions:

- If the DDL or DML statement references a remote object, the query part can't be parallelized.

- If a query involves joins and sorts on tables having object types, the query will not be parallelized if the object definitions do not have a MAP function.

- Queries on nested tables can't be parallelized.

If you ask Oracle to execute a query in parallel, and it can't run in parallel because of these restrictions, Oracle will run the query serially without raising any error or warning.

Parallel DML

Data Manipulation Language (DML) operations such as INSERT, UPDATE, and DELETE can be parallelized by Oracle. Parallel execution can speed up large DML operations and is particularly advantageous in data warehousing environments where it's necessary to maintain large summary or historical tables. In OLTP systems, parallel DML sometimes can be used to improve the performance of long-running batch jobs.

Deciding to Parallelize a DML Statement

When you issue a DML statement such as an INSERT, UPDATE, or DELETE, Oracle applies a set of rules to determine whether that statement can be parallelized. For UPDATE and DELETE statements, the rules are identical. INSERT statements, however, have their own set of rules.

To parallelize DML (INSERT, UPDATE, and DELETE) statements, you must enable parallel DML. Refer to the section later in this chapter titled "Enabling Parallel DML" for details.

UPDATE and DELETE statements

Oracle can parallelize UPDATE and DELETE statements on partitioned tables, but only when multiple partitions are involved. You cannot parallelize UPDATE or DELETE operations on a nonpartitioned table or when such operations affect only a single partition. If such a statement includes a subquery, then the decision to parallelize the UPDATE or DELETE operation is made independently of the decision to parallelize the subquery.

UPDATE or DELETE operations are parallelized only if the table being updated or deleted has a parallel specification or if a PARALLEL hint is included after the UPDATE or DELETE keyword in the statement.

INSERT statements

Standard INSERT statements using a VALUES clause cannot be parallelized. Oracle can parallelize only INSERT . . . SELECT . . . FROM statements. The decision to parallelize the INSERT operation is made independently from the decision to parallelize the SELECT operation.

The INSERT operation can be parallelized only if the table being inserted into has a parallel specification or if a PARALLEL hint is included after the INSERT keyword in the statement.

Setting the Degree of Parallelism

As we discussed in Chapter 3, the degree of parallelism can be specified at the statement level, the object definition level, or the instance level. The PARALLEL and PARALLEL_INDEX hints discussed in relation to the SELECT statements apply to other DML statements as well. The following sections describe the rules used to determine the degree of parallelism for DML statements.

UPDATE and DELETE statements

The degree of parallelism to use for an UPDATE or DELETE statement is determined by the following precedence rules:

1. Oracle first retrieves the DEGREE and INSTANCES specifications from the definition of the target table.

2. If the statement contains a parallel hint associated with the UPDATE or DELETE, the hint overrides the specification in the table definition.

The number of partitions in the target table determines the maximum degree of parallelism achievable, because while one parallel slave process can update or delete multiple partitions, only one slave process can update any specific partition. If the specified degree of parallelism is less than the number of partitions, then some parallel slave processes work on more than one partition. As soon as a slave process finishes work on one partition, it will take up one of the remaining partitions. This process continues until the work on the statement is complete. If the specified degree of parallelism is more than the number of partitions targeted, the extra parallel slave processes will sit idle.

INSERT statements

Remember that the only type of INSERT statement that Oracle can parallelize is the INSERT . . . SELECT . . . FROM statement. When Oracle parallelizes such an INSERT statement, the same degree of parallelism is always applied to both the INSERT and the SELECT parts of the statement. The degree of parallelism is determined by the following precedence rules:

1. Oracle retrieves the DEGREE and INSTANCES specifications from all the tables and indexes involved in the SELECT part of the statement. Oracle then chooses the maximum values for those two settings.

2. The DEGREE and INSTANCES specifications from the table into which rows are being inserted overrides the degree of parallelism obtained from Step 1.

3. If the INSERT part of the statement contains a parallel hint, that hint overrides the degree of parallelism obtained from Step 2.

Enabling Parallel DML

Oracle's parallel DML features are not enabled by default. Before you can execute DML statements in parallel, you must enable the parallel DML feature. You do this at the session level, using the following ALTER SESSION command:

```
ALTER SESSION ENABLE PARALLEL DML;
```

After enabling parallel DML support at the session level, you can issue DML statements that execute in parallel. In order for parallel execution to actually occur, at least one of the following must be true:

- The target table in your DML statement must have values greater than 1 for its DEGREE and/or INSTANCES specifications.

- The DML statement must include a parallel hint.

UPDATE and DELETE statements can be parallelized for partitioned tables only.

If a session has pending transactions, you can't enable or disable parallel DML in the session. For example, in a SQL*Plus session you will see the following error message shown in the following example if you attempt to alter the session to enable (or disable) parallel DML within a transaction:

```
SQL> UPDATE emp SET COMM = 100 WHERE empno = 7369;

1 row updated.

SQL> ALTER SESSION ENABLE PARALLEL DML;
ERROR:
ORA-12841: cannot alter the session parallel DML state within a transaction
```

The enabling or disabling of parallel DML in a session does not affect parallel DDL statements nor does it affect parallel SELECT statements. You can execute parallel DDL statements and parallel SELECT statements in a session, regardless of whether parallel DML is enabled or disabled.

Parallel DML Transactions

Transactions involving parallel DML statements differ from those involving only serial statements in at least three areas:

- The visibility of changes made by parallel DML statements

- The amount of rollback information generated

- The number of locks held

Normally, when you use DML statements in a transaction to change data in the database, those changes are visible to subsequent SELECT statements that participate in the transaction. With parallel DML, that's not the case. The results of parallel DML are not visible to subsequent statements in the same transaction. Not only are the changes not visible, you are not even allowed to select from the tables involved. If you modify (insert, update, or delete) a table using parallel DML, no other query or DML statement (whether serial or parallel) can access the same table in that transaction. Oracle will generate an error if you try to access any table that has been modified previously, in the same transaction, using parallel DML. Here is an example:

```
SQL> ALTER SESSION ENABLE PARALLEL DML;

Session altered.

SQL> INSERT /*+ PARALLEL (emp_temp,4,1) */
  2  INTO emp_temp SELECT * FROM emp;

14 rows created.

SQL> SELECT * FROM emp_temp;
select * from emp_temp
              *
ERROR at line 1:
ORA-12838: cannot read/modify an object after modifying it in parallel
```

Parallel DML statements require more rollback segments than equivalent serial DML statements. When DML statements are executed using parallel DML, each parallel slave process creates a separate transaction within Oracle. In addition, the parallel coordinator also creates a transaction for itself. All of these transactions need rollback segments. Therefore, when you are using parallel DML, the rollback segment requirements are much greater than when you are using serial DML. You need to plan ahead for a sufficient number and size of rollback segments when using parallel DML.

Parallel DML statements also require more locks than serial DML statements. When a DML statement is being executed in parallel, each parallel slave process acquires its own locks on the table being modified. The parallel coordinator also acquires locks on the table. The result is that parallel DML statements hold many more locks than comparable serial DML statements. To compensate for this, when using parallel DML, you should increase the values for the DML_LOCKS and ENQUEUE_ RESOURCES initialization parameters.

Restrictions on Parallel DML

Parallel DML cannot be used in all circumstances. There are a number of restrictions governing when a given statement can be executed in parallel. Certain table types simply do not support parallel operations. There is also a fairly long list of specific cases in which parallel DML is not an option.

Parallel DML is not supported for the following types of tables:

- Clustered tables

- Tables having object columns or LOB (large object) columns

- Index-organized tables

- Nonpartitioned tables when DELETE or UPDATE statements are being executed

---

 INSERT . . . SELECT . . . FROM statements can be performed in parallel even on nonpartitioned tables.

In addition to the restrictions on table types, there are a number of specific situations in which a DML statement cannot be parallelized. The restrictions are the following:

- A DML statement that may fire a trigger on a table cannot be parallelized. You must disable the triggers that may be fired by your DML statement if you want to use parallel DML.

Triggers defined with a WHEN clause are still considered to have fired, even if the WHEN clause prevents the body of the trigger from executing.

- You cannot use parallel DML on tables being replicated.

- A DML statement cannot be parallelized if it encounters any of the following types of table or column constraints:

  — Referential integrity constraints involving DELETE CASCADE

  — Self-referential integrity constraints

  — Deferrable integrity constraints

- A DML statement cannot be parallelized if it modifies or queries a remote object. Also, you cannot access a remote table within a parallel transaction. Here is an example that demonstrates this point:

```
SQL> ALTER SESSION ENABLE PARALLEL DML;

Session altered.

SQL> INSERT /*+ PARALLEL(empx,4) */ INTO empx SELECT * FROM emp;

14 rows created.

SQL> SELECT * FROM dept@test;
SELECT * FROM dept@test
                      *
ERROR at line 1:
ORA-12840: cannot access remote table in a parallel transaction
```

The INSERT statement in this example starts a parallel transaction. The next statement within the transaction accesses the remote table dept@test. This is not allowed and Oracle returns an appropriate error.

- Once you modify a table, regardless of whether it was modified in parallel or serially, you cannot use parallel DML on the same table within the same transaction. For example:

```
SQL> ALTER SESSION ENABLE PARALLEL DML;

Session altered.

SQL> UPDATE empx SET sal = sal * 1.1;

28 rows updated.

SQL> INSERT /*+ PARALLEL(empx,4) */ INTO empx SELECT * FROM emp;
INSERT /*+ PARALLEL(empx,4) */ INTO empx SELECT * FROM emp
                      *
```

```
ERROR at line 1:
ORA-12839: cannot modify an object in parallel after modifying it
```

- Parallel DML cannot be used if the initialization parameter ROW_LOCKING is set to INTENT.

Parallel DDL

Parallel DDL works for both tables and indexes, whether partitioned or nonpartitioned. For nonpartitioned tables and indexes, only the following types of DDL statements can be parallelized:

```
CREATE TABLE...AS SELECT
CREATE INDEX
ALTER INDEX...REBUILD
```

If you're working with partitioned tables and indexes, the scope of Oracle's parallel DDL support broadens. The following statements can be parallelized for partitioned tables and indexes:

```
CREATE TABLE...AS SELECT
ALTER TABLE...MOVE PARTITION
ALTER TABLE...SPLIT PARTITION
CREATE INDEX
ALTER INDEX...REBUILD PARTITION
ALTER INDEX...SPLIT PARTITION
```

Not all tables allow these operations to be executed in parallel. Tables with object columns or LOB columns don't allow parallel DDL.

Setting the Degree of Parallelism

With DDL statements, you do not specify the degree of parallelism using hints. Instead, you use the PARALLEL clause. The PARALLEL clause takes the following form:

```
{NOPARALLEL |
PARALLEL (DEGREE {degree | DEFAULT}
   [INSTANCES {instances | DEFAULT}] )}
```

Here's an example that shows the PARALLEL clause being used in a CREATE INDEX statement. The specified DEGREE is 4, so 4 parallel slave processes will be used to create the index:

```
CREATE INDEX customer_ix ON customers (customer_id)
   TABLESPACE ind01
   STORAGE (INITIAL 100M NEXT 100M PCTINCREASE 0 MAXEXTENTS 20)
   PARALLEL (DEGREE 4);
```

Storage Issues for Parallel DDL

When you create a table or index using parallel DDL, two or more parallel slave processes work on behalf of your statement to create the object. Each parallel slave process creates a temporary segment during the creation process. At the end, the parallel coordinator trims each of these temporary segments to release any free space and then combines these segments into one segment.

When you are using parallel DDL to create an object such as a table or an index, you need to be aware of two issues:

- How space is allocated
- The potential for fragmentation

You should be careful while specifying the storage clause for tables or indexes being created in parallel, because the amount of space allocated may be much greater than what you would otherwise expect. When you create a table or an index using parallel DDL, each parallel slave process allocates space based on the table or index's storage clause. For example, if you create a table with INITIAL 10 MB and a degree of parallelism of 4, then each of the four parallel slave processes allocates an extent of 10 MB. The result is that a total of 40 MB will be allocated for the table during creation.

When you create a table or index using parallel DDL, it is possible to introduce fragmentation into the object during creation. If all the space in the temporary segments allocated by the parallel slave processes is not used, the unused space will be trimmed out of the temporary segments and returned to the database as free space. When the temporary segments are merged, that free space remains in between the extents, causing the table or index to be fragmented.

Parallel Data Loading

Oracle's SQL*Loader utility loads data into Oracle tables from external files. With some restrictions, SQL*Loader supports the loading of data in parallel. If you have a large amount of data to load, SQL*Loader's parallel support can dramatically reduce the elapsed time needed to perform that load.

Initiating Parallel Data Loading

SQL*Loader supports parallel loading by allowing you to initiate multiple concurrent direct path load sessions that all load data into the same table or into the same partition of a partitioned table. Unlike the case when you execute a SQL statement in parallel, the task of dividing up the work falls on your shoulders. Follow these steps to use parallel data loading:

1. Create multiple input datafiles.

2. Create a SQL*Loader control file for each input datafile.

3. Initiate multiple SQL*Loader sessions, one for each control file and datafile pair.

When you initiate the SQL*Loader sessions, you must tell SQL*Loader that you are performing a parallel load. You do that by adding the PARALLEL=TRUE parameter to the SQL*Loader command line. For example, the following commands could be used to initiate a load performed in parallel by four different sessions:

```
SQLLOAD scott/tiger CONTROL=part1.ctl DIRECT=TRUE PARALLEL=TRUE
SQLLOAD scott/tiger CONTROL=part2.ctl DIRECT=TRUE PARALLEL=TRUE
SQLLOAD scott/tiger CONTROL=part3.ctl DIRECT=TRUE PARALLEL=TRUE
SQLLOAD scott/tiger CONTROL=part4.ctl DIRECT=TRUE PARALLEL=TRUE
```

Note that the commands here should be executed from four different operating system sessions. The intent is to get four SQL*Loader sessions going at once, not to run four sessions one at a time. For example, if you are using the Unix operating system, you might open four command-prompt windows and execute one SQL*Loader command in each window.

Another important thing to note here is that you need to use the direct path in order to perform a load in parallel, as explained in the next section. This is achieved by the command-line argument DIRECT=TRUE. Parallel loads are not possible using the conventional path option.

How Parallel Data Loading Works

Parallel loads must be done using the direct path. When you initiate a direct path load, SQL*Loader formats the input data into Oracle data blocks and writes those blocks directly to the datafiles. The blocks are always added above the target table's high-water mark (HWM). Direct path loads bypass SQL command processing, and they bypass the database buffer cache in the SGA. The result is much higher performance than you can get using a conventional path load.

Each parallel load session inserts into the table by allocating one or more new extents, as illustrated in Figure 4-1.

The extents used by SQL*Loader are marked as TEMPORARY during the load process. After the loading is complete, the last loaded extent from each parallel load process is trimmed to release any free space. Then the extents are added to the existing segment of the table or partition above the high-water mark. The HWM is then adjusted to reflect the added data. You need to consider two important issues with respect to parallel data loading:

- Free space below the high-water mark will not be used.

- A table's initial extent can never be used.

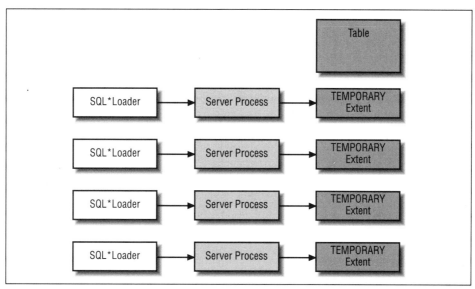

Figure 4-1. Parallel direct path load

Parallel direct path loads do not use any space below the high-water mark. Therefore, if you have significant unused space below the HWM prior to loading, you should consider rebuilding the table in order to reset the HWM before you start the load.

Parallel direct path loads insert data into new extents and do not use any existing extents. Therefore, the initial extent of a table can never be used by a parallel load. If all the data in a table is to come from parallel loads, you should create a very small initial extent in order to conserve disk space. If you feel that you must use the space in the initial extent, you'll have to load the data into the table without using SQL*Loader's parallel feature.

Restrictions on Parallel Data Loading

Parallel direct path loading significantly improves data loading performance. However, that performance improvement comes with a price. The following restrictions apply to parallel direct path loads:

- Indexes are not maintained when a parallel direct path load is performed. You will need to rebuild all indexes on the table being loaded after the load is complete.

- There is no communication between the concurrent load sessions. Therefore, you can only append rows to a table. The TRUNCATE, REPLACE, and INSERT options of SQL*Loader cannot be used for a parallel direct path load.

- All referential integrity and CHECK constraints on the table being loaded must be disabled for the duration of the load.

- All triggers on the table being loaded must be disabled for the duration of the load.

Since parallel data loading uses the direct path, all the restrictions of a direct path load also apply to parallel loads. For example, you can't use direct path loads on clustered tables. Also, the table being loaded must not be involved in any active transactions. For more information on direct path load and its restrictions, please refer to Oracle Corporation's *Oracle8 Utilities* manual.

Improving the Performance of Parallel Loads

There are several things you can do to improve the performance of a parallel load. Consider doing the following:

- Spreading the table to be loaded across multiple disk drives

- Using SQL*Loader's UNRECOVERABLE option

I/O bottlenecks are a prime source of performance degradation. Spreading the data to be loaded across multiple disk drives reduces I/O contention between the load processes and helps ensure that the load process is not limited by the throughput of a single disk. First, you must have multiple datafiles for your table, and these datafiles must be on separate disks. Then you can specify a database filename using the FILE keyword of the OPTIONS clause in the SQL*Loader control file. Note the fourth line in this example:

```
LOAD DATA
INFILE 'load1.dat'
INSERT INTO TABLE emp
OPTIONS (FILE='/u06/oradata/TPRD/data1.dbf')
(empno POSITION(01:04) INTEGER EXTERNAL NULLIF empno=BLANKS
...
```

SQL*Loader then will allocate the extents for each load session in the datafile specified. To maximize throughput, make sure that the control file for each SQL*Loader session specifies a different datafile.

You can specify the UNRECOVERABLE option for the SQL*Loader sessions involved in a parallel load to avoid the generation of redo for that load. This saves a lot of time and redo log space. However, it also makes the table unrecoverable in the event of a media failure. For this reason, you should back up the tables that were loaded after the load completes.

Parallel Recovery

Parallel recovery can speed up both instance recovery and media recovery. In parallel recovery, multiple parallel slave processes are used to perform recovery operations. The SMON background process reads the redo log files, and the parallel slave processes apply the changes to the datafiles. Parallel recovery is most beneficial when several datafiles on different disks are being recovered.

In a serial recovery scenario, the SMON background process both reads the redo log files and applies the changes to the datafiles. This may take a considerably long time when multiple datafiles need to be recovered. However, when parallel recovery is being used, the SMON process is responsible only for reading the redo log files. The changes are applied to the datafiles by multiple parallel slave processes, thereby reducing the recovery time.

Recovery requires that the changes be applied to the datafiles in exactly the same order in which they occurred. This is achieved by single-threading the read phase of the recovery process by the SMON process. SMON reads the redo log files and serializes the changes before dispatching them to the parallel slave processes. The parallel slave processes then apply those changes to the datafiles in the proper order. Therefore, the reading of the redo log files is performed serially even during a parallel recovery operation.

The RECOVERY_PARALLELISM initialization parameter controls the degree of parallelism to use for a recovery. You can override that setting for a specific situation by using the RECOVER command's PARALLEL clause. Both options are described in the following sections.

Specifying the RECOVERY_PARALLELISM Parameter

The initialization parameter RECOVERY_PARALLELISM specifies the number of parallel slave processes to participate in a recovery process. It applies to both instance recovery and media recovery. A value of 0 or 1 indicates serial recovery—no parallelism will be used. The RECOVERY_PARALLELISM parameter setting cannot exceed the PARALLEL_MAX_SERVERS setting.

Specifying the PARALLEL Clause

The PARALLEL clause can be used with the RECOVER command to parallelize media recovery. You use it to specify the degree or the number of parallel slave processes that will be used. The syntax for the PARALLEL clause is discussed in the "Parallel DDL" section of this chapter. You can use the PARALLEL clause with the RECOVER DATABASE, RECOVER TABLESPACE, and RECOVER DATAFILE commands. Here are some examples:

```
RECOVER DATABASE PARALLEL (DEGREE d INSTANCES DEFAULT);
RECOVER TABLESPACE tablespace_name PARALLEL (DEGREE d INSTANCES i);
RECOVER DATAFILE 'datafile_name' PARALLEL (DEGREE d);
RECOVER DATABASE PARALLEL (DEGREE DEFAULT);
```

When you specify DEFAULT for DEGREE, it takes a value equal to twice the number of datafiles being recovered. When you specify DEFAULT for INSTANCES, it takes the instance-level default value specified by the initialization parameter PARALLEL_DEFAULT_MAX_INSTANCES.

The specification in the PARALLEL clause used with the RECOVER command overrides any RECOVER_PARALLELISM parameter setting. If you've enabled parallel recovery by setting RECOVER_PARALLELISM, you can disable it for a specific recovery operation by using the RECOVER command's NOPARALLEL clause. For example:

```
RECOVER DATABASE NOPARALLEL;
```

In this case, since you used the NOPARALLEL keyword, the recovery would be done serially.

Parallel Replication Propagation

Oracle provides replication mechanisms allowing you to maintain copies of database objects in multiple databases. Changes are propagated among these databases over database links. The SNP (snapshot) background processes perform the replication process. For large volumes of replicated data, parallel propagation can be used to enhance throughput.

With serial replication, Oracle propagates replicated transactions one at a time in the same order in which they are committed in the source database. With parallel propagation, Oracle enlists multiple parallel slave processes to propagate replicated transactions using multiple parallel streams. Oracle orders the dependent transactions properly based on the System Change Number (SCN). During parallel propagation, you can see multiple connections to the destination database.

You enable parallel replication propagation at the database link level. A database link is created for a particular destination database. When you enable parallel propagation for a database link, Oracle uses multiple parallel slave processes to replicate to the corresponding destination. If you're using Replication Manager, edit the property sheet for the link, enable the "Parallel Propagation" setting, and then specify the desired degree of parallelism in the "Processes" field.

To enable parallel replication propagation from the SQL*Plus command line, you need to use the Oracle built-in package DBMS_DEFER_SYS. Execute the DBMS_

DEFER_SYS.SCHEDULE_PUSH procedure for the destination database link, and pass the desired degree of parallelism as the value for the parallelism argument. The following shows an example of setting the degree of parallelism for replication propagation using the DBMS_DEFER_SYS.SCHEDULE_PUSH procedure:

```
SQL> EXECUTE DBMS_DEFER_SYS.SCHEDULE_PUSH (-
> DESTINATION => 'finprod.world', -
> INTERVAL => 'SYSDATE+1/24', -
> NEXT_DATE => 'SYSDATE+1/24', -
> PARALLELISM => 6);
```

This example sets the degree of parallelism to 6 for propagating to the "finprod. world" destination database. It also specifies the time when the first propagation will start (NEXT_DATE) and the frequency of propagation (INTERVAL). For a detailed discussion of replication, refer to *Oracle Distributed Systems* by Charles Dye (O'Reilly & Associates, 1999).

5

Monitoring and Tuning Parallel Execution

Parallel execution can significantly reduce the processing time required for queries and other SQL statements, but only if it is properly implemented and tuned. You must monitor and tune the performance of parallel execution in your environment on a regular basis. In this chapter you'll learn about the various tools and procedures at your disposal for monitoring the parallel execution performance of a database. You'll also find some tuning tips and information on some important Oracle8i enhancements related to parallel execution performance.

Tuning Overview

Oracle tuning in general is a very large area, but when you focus strictly on parallel execution, there are only a few tuning-related adjustments that you can make. These include:

- Changing the PARALLEL_MIN_SERVERS initialization parameter, which controls the minimum number of parallel slave processes maintained in the parallel slave process pool

- Changing the PARALLEL_MAX_SERVERS initialization parameter, which controls the maximum number of parallel slave processes maintained in the parallel slave process pool

- Changing the PARALLEL_SERVER_IDLE_TIME initialization parameter, which controls the amount of time a slave process is kept around when it's not being used

- Changing the degree of parallelism, using the DEGREE and INSTANCES keywords, for either a statement or a table

- Changing your statements to avoid "parallel from serial" bottlenecks (i.e., those caused by your execution plan's having to perform the PARALLEL_FROM_ SERIAL step, described in the discussion of EXPLAIN PLAN later in this chapter)

- Using Oracle8*i*'s new automatic parallel execution tuning feature

Of course, to tune something, you need a way to gather statistics and measure performance. As you might have guessed already, Oracle's dynamic performance views (the V$ views) are your prime source of information on parallel execution performance. Another useful source of information is the EXPLAIN PLAN statement, which can tell you if the execution plan for a given SQL statement contains any "parallel from serial" bottlenecks.

Dynamic Performance Views

Several Oracle dynamic performance views provide important information that's useful for monitoring and tuning parallel SQL execution. The views that you need to be aware of are shown in the following list:

V$PQ_SYSSTAT
V$PQ_SESSTAT
V$PQ_SLAVE
V$PQ_TQSTAT
V$SYSSTAT
V$SESSTAT
V$PX_PROCESS
V$PX_SESSION
V$PX_SESSTAT
V$PX_PROCESS_SYSSTAT

Several of these views are new with the release of Oracle8*i*. V$SYSSTAT and V$SESSTAT have been around for a while; they contain general statistics, some of which apply to parallel execution. The other views return information specific to parallel execution. The names of the new parallel execution views all begin with V$PX, while the names of older parallel query views begin with V$PQ. For the most part, the new V$PX views will eventually replace the older V$PQ views. Table 5-1 describes the relationship between these two sets of views.

Table 5-1. Relationship of V$PX Views to V$PQ Views

New in Oracle8*i*	Oracle8	Comments
V$PX_SESSION	N/A	—
V$PX_SESSTAT	N/A	—
N/A	V$PQ_SESSTAT	V$PQ_SESSTAT eventually will be dropped.

Table 5-1. Relationship of V$PX Views to V$PQ Views (continued)

New in Oracle8*i*	Oracle8	Comments
V$PX_PROCESS	V$PQ_SLAVE	V$PQ_SLAVE eventually will be dropped.
V$PX_PROCESS_SYSTAT	V$PQ_SYSSTAT	V$PQ_SYSSTAT eventually will be dropped.
N/A	V$PQ_TQSTAT	V$PQ_TQSTAT eventually will be renamed V$PX_TQSTAT.

The following sections explain how to use the information from the dynamic performance views to make parallel execution tuning decisions.

Only the most important information returned by each view is described in this chapter. For detailed information on all the statistics, refer to Oracle Corporation's *Oracle8i Reference Manual.*

The V$PQ_SYSSTAT View

The V$PQ_SYSSTAT view provides instance-wide statistics related to parallel execution. You can use these statistics to help determine appropriate values for the PARALLEL_MAX_SERVERS and PARALLEL_MIN_SERVERS initialization parameters.

The following example shows the types of statistics that you can get from the V$PQ_SYSSTAT view:

```
SQL> SELECT * FROM v$pq_sysstat;

STATISTIC                       VALUE
------------------------------ ---------
Servers Busy                        4
Servers Idle                        0
Servers Highwater                   5
Server Sessions                     5
Servers Started                    10
Servers Shutdown                    6
Servers Cleaned Up                  0
Queries Initiated                   5
DML Initiated                       0
DFO Trees                           5
Sessions Active                     1
Local Msgs Sent                   163
Distr Msgs Sent                     0
Local Msgs Recv'd                 505
Distr Msgs Recv'd                   0

15 rows selected.
```

The most useful of the statistics returned from this view are the Servers Busy, Servers Started, and Servers Shutdown statistics. These can be used to optimize the settings for the PARALLEL_MIN_SERVERS, PARALLEL_MAX_SERVERS, and PARALLEL_SERVER_IDLE_TIME initialization parameters.

Servers Busy

The Servers Busy statistic tells you the number of parallel slave processes that are currently busy executing parallel SQL statements. You can use this statistic to adjust the values of PARALLEL_MIN_SERVERS and PARALLEL_MAX_SERVERS.

If the Servers Busy statistic is consistently higher than the value of the PARALLEL_MIN_SERVERS initialization parameter, then you should increase the value of PARALLEL_MIN_SERVERS to match the Servers Busy value. There's no point in allowing the number of servers to drop below what you are consistently using.

If the Servers Busy statistic is consistently equal to the value of the PARALLEL_MAX_SERVERS initialization parameter, then your parallel execution operations are being constrained by that parameter, and you should consider increasing its value. However, before increasing PARALLEL_MAX_SERVERS, make sure that you have sufficient CPU resources to run the additional parallel slave processes that will result. If your CPU is heavily loaded, increasing the number of parallel slave processes may cause CPU bottlenecks to occur.

Servers Started and Servers Shutdown

The Servers Started statistic indicates the total number of parallel slave processes started on the instance. Likewise, the Servers Shutdown statistic indicates the total number of parallel slave processes shut down on the instance. If the values for these statistics are increasing consistently over time, that's an indication that Oracle is stopping parallel slave processes that are later going to be needed again. You'll take a performance hit from all the startup and shutdown activity. In such a case, you should consider increasing the value of the PARALLEL_SERVER_IDLE_TIME initialization parameter. This will cause Oracle to wait longer before stopping idle parallel slave processes and should reduce the constant need to start new ones.

The V$PQ_SESSTAT View

The V$PQ_SESSTAT view provides summary statistics about the parallel statements executed in your session. The following example shows the statistics returned when you query this view:

```
SQL> SELECT * FROM v$pq_sesstat;

    STATISTIC                    LAST_QUERY SESSION_TOTAL
    --------------------------- ---------- -------------
    Queries Parallelized                 1             1
    DML Parallelized                     0             0
    DFO Trees                            1             1
    Server Threads                       4             0
    Allocation Height                    4             0
    Allocation Width                     0             0
    Local Msgs Sent                      0             0
    Distr Msgs Sent                     18            18
    Local Msgs Recv'd                    0             0
    Distr Msgs Recv'd                   18            18

    10 rows selected.
```

Columns have the following meanings:

STATISTIC

This column shows the name of each statistic.

LAST_QUERY

This column provides the value of the statistic for the previous SQL statement that you executed. If your SQL statement didn't execute in parallel, this view will return 0 in the LAST_QUERY column for all the statistics. A query to a data dictionary view does not affect the value in the LAST_QUERY column. Therefore, if you query the V$PQ_SESSTAT view twice in succession, you will still get the same result. Also, if you query any other data dictionary view between two queries to this view, the values in the LAST_QUERY column will not be affected.

SESSION_TOTAL

This column provides the value of each statistic for the entire session. It's essentially the total of the statistic values from each SQL statement executed from the time the session was created.

Table 5-2 describes the most important of the V$PQ_SESSTAT statistics in terms of monitoring parallel execution.

Table 5-2. Important V$PQ_SESSTAT Statistics

Statistic	Description
Queries Parallelized	The number of queries that were run in parallel
DML Parallelized	The number of DML operations that were run in parallel
Server Threads	The total number of parallel slave processes used
Allocation Height	The requested number of slave processes per instance
Allocation Width	The requested number of instances

These statistics provide information on the number of queries and DML statements that have been parallelized in your session, the number of parallel slave processes requested per instance, and the number of instances requested. After executing a parallel SQL statement, you can query the V$PQ_SESSTAT view to determine whether the statement ran in parallel. Assuming that it did run in parallel, you then can see the number of parallel slave processes that were requested and used.

If you expect a SQL statement to run in parallel, and it doesn't do so, you need to find out why parallelism wasn't used. Refer to Chapter 4, *Using Parallel Execution*, to learn about restrictions on the use of parallel execution with various types of SQL statements and about the conditions that force a parallel SQL statement to run serially. If the statement doesn't execute with the expected degree of parallelism, you need to check the hints or parallel clauses in the statement and/or in the definition of the associated tables and indexes.

The V$PQ_SLAVE View

The V$PQ_SLAVE dynamic performance view returns one row for each parallel query slave process currently active for an instance. Various statistics are returned on each slave process, including the status, busy time, idle time, CPU used, and so on. Table 5-3 describes each column in this view.

Table 5-3. V$PQ_SLAVE Statistics

Column	Description
SLAVE_NAME	Name of the parallel slave process
STATUS	Current status (BUSY or IDLE) of the parallel slave process
SESSIONS	Number of sessions that have used this parallel slave process
IDLE_TIME_CUR	Amount of time spent idle while processing statements in the current session
BUSY_TIME_CUR	Amount of time spent busy while processing statements in the current session
CPU_SECS_CUR	Amount of CPU time spent on the current session
MSGS_SENT_CUR	Number of messages sent while processing statements for the current session
MSGS_RCVD_CUR	Number of messages received while processing statements for the current session
IDLE_TIME_TOTAL	Total amount of time this slave process has been idle
BUSY_TIME_TOTAL	Total amount of time this slave process has been active
CPU_SECS_TOTAL	Total amount of CPU time this slave process has used to process statements
MSGS_SENT_TOTAL	Total number of messages this slave process has sent
MSGS_RCVD_TOTAL	Total number of messages this slave process has received

The important statistics returned by the V$PQ_SLAVE view are SESSIONS, CPU_SECS_TOTAL, MSGS_SENT_TOTAL, and MSGS_RCVD_TOTAL. Together, these statistics indicate how evenly the processing load is being distributed when parallel execution is being used.

Here's an example of the output that you'll get when you query the V$PQ_SLAVE view:

```
SQL> SELECT slave_name, status, sessions, cpu_secs_total,
  2  msgs_sent_total, msgs_rcvd_total
  3  FROM  v$pq_slave;

SLAV STAT    SESSIONS CPU_SECS_TOTAL MSGS_SENT_TOTAL MSGS_RCVD_TOTAL
---- ----  ---------- -------------- --------------- ---------------
P000 BUSY         53              0            2351            4627
P001 BUSY         53              0            2351            4627
P002 BUSY         25              0              73             153
P003 BUSY         25              0              73             153
```

The values for the four statistics returned by this query should not vary too much between processes. Too much variation indicates an unbalanced workload among the slave processes. Some processes are doing more work than others, which lowers your overall efficiency.

One possible cause of an unbalanced workload is a mismatch between the degree of parallelism used for a DML statement and the number of partitions accessed by that statement. When DML statements access data in a partitioned table or index, a parallel slave process is assigned to each partition. The number of slave processes is limited by the degree of parallelism in effect for the statement. If the degree of parallelism is greater than the number of partitions, then the extra slave processes remain idle throughout the processing of the statement. If there are fewer processes than there are partitions, then some processes will have to process two or more partitions. To balance the workload properly, you should choose a degree of parallelism such that the number of partitions is a multiple of the degree of parallelism. Otherwise, you'll have an imbalance that results in a loss of efficiency.

For example, consider what happens if a table has four partitions, but the degree of parallelism for a DML statement against that table is only 3. Three slave processes will be assigned to the statement, each process working on one partition. The slave process that finishes processing its assigned partition first will be assigned to the fourth partition. That means one slave process will have to handle two partitions. While that one process is working with the fourth partition, the other two slave processes will be sitting idle. This wastes resources. Therefore, it's important to choose carefully the degree of parallelism used for a statement.

The V$PQ_TQSTAT View

The V$PQ_TQSTAT dynamic performance view provides detailed statistics on each parallel slave process currently running for an instance. This view shows the producer/consumer relationship between the parallel slave processes and the query coordinator. In cases in which inter-operational parallelism is being used, this view also shows the producer/consumer relationship between different sets of parallel slave processes. The important statistics to note from this view are NUM ROWS (number of rows) and BYTES (number of bytes), processed by each of the parallel slave processes.

As discussed in Chapter 3, *Parallel Execution Concepts*, the query coordinator divides the work of executing a query into multiple tasks and assigns each task to a parallel slave process. This complete process structure, consisting of the query coordinator and associated parallel slave processes, is called a *data flow operation* (DFO). Oracle assigns a DFO number to each data flow operation. That DFO number shows up in the V$PQ_TQSTAT view's DFO_NUMBER column.

The slave processes act as producers and the query coordinator acts as a consumer. The following example shows some useful information from V$PQ_TQSTAT for a parallel SELECT statement:

```
SQL> SELECT /*+ PARALLEL(emp,4) */ * FROM emp;

    EMPNO ENAME      JOB          MGR HIREDATE        SAL      COMM    DEPTNO
--------- ---------- ---------- ------- --------- --------- --------- ---------
     7654 MARTIN     SALESMAN      7698 28-SEP-81      1250      1400        30
     7698 BLAKE      MANAGER       7839 01-MAY-81      2850                  30
     .
     .
     .

7168 rows selected.

SQL> SELECT dfo_number, tq_id, server_type, process, num_rows, bytes
  2  FROM v$pq_tqstat
  3  ORDER BY dfo_number, tq_id, server_type;

DFO_NUMBER     TQ_ID SERVER_TYP PROCESS    NUM_ROWS     BYTES
---------- --------- ---------- ---------- --------- ---------
         1         0 Consumer   QC              7168    329464
         1         0 Producer   P001            1777     81658
         1         0 Producer   P003            1804     82941
         1         0 Producer   P002            1804     82935
         1         0 Producer   P000            1783     81930
```

In this example, the query was executed using four parallel slave processes. As you can see from the SERVER_TYP column, the parallel slave processes act as producers, and the query coordinator acts as the consumer. The producers and consumers communicate using a queue known as a *table queue* (TQ). Table queues are identified by ID numbers that are returned in the TQ_ID column. The NUM_ROWS and BYTES columns provide information on the number of rows and bytes handled by each process.

When inter-operational parallelism is used, one set of slave processes acts as producers to a second set of consumer slave processes. The processes in that second set then act as producers to the query coordinator. Thus, you can have multiple layers of producers and consumers. Each layer is represented by a unique TQ_ID value.

The following example shows useful information from the V$PQ_TQSTAT view for a parallel SELECT statement involving inter-operational parallelism:

```
SQL> SELECT /*+ PARALLEL(emp_test,4) */ * FROM emp_test ORDER BY ename;

    EMPNO ENAME      JOB           MGR HIREDATE       SAL      COMM    DEPTNO
--------- ---------- --------- --------- --------- --------- --------- ---------
     7698 BLAKE      MANAGER      7839 01-MAY-81     2850                    30
     7654 MARTIN     SALESMAN     7698 28-SEP-81     1250      1400          30
       .
       .
       .

14 rows selected.

SQL> SELECT dfo_number, tq_id, server_type, process, num_rows, bytes
  2  FROM v$pq_tqstat
  3  ORDER BY dfo_number, tq_id, server_type;

DFO_NUMBER      TQ_ID SERVER_TYP PROCESS      NUM_ROWS      BYTES
---------- ---------- ---------- ---------- ---------- ----------
         1          0 Consumer   P003                4        197
         1          0 Consumer   P002                3        159
         1          0 Consumer   P001                3        165
         1          0 Consumer   P000                4        208
         1          0 Producer   P007                0         20
         1          0 Producer   P006                0         20
         1          0 Producer   P005                0         20
         1          0 Producer   P004               14        657
         1          0 Ranger     QC                 14       1446
         1          1 Consumer   QC                 14        717
         1          1 Producer   P003                4        194
         1          1 Producer   P000                4        205
         1          1 Producer   P001                3        162
         1          1 Producer   P002                3        156

14 rows selected.
```

In the preceding output, layer 0 (TQ_ID = 0) is responsible for the table scan, and layer 1 (TQ_ID = 1) is responsible for the sort. After the table is scanned by four slave processes (P004, P005, P006, and P007), the output is distributed among the other parallel slave processes (P000, P001, P002, and P003) for sorting. The query coordinator divides the sort operation into four ranges and assigns one range to each parallel slave process. Each slave process then takes the input that falls within its range and sorts it. The role of dividing the sort into four ranges is called "Ranger" (note this under SERVER_TYP in the previous output). In the output you can see the query coordinator (QC) taking the role of Ranger in layer 0.

In a given layer, if the producers process too many rows as compared to the consumers, that indicates inefficient query processing. This may be caused by a badly written query or by an uneven distribution of data. For example, if you are using a GROUP BY operation and the number of rows processed for one distinct value for the columns in the GROUP BY clause differ widely from the number of rows processed for another distinct value, then you will observe a large variance.

The V$SYSSTAT and V$SESSTAT Views

The V$SYSSTAT and V$SESSTAT views provide a large number of generic statistics on database performance. Some of those statistics apply to parallel execution. V$SYSSTAT provides these statistics for the entire system, whereas V$SESSTAT provides them for the current session. The statistics to look at that are relevant to parallel execution all have the string "parallel" somewhere in their names. You can retrieve them using a query like the one shown in this example, which queries V$SYSSTAT:

```
SQL> SELECT * FROM v$sysstat WHERE name LIKE '%parallel%';

STATISTIC# NAME                                     CLASS      VALUE
---------- ------------------------------------ ---------- ----------
       167 queries parallelized                     32         97
       168 DML statements parallelized             32          0
       169 DDL statements parallelized             32          0
```

While V$SYSSTAT returns statistics by name, V$SESSTAT returns them only by number. As the output from V$SYSSTAT shows, the parallel execution statistics are numbers 167, 168, and 169. These represent, respectively, the number of queries parallelized, the number of DML statements parallelized, and the number of DDL statements parallelized. Using the numbers, you can query V$SESSTAT as follows:

```
SQL> SELECT statistic#, sum(value) from v$sesstat
  2  WHERE statistic# IN (167,168,169)
  3  GROUP BY statistic#;

STATISTIC#      VALUE
---------- ----------
       167         60
       168          0
       169          0

3 rows selected.
```

The information provided by these views is useful for informational purposes but doesn't really lead to any tuning activity.

The V$PX_PROCESS View

The V$PX_PROCESS view provides one row of information for each parallel slave process. The information returned includes the session ID, the serial number, and the status of each of those processes. Here is a sample of the output that you'll get when querying V$PX_PROCESS:

```
SQL> SELECT * FROM v$px_process;

SERV STATUS         PID SPID         SID   SERIAL#
---- --------- --------- --------- --------- ---------
P001 IN USE          15 119          10       146
P000 IN USE          14 223          15        35
P003 IN USE          17 236          14       215
P002 IN USE          16 64           13       990
```

This view will replace V$PQ_SLAVE in a future release. As of the current release of Oracle (release 8.1.6), the V$PX_PROCESS view does not provide all of the information provided by V$PQ_SLAVE. We expect more information to be added to V$PX_PROCESS before V$PQ_SLAVE is made obsolete.

The V$PX_SESSION View

The V$PX_SESSION dynamic performance view provides real-time information on busy parallel slave processes in the instance. This view provides the session ID and the serial number of the query coordinator and of the parallel slave processes. This view also provides information about the requested and actual degrees of parallelism. Here is an example of a query against V$PX_SESSION:

```
SQL> SELECT sid, serial#, qcsid, qcserial#, server#,
  2  degree, req_degree
  3  FROM v$px_session;

     SID   SERIAL#     QCSID QCSERIAL#   SERVER#    DEGREE REQ_DEGREE
--------- --------- --------- --------- --------- --------- ----------
      11      7275        11
      14       211        11      7275         1         4          4
       9         9        11      7275         2         4          4
      10       135        11      7275         3         4          4
      13       669        11      7275         4         4          4
```

When you look at the output from this view, check the requested versus the actual degrees of parallelism. If they don't match, you should check the number of parallel slave processes available, the maximum number of parallel slave processes allowed (PARALLEL_MAX_SERVERS), and the PARALLEL_MIN_PERCENT setting.

The V$PX_SESSTAT View

The V$PX_SESSTAT view provides session statistics for all sessions using parallel execution. This view is a join between V$PX_SESSION and V$SESSTAT. V$PX_SESSTAT provides the session identifier, statistics number, and value for the parallel coordinator and for each of the busy parallel slave processes. Here is an example of a query against V$PX_SESSTAT:

```
SQL> SELECT sid, serial#, qcsid, qcserial#, qcinst_id, degree, req_degree,
statistic#, value FROM v$px_sesstat;

SID SERIAL# QCSID QCSERIAL# QCINST_ID DEGREE REQ_DEGREE STATISTIC#  VALUE
--- ------- ----- --------- --------- ------ ---------- ---------- ------
 10      43    12        41         1      4          4         22      0
 10      43    12        41         1      4          4         21 144048
 10      43    12        41         1      4          4         20 144048
 10      43    12        41         1      4          4         19      0
 10      43    12        41         1      4          4         18      0
  .
  .
  .
```

The statistics provided by this view include the amount of CPU time used by each session, the number of DDL and DML statements parallelized for each session, and more. You can use the statistics provided by V$PX_SESSTAT in the same way you use the statistics from V$SESSTAT.

The V$PX_PROCESS_SYSSTAT View

The V$PX_PROCESS_SYSSTAT view provides statistics on parallel execution. Some of these statistics are the same as those provided by V$PQ_SYSSTAT. The following example shows the results of a query against V$PX_PROCESS_SYSSTAT:

```
SQL> SELECT * FROM v$px_process_sysstat;

STATISTIC                        VALUE
------------------------------ ---------
Servers In Use                       4
Servers Available                    0
Servers Started                     10
Servers Shutdown                     6
Servers Highwater                    5
Servers Cleaned Up                   0
Server Sessions                      5
Memory Chunks Allocated              1
Memory Chunks Freed                  0
Memory Chunks Current                1
Memory Chunks HWM                    1
Buffers Allocated                   88
Buffers Freed                       76
```

```
Buffers Current                    12
Buffers HWM                        16

15 rows selected.
```

Most of the useful information provided by this view corresponds to the information returned by the V$PQ_SYSSTAT view and can be used to tune the settings for the following initialization parameters:

> PARALLEL_MIN_SERVERS
> PARALLEL_MAX_SERVERS
> PARALLEL_SERVER_IDLE_TIME

See the section on V$PQ_SYSSTAT for details.

Using EXPLAIN PLAN to View Parallel Execution

The sequence of operations that Oracle performs to execute a SQL statement is called an *execution plan*. Sometimes it's useful to look at the execution plan for a statement, in order to determine whether the plan picked by the optimizer is an efficient one. You can use Oracle's EXPLAIN PLAN statement for this purpose. EXPLAIN PLAN takes a SQL statement, determines the execution plan, and stores that plan in a special table known as the *plan table*.

 If you are not familiar with the use of EXPLAIN PLAN, you may want to consult Oracle Corporation's *Oracle8 Tuning* manual, *Oracle SQL*Plus: The Definitive Guide* by Jonathan Gennick (O'Reilly & Associates, 1998), or *Oracle SQL: The Essential Reference* by David Kreines (O'Reilly & Associates, 2000).

The plan table used by EXPLAIN PLAN is most often named PLAN_TABLE. The columns of the table describe various aspects of the execution plan. Two columns are of special importance for parallel execution:

OBJECT_NODE
> Describes the order in which the output from execution plan operations is consumed.

OTHER_TAG
> Describes the parallel or serial relationships between steps. The possible values for the OTHER_TAG column are described in Table 5-4.

Table 5-4. Values of the OTHER_TAG Column in the Plan Table

Value	Meaning
SERIAL	A serial operation
No value; the column is null	A serial operation
SERIAL_FROM_REMOTE	A serial operation at a remote site
PARALLEL_FROM_SERIAL	A serial operation that passes output to a set of parallel slave processes
PARALLEL_TO_PARALLEL	A parallel operation that passes output to a second set of parallel slave processes
PARALLEL_TO_SERIAL	A parallel operation that passes output to the parallel coordinator
PARALLEL_COMBINED_WITH_PARENT	A parallel operation, the parent step of which also was executed in parallel by the same set of slave processes
PARALLEL_COMBINED_WITH_CHILD	A parallel operation, the child step of which also was executed in parallel by the same set of slave processes

When a query is executed in parallel, make sure that you don't have any serial execution steps in the execution plan. You can check for that by using EXPLAIN PLAN to view the execution plan of your parallel SQL statements and checking the values for the OTHER_TAG column. The values that you want to see are the following:

> PARALLEL_TO_PARALLEL
> PARALLEL_TO_SERIAL
> PARALLEL_COMBINED_WITH_PARENT
> PARALLEL_COMBINED_WITH_CHILD

Any other value indicates a serial operation, which may represent a bottleneck. The following example shows an execution plan for a statement with just such a bottleneck. Notice the DEGREE values for the two tables involved in the query. You'll see that these have a drastic effect on the query's performance:

```
SQL> SELECT table_name, degree, instances FROM user_tables;

TABLE_NAME                      DEGREE  INSTANCES
------------------------------- ------- ---------
DEPTTEST                             1          1
EMPTEST                              4          1

2 rows selected.

SQL> EXPLAIN PLAN SET statement_id = 's1' FOR
  2  SELECT empno, ename, sal, comm, dname FROM
  3  emptest e, depttest d
  4  WHERE e.deptno = d.deptno
  5  ORDER BY empno;
```

```
Explained.

SQL> SELECT LPAD(' ',2*(level-1))||operation||' '||options
  2  ||' '||object_name
  3  || DECODE(other_tag,NULL,'','(') || other_tag
  4  || DECODE(other_tag,NULL,'',')') "Query Plan"
  5  FROM plan_table
  6  START WITH id = 0 AND statement_id = '&stid'
  7  CONNECT BY PRIOR id = parent_id AND statement_id ='&stid';
Enter value for stid: s1
old   5: START WITH id = 0 AND statement_id = '&stid'
new   5: START WITH id = 0 AND statement_id = 's1'
Enter value for stid: s1
old   6: CONNECT BY PRIOR id = parent_id AND statement_id ='&stid'
new   6: CONNECT BY PRIOR id = parent_id AND statement_id ='s1'

Query Plan
-------------------------------------------------------------------
SELECT STATEMENT
  SORT ORDER BY (PARALLEL_TO_SERIAL)
    MERGE JOIN  (PARALLEL_TO_PARALLEL)
      SORT JOIN (PARALLEL_COMBINED_WITH_PARENT)
        TABLE ACCESS FULL EMPTEST(PARALLEL_TO_PARALLEL)
      SORT JOIN (PARALLEL_COMBINED_WITH_PARENT)
        TABLE ACCESS FULL DEPTTEST(PARALLEL_FROM_SERIAL)

7 rows selected.
```

This execution plan indicates that the table scan of the depttest table is being performed in serial. You can tell this because the other_tag for that step is PARALLEL_FROM_SERIAL. The reason for this step is because the depttest table has DEGREE set to 1 in its definition. The problem, though, is that the results of this serial operation are being fed into a parallel operation. It's unlikely that a serial table scan will be able to feed a parallel operation fast enough to take full advantage of that parallelism.

One way to fix the problem, and get rid of the PARALLEL_FROM_SERIAL step, is to increase the DEGREE setting for the depttest table. This example shows how to do this and then shows the resulting change in the execution plan:

```
SQL> ALTER TABLE depttest PARALLEL (DEGREE 4);

Table altered.

SQL> EXPLAIN PLAN SET statement_id = 's4' FOR
  2  SELECT empno, ename, sal, comm, dname FROM
  3  emptest e, depttest d
  4  WHERE e.deptno = d.deptno
  5  ORDER BY empno
  6  /

Explained.
```

```
SQL> SELECT LPAD(' ',2*(LEVEL-1))||operation||' '||options
  2  ||' '||object_name
  3  || DECODE(other_tag,NULL,'','(') || other_tag
  4  || DECODE(other_tag,NULL,'',')') "Query Plan"
  5  FROM plan_table
  6  START WITH id = 0 AND statement_id = '&stid'
  7  CONNECT BY PRIOR id = parent_id AND statement_id ='&stid';
Enter value for stid: s4
old   6: START WITH id = 0 AND statement_id = '&stid'
new   6: START WITH id = 0 AND statement_id = 's4'
Enter value for stid: s4
old   7: CONNECT BY PRIOR id = parent_id AND statement_id ='&stid'
new   7: CONNECT BY PRIOR id = parent_id AND statement_id ='s4'

Query Plan
-------------------------------------------------------------------
SELECT STATEMENT
  SORT ORDER BY (PARALLEL_TO_SERIAL)
    MERGE JOIN  (PARALLEL_TO_PARALLEL)
      SORT JOIN (PARALLEL_COMBINED_WITH_PARENT)
        TABLE ACCESS FULL EMPTEST(PARALLEL_TO_PARALLEL)
      SORT JOIN (PARALLEL_COMBINED_WITH_PARENT)
        TABLE ACCESS FULL DEPTTEST(PARALLEL_TO_PARALLEL)

7 rows selected.
```

Notice the change in the execution plan. The PARALLEL_TO_PARALLEL value in the last step indicates that the depttest table now will be scanned in parallel. You now have one parallel operation feeding another parallel operation, and the potential serial bottleneck has been removed.

 Oracle8*i* comes with a script named *utlxplp.sql* that displays the execution plan of parallel SQL statements in a useful manner. You can find this script in your *$ORACLE_HOME/rdbms/admin* directory, and you can use it to analyze the EXPLAIN PLAN outputs of your parallel SQL statements. For more information on the *utlxplp.sql* script, refer to Oracle Corporation's *Oracle8i Tuning* manual.

Tuning Tips for Parallel Execution

So far in this chapter, we've discussed various tools and techniques that you can use to monitor and tune parallel execution performance. In this section, we'll pass on some general tips that you also can use to improve the performance of parallel execution on your database:

Use parallel execution properly

Parallel execution helps improve performance for operations involving large amounts of data. The performance of large queries and bulk data loads, for example, can benefit immensely from parallel execution. Parallel execution usually is not helpful for operations involving a small amount of data. That's because, for a small amount of data, the overhead of breaking the operation into subtasks and coordinating the execution of those subtasks among parallel slave processes far exceeds the actual processing time required to execute the query in serial. Decision support system (DSS) applications gain maximum benefit from parallel execution, because these applications usually handle large amounts of data, complex queries, and bulk data loading. Online transaction processing (OLTP) applications can benefit from parallel execution for batch processing.

Another thing to keep in mind is that parallel execution requires a multiprocessor system with spare CPU and memory resources. On a single-processor system, there is no reason to use parallel execution, as the parallel slave processes will contend for the same CPU and degrade performance. On an over-utilized system, parallel execution can cause bottlenecks and degrade performance even further.

Analyze tables and indexes regularly

Oracle's cost-based optimizer bases its decisions on the table and index statistics that you collect using the ANALYZE command. It's important to keep these statistics up to date. With outdated statistics, the optimizer might choose a poor execution plan, thereby adversely affecting performance. Analyze your tables and indexes regularly to keep their statistics up to date. Also, be sure to reanalyze after performing large data loads, bulk inserts, and index creations.

Use the UNRECOVERABLE option in parallel load and table creation operations

You can specify the UNRECOVERABLE option for SQL*Loader sessions involved in a parallel load to avoid the generation of redo for that load. This saves a lot of time and redo log space. You also can use the UNRECOVERABLE option while creating tables in parallel using CREATE TABLE . . . AS SELECT statements or while using INSERT INTO . . . SELECT statements to do bulk inserts into a table.

 Use of the UNRECOVERABLE option means that the affected tables and indexes can't be recovered in the event of a media failure. Always back up the affected tables immediately after completing an UNRECOVERABLE operation.

Drop indexes while loading data

Large tables often have several indexes on them to improve query performance. However, maintaining these indexes while loading data is resource-intensive and has a detrimental effect on the performance of the load. You can minimize the performance impact of this index maintenance by dropping all nonunique indexes before performing any large data load. After the load is complete, you can use Oracle's parallel index creation feature to re-create those indexes efficiently.

Choose the appropriate degree of parallelism

Oracle sets default values for the degree of parallelism at the instance level. However, those default values may not be appropriate for all queries. Therefore, you should override the default values by specifying the degree of parallelism at the table or index level or at the statement level. For operations on a partitioned table, for example, you should set the degree of parallelism to a value equal to the number of partitions or to a value such that the number of partitions is a multiple of the degree of parallelism.

Take advantage of disk striping

In Chapter 3 you learned that Oracle parallel execution is beneficial when the data being accessed is spread across multiple disk drives. I/O bottlenecks are avoided because all the parallel slave processes can read data from different disks. You should stripe the tablespaces used for tables, indexes, and temporary segments over multiple devices.

You can use either operating system striping or Oracle striping. Many operating systems provide utilities to stripe physical disks and create logical drives. To use Oracle striping, you should allocate multiple datafiles to each tablespace, where each datafile resides on a separate physical drive. Parallel SQL*Loader can take advantage of Oracle striping through the use of the FILE clause in the SQL*Loader control file.

Partition your data

Oracle8 and Oracle8i allow you to partition tables and indexes. Partitioning provides a variety of benefits and is useful for parallel execution too. On a partitioned table, the parallel coordinator divides the work by partition and assigns a parallel slave process to each partition. Each slave process works independently on the partition to which it is assigned. Also, to improve I/O performance, you can put partitions of a table on separate tablespaces, with each residing on a separate disk. Some operations, such as UPDATE and DELETE statements, can be parallelized only on partitioned tables.

Automatic Tuning of Parallel Execution in Oracle8i

With the release of Oracle8i, Oracle has provided some significant additional support for tuning parallel execution environments. Specifically, Oracle now has the ability to make some tuning decisions automatically. If you've already manually tuned your application, and it's performing satisfactorily, automatic tuning may not be beneficial. However, new applications that run on Oracle8*i* and use Oracle8*i*'s parallel execution features can benefit from automatic tuning.

To enable automatic tuning of parallel execution, set the initialization parameter PARALLEL_AUTOMATIC_TUNING to TRUE. At this point, you need to be aware of three effects of automatic tuning:

- The effect of automatic tuning on the default value of the initialization parameters listed in Table 5-5

- The effect of automatic tuning on the adaptive multiuser algorithm

- The effect of the PARALLEL_THREADS_PER_CPU initialization parameter setting

When you set PARALLEL_AUTOMATIC_TUNING = TRUE (thereby enabling automatic tuning of parallel execution), that has an effect on the default values of several initialization parameters. Table 5-5 shows the changes in default values that occur when automatic tuning is used. Remember that you can always override these defaults by explicitly setting the parameters in your initialization file.

Table 5-5. The Effect of Automatic Tuning on Initialization Parameter Defaults

Parameter	Default Value When PARALLEL_AUTOMATIC_ TUNING = FALSE	Default Value When PARALLEL_AUTOMATIC_ TUNING = TRUE
PARALLEL_ADAPTIVE_ MULTI_USER	FALSE	TRUE
PARALLEL_MAX_SERVERS	5	10×number of CPUs
LARGE_POOL_SIZE	0	Based on a complicated computation using various other parameters
PARALLEL_EXECUTION_ MESSAGE_SIZE	2 K	4 K

When PARALLEL_ADAPTIVE_MULTI_USER = TRUE, Oracle determines the degree of parallelism based on the system's current workload. For example, consider a table with DEGREE set to 8. Under a normal system load, a full table scan on the table entails eight parallel slave processes. However, under a heavy load, when many users are executing processes on the system, Oracle automatically reduces the degree of parallelism. For example, it may reduce the degree of parallelism from 8 to 4. This reduces the CPU and memory requirements of the statement, which helps in reducing CPU and memory bottlenecks for the instance, which, in turn, improves performance.

The default value on most platforms for PARALLEL_THREADS_PER_CPU is 2. Oracle uses this parameter to compute the default degree of parallelism for the instance. It does this by multiplying the number of CPUs on the system by the value of the PARALLEL_THREADS_PER_CPU parameter.

When using automatic tuning, you should leave the parameters shown in Table 5-5 set to their default values and then monitor performance over a reasonable period of time using the dynamic performance views. If you then determine that some parameters need manual tuning, you can explicitly set them. Oracle recommends that you leave the LARGE_POOL_SIZE and PARALLEL_EXECUTION_ MESSAGE_SIZE parameters at their default values. You should, however, tune PARALLEL_MAX_SERVERS based on the statistics from V$PQ_SYSSTAT or V$PX_ PROCESS_SYSSTAT.

III

Oracle Parallel Server

This part of the book describes the Oracle Parallel Server (OPS) product and describes how to create and manage OPS databases. It consists of the following chapters:

- Chapter 6, *Oracle Parallel Server Architecture*, describes the overall architecture of the product and how OPS instances coordinate activities against a single database.

- Chapter 7, *Administering an OPS Database*, explains what you need to know about creating and managing an OPS database.

- Chapter 8, *Locking Mechanisms in OPS*, describes the locking mechanisms that are fundamental to Oracle Parallel Server operations.

- Chapter 9, *Storage Management in OPS*, explains how to use free lists and other memory structures to optimize performance in OPS.

- Chapter 10, *Monitoring and Tuning OPS*, discusses how you can get the best performance out of OPS.

- Chapter 11, *Partitioning for OPS*, describes application, data, and transaction partitioning techniques for OPS.

- Chapter 12, *Application Failover*, discusses how you can use Oracle Parallel Server to support high availability.

- Chapter 13, *Parallel Execution in OPS*, describes how you can combine both sets of Oracle's parallel features by using parallel execution in OPS environments.

6

Oracle Parallel Server Architecture

Before you can install and configure Oracle Parallel Server (OPS) successfully, you need to understand its various architectural components. If you are new to OPS, this chapter is definitely for you. If you are familiar with OPS concepts, this chapter will serve as a review of the OPS features and components before you move on to the details in subsequent chapters. This chapter introduces Oracle Parallel Server and discusses the OPS features related to instance and database architecture. It also describes how datafiles, the Integrated Distributed Lock Manager (IDLM), and rollback segments work with OPS.

Remember that parallel execution and Oracle Parallel Server are two separate feature sets available from Oracle. They are independent of each other but can work together. Most OPS environments also run parallel execution. Parallel server adds some additional features to parallel execution. Chapter 13, *Parallel Execution in OPS*, explains how you can exploit parallel execution features in an Oracle Parallel Server environment.

 For simplicity, most of the diagrams in this chapter use a two-instance OPS environment to illustrate the concepts being described. However, remember that the discussions here are applicable to OPS with any number of instances.

OPS and Oracle Instances

One of the key differences between an OPS database and a standalone Oracle database is that with OPS, you have multiple instances opening the database at the same time. This is a crucial point to understand. Before discussing the complexities of multiple instances, however, let's review the concept of a *standalone Oracle instance.* A standalone instance represents the traditional case in which you have one instance opening one database.

A Standalone Oracle Instance

An Oracle instance consists of a shared area in memory and a set of background processes. The shared memory area is shared by many user connections and transactions and is called the System Global Area (SGA). The background processes centralize database functions on behalf of many user connections.

The SGA consists of the database buffer cache, the redo log buffer, and the shared pool. Briefly, these structures have the following functions:

Database buffer cache
> Holds database blocks read from the datafiles

Redo log buffer
> Holds information about changes made to the database

Shared pool
> Contains data dictionary cache and shared SQL areas

The background processes for an instance usually include the following:

Database Writer (DBWn)
> Writes database changes out to the datafiles

Log Writer (LGWR)
> Writes the redo log to the redo log files

Process Monitor (PMON)
> Cleans up after processes that terminate abnormally

System Monitor (SMON)
> Performs crash recovery and cleans up temporary segments

Checkpoint Process (CKPT)
> Records checkpoint information in database file headers

In addition to the processes shown in the previous list, there are several other, optional processes that you can start by setting various initialization parameters. These optional processes include:

Archiver (ARCH)
> Copies filled redo log files to the archive log destination

Recoverer (RECO)
> Resolves distributed transactions that have failed

Job Queue Processes (SNPn)
Run PL/SQL jobs at scheduled times

Dispatchers (Dnnn)
Are used in a multithreaded server (MTS) environment to distribute user connections to shared server processes

Server Processes (Snnn)
Run on the server and perform work on behalf of users connected remotely

Figure 6-1 shows some of these required and optional processes. The arrangement shown in Figure 6-1, showing one instance per database, is the configuration when the Oracle Parallel Server Option is not being used. As we mentioned, such a configuration is referred to as a standalone Oracle instance.

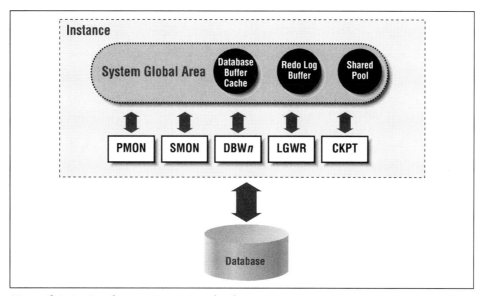

Figure 6-1. An Oracle instance opens a database

Multiple Oracle Instances

With Oracle Parallel Server, one database is mounted and opened by multiple instances concurrently. Each OPS instance is like any standalone Oracle instance in that it consists of a System Global Area (SGA) and several background processes. Each Oracle instance runs on a separate node having its own CPU and memory. Nodes may be Symmetric Multiprocessor (SMP) nodes with multiple CPUs, or they may have only a single CPU. The amount of memory and the number of CPUs on the various nodes do not need to match. The database resides on a disk subsystem shared by all nodes. Figure 6-2 shows an OPS configuration running on two nodes.

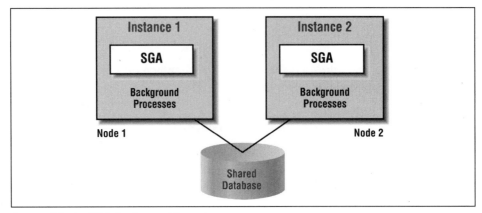

Figure 6-2. An OPS database with two instances

Instance and Database Names

In a standalone Oracle database, the instance and the database usually have the same name. This name is the same as the ORACLE_SID. In an OPS configuration, each instance usually has its own ORACLE_SID. These SIDs are named to indicate that multiple instances are being used for one database. For example, the instances mounting an OPS database TEST might be named TEST1, TEST2, TEST3, and so on.

OPS characteristics

Because OPS is a multi-instance architecture, an OPS configuration has some unique characteristics that differentiate it from a single-instance configuration of Oracle:

- The datafiles and control files are shared by all instances.

- Each instance has its own set of redo log files.

- An OPS environment has the Integrated Distributed Lock Manager (IDLM) for inter-instance synchronization. IDLM consists of some additional background processes.

- An OPS environment has a Group Membership Service (GMS) to communicate with the operating system's cluster manager, a component that coordinates the activities of the various nodes in a cluster. GMS is part of the Oracle8 OPS environment. Oracle8*i* OPS does not have GMS. In Oracle8*i*, GMS functionality is incorporated into the Oracle kernel as Cluster Group Services (CGS).

- Each instance has its own rollback segments.

Enabling and Disabling Oracle Parallel Server

Oracle provides an initialization parameter named PARALLEL_SERVER that allows you to enable or disable the Oracle Parallel Server Option. Set the parameter to TRUE (to enable) or FALSE (to disable).

Only one instance can mount and open the database when the Oracle Parallel Server Option is disabled. One or more instances can mount the same database in shared mode when the option is enabled.

OPS requirements

If you are going to install and run Oracle Parallel Server in your environment, the following requirements must be met:

- You must license Oracle's Parallel Server Option.

- The hardware platform and operating system must support a shared disk architecture.

- The operating system software must support clustering, and it must have a component to manage nodes participating in the OPS environment. As we mentioned, this component typically is referred to as a cluster manager.

- Each node in the cluster should have its own ORACLE_HOME directory with its own copy of the Oracle Server software. The Oracle software release must be identical on all nodes. For example, you cannot run release 8.1.5 on one node while running 8.0.5 on another.

 We strongly recommend using identical directory structures for the Oracle software and related files (such as parameter files, alert log files, etc.) on all nodes. Oracle's Optimal Flexible Architecture (OFA) is the most commonly used directory structure and is what we recommend. You should be able to find a description of the OFA in your system-specific *Getting Started* manual. For example, if you're using Windows NT, look for OFA information in Oracle Corporation's *Oracle8i Enterprise Edition for Windows NT Getting Started* manual.

- For Unix systems, all database files (datafiles, control files, and redo log files) must be on raw devices.

Comparing OPS and standalone configurations

Table 6-1 compares the features of a standalone Oracle instance configuration with those of an Oracle Parallel Server configuration. Some of the terms and concepts may not make sense now, but all of them will be explained later in this chapter.

Table 6-1. Comparison of Standalone Configuration with OPS Configuration

Standalone Oracle Instance	Oracle Parallel Server
One instance mounts one database.	Multiple instances mount one database in shared mode.
One System Global Area (SGA) and one set of background processes.	Multiple SGAs and multiple sets of background processes—one set on each node.
	Additional background processes required—LCKn, LMON, LMDn.
	Integrated Distributed Lock Manager (IDLM) required to coordinate between multiple instances.
All locks are acquired and resolved at the instance level.	Global locks must be managed across multiple instances to ensure cache coherency.
No overhead of synchronization.	Overhead of synchronization exists.
Runs on single processor or SMP machines.	Runs on cluster or MPP machines.
	Global constant parameters required.
V$ views to monitor the instance.	V$ views to monitor the local instance; GV$ views to monitor all instances.
Suitable for almost all types of applications.	May not be suitable for some applications because of high synchronization overhead requirements.
Availability limited to one instance.	Multiple instances provide high availability.
Scalability limited to one instance.	Scalability extended by adding new instances.

Users in an OPS environment

Oracle Parallel Server is transparent to database users. Users log on to individual OPS instances just as they would to a standalone Oracle instance. Because all instances access the same database, user accounts need be created only once. Users have identical privileges across all instances, because user access is controlled through one common data dictionary residing in the database. A user can connect to any instance, and a user can connect to many instances at the same time.

Synchronization Between Instances

In an Oracle Parallel Server configuration, multiple instances mount and open the database in shared mode. Since multiple instances share one database, it is likely that copies of the same object will end up in the SGA of more than one instance. For example, when instance 1 needs to modify rows contained in block B1, it reads the block B1 from disk into its buffer cache and then modifies the block. Now, if instance 2 also needs to modify block B1, it needs a copy of that block in *its* buffer cache. In order for instance 2 to get the latest copy of the block, instance 1 first must write that block back to disk. Instance 2 then can read it and proceed to modify it.

Because two instances can modify the copy of a block held in their respective buffer caches, there is a need to maintain consistency between these two copies. In other words, in terms of the previous example, instance 2 needs some way to know that instance 1 has already read and modified the same block that it also needs to change. Maintaining consistency among cached versions of database blocks in buffer caches of multiple instances is called *cache coherency* and is illustrated in Figure 6-3. Oracle uses global locks to ensure cache coherency. These locks are referred to as *global locks* because they are managed across all the instances associated with the OPS database. An Oracle component called the Integrated Distributed Lock Manager (IDLM) coordinates these inter-instance locking activities.

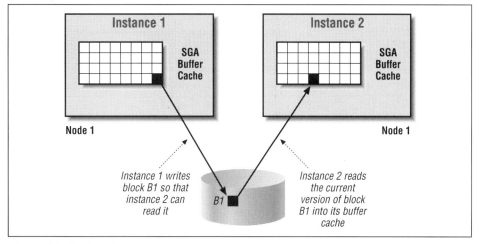

Figure 6-3. Cache coherency

With the release of Oracle8*i*, a new technique called *cache fusion* has been introduced to maintain cache coherency. When one instance needs a block held by another, cache fusion enables the block to be transferred directly between the two instances without first being written to disk. This buffer-to-buffer transfer of blocks allows synchronization to occur much faster than when the blocks are transferred via disk and greatly improves Oracle Parallel Server's performance in Oracle8*i*.

Directly related to cache fusion, a new Oracle8*i* background process called the *Block Server Process* (BSP) has been added to facilitate the transfer of buffer cache blocks from one instance to another. The BSP creates a consistent-read image of the blocks to be transferred and sends them to the requesting instance. The cache fusion technique has been implemented only for a subset of the cases in which cache coherency is necessary. Chapter 8, *Locking Mechanisms in OPS*, discusses in detail the mechanism used to maintain cache coherency.

OPS Impact on Database Files

Installing Oracle Parallel Server has an impact on how database files are used. Some files—for example, the datafiles—are shared among all instances. Other files are not. This section discusses each type of file in terms of how it is used in an OPS configuration.

Initialization Parameter Files

In an OPS configuration, you need to be concerned about three types of initialization parameters:

- Some parameters, such as GC_FILES_TO_LOCK, must be the identical across all instances. These are known as *global constant parameters*.

- Certain other parameters, such as DB_BLOCK_BUFFERS, do not need to be the same for each instance.

- Still other parameters, such as ROLLBACK_SEGMENTS, actually must be different for each instance.

Because the parameters for each instance in an OPS configuration won't all match, each instance must have its own initialization parameter file (*INIT.ORA*). When you change a parameter in an OPS configuration, make sure to consider whether that parameter is a global constant parameter. If it is a global constant parameter and you change it, you must remember to change it in all of the parameter files. Chapter 7, *Administering an OPS Database*, goes into detail on the subject of OPS initialization parameters and the files used to manage them.

Place all common initialization parameters in one common parameter file. Then, use the IFILE directive in each instance-specific parameter file to include this common file. This eases the administrative burden of keeping the global common parameters in sync. For this scheme to work, the common parameter file must reside on a filesystem that's accessible from all OPS nodes.

Datafiles

Datafiles are shared by all instances. Each instance in an OPS configuration must have access to all of the datafiles that make up a database. Each instance will verify access to all online datafiles at startup. In addition, whenever you add a new datafile, all instances verify access to that file. If an instance cannot access all online datafiles, it won't be able to open the database, and Oracle will display an error message.

Control Files

Under OPS, all instances share the control files for a database, and each instance must have access to *all* the control files. Control files for an OPS database contain some additional information not found in control files used with a single-instance database. When OPS is being used, the control files are used to keep track of the global constant parameters discussed earlier. When you start a new instance, the global constant parameters from the initialization file for that instance are compared to the values in the control file. If they don't match, the instance will not start and an error will be reported. This prevents you from mistakenly getting these parameters out of sync.

Online Redo Log Files

Each instance in an OPS configuration has its own set of redo log files. However, each instance must have access to the redo log files used by all other instances. The reason for this is that if an instance fails, one of the other instances accessing the database will read the redo logs from the failed instance and recover any committed changes made by the failed instance that have not yet been written to the datafiles.

As with a standalone instance, each OPS instance must have at least two groups of redo log files. Further, in an OPS database, the redo log files are organized into threads. A *thread* is a set of two or more redo log groups. In a standalone configuration, all the redo log groups for a database are in one thread, and the instance cycles through each group in the thread as changes are made to the database. In an OPS configuration, you must have multiple threads—one for each instance. When an OPS instance starts, it is assigned one thread of the redo log. For an illustration, refer to Figure 6-4, which shows an OPS configuration in which each instance has its own thread of redo log.

Just as redo log groups are numbered, so are redo log threads. Each thread is identified by a thread number. Threads can have different numbers of redo log groups (at least two). The redo log files can be mirrored within a group, and the number of mirrored redo log members in each group may vary from group to group and thread to thread. However, for ease of administration, we recommend having the same number of redo log groups in each thread and the same number of members in each group.

When an instance starts, it acquires a thread of redo log. The specific thread acquired is the one specified by the initialization parameter THREAD. If THREAD is not specified (the default value is 0), the instance may acquire any one of the threads. In such a case, because the threads change, the specific redo log files used by an instance will change each time the instance is stopped and restarted.

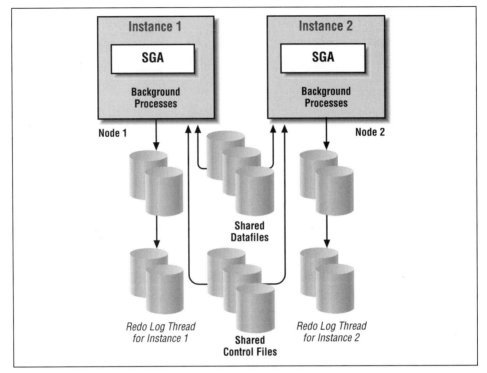

Figure 6-4. OPS instances with database files

For a detailed discussion of redo threads and how to create and enable them, see Chapter 7.

Archived Redo Log Files

Archiving of redo log files for each OPS instance is handled just as a standalone instance is. Each instance has its own ARCH process and writes to its own archive log destination. Since online redo logs are local to each instance, archived redo logs also are local to each instance. During normal operation, archived log files of one instance need not be accessible to other instances. However, when performing recovery using archived logs, archived log files of all instances must be accessible to the instance doing the recovery.

Alert Log and Trace Files

Each instance has its own alert log file and generates its own trace files. The locations of these files are set by initialization parameters specific to each instance. Each instance has its own destination for these files, and the directory for these files resides on the local node for that instance.

Integrated Distributed Lock Manager

Database resources such as data blocks, index blocks, rollback segments, and the data dictionary are shared among all OPS instances. To prevent conflicts, a locking mechanism is needed to control access to these resources. The Integrated Distributed Lock Manager (IDLM) provides this locking mechanism and does the following:

- Maintains a list of shared database resources

- Allocates locks on these resources

- Coordinates lock requests

- Keeps track of granted locks on resources

Two background processes, the Lock Manager Daemon (LMD) and the Lock Monitor (LMON), together with a distributed lock area in the SGA, constitute the Integrated Distributed Lock Manager. These components are shown in Figure 6-5.

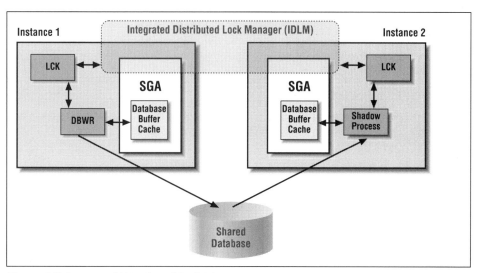

Figure 6-5. Integrated Distributed Lock Manager

The locking status of various database resources is maintained in an area of the SGA referred to as the *distributed lock area*. This lock information is distributed across all OPS nodes. Each node maintains locking status for a subset of database resources. The node that maintains information on a particular database resource is called the *master node* for the particular resource. Lock requests by any node for a resource are referred to the master node for that resource. Distributing lock information across many nodes provides fault tolerance. If one node fails, only a subset of the lock information needs to be redistributed among the surviving nodes. Similarly, when instances are started or stopped, lock information is redistributed among the running nodes.

IDLM is one of the major differences between Oracle7 Parallel Server and Oracle8 Parallel Server. The lock management subsystem used in Oracle7 is external to Oracle and is referred to as the Distributed Lock Manager (DLM). DLM historically has been supplied by the operating system vendor as an OS component. Because each operating system vendor provided its own implementation of DLM, the functionality tended to be different on each platform. Understandably, these differences led to problems. So with the release of Oracle8, the lock management functionality has been integrated into the Oracle software. IDLM in Oracle8 provides consistency across platforms. Chapter 8 discusses the IDLM in more detail.

Background Processes Specific to OPS

A standalone instance has a set of background processes, including DBW*n*, LGWR, SMON, PMON, CKPT, and a few other optional processes. A parallel server instance has all of these, plus a few extra processes that are specific to OPS; these are LCK*n*, LMD*n*, and LMON. Oracle8*i* has introduced a new process named BSP. The following sections describe these OPS-specific processes.

Lock processes (LCKn)

Each OPS instance has at least one background lock process (LCK0) to handle its locking requests, and may have as many as 10. The processes are always numbered LCK0, LCK1, and so on, up to LCK9. The LCK processes manage the locks used by an instance. They are responsible for maintaining the distributed lock area in the SGA, and for communicating with the Integrated Distributed Lock Manager.

The GC_LCK_PROCS initialization parameter controls the number of LCK processes. The default value for this parameter is 1. You can increase the number of LCK processes by increasing the value of this parameter. All instances in an OPS environment must have the same number of LCK processes and, consequently, must have the same setting for GC_LCK_PROCS. For most environments, one lock process, LCK0, is sufficient. However, you may want to start more LCK processes to improve performance if either of the following scenarios applies:

- You need to manage more locks than one LCK process can handle. There is a limit to the number of locks that one LCK process can manage. The limit depends on the operating system. If more locks are required, then additional LCK processes must be started.

- The LCK0 process is consuming too much CPU.

GC_LCK_PROCS is obsolete in Oracle8*i*.

Lock Manager Daemon process (LMDn)

Each OPS instance has at least one Lock Manager Daemon process (LMD*n*). This process, which is a component of the IDLM, handles remote locking requests. Lock requests from remote instances are sent to the LMD process of the holding instance. The LMD process communicates with the LCK process to release the lock requested by the remote instance.

Lock Monitor process (LMON)

Each OPS instance has one Lock Monitor process (LMON). This process is responsible for cleaning up global locks in the event that an Oracle server process, or an entire instance, terminates abnormally. This is necessary, because otherwise all the resources held by the failed process or instance would remain locked as long as the database remained open.

As we've mentioned, lock information is distributed across all OPS instances, and each instance keeps information for a subset of locks. LMON also is responsible for redistributing global locks whenever an OPS instance is started or stopped.

Block Server process (BSP)

The Block Server process (BSP) is required only in Oracle8*i* and is needed to implement cache fusion. This process is responsible for preparing a consistent read (CR) version of a block in the holding instance and then transmitting that block to the corresponding BSP process of the requesting instance over the fast interconnect, in order to maintain cache coherency.

Interaction of IDLM with Other Oracle Components

Let's use an example to explain how various components of OPS interact to control access to a shared database resource. For this example, let's assume that two nodes are configured in an OPS installation. Instance 1 is updating a block in its buffer cache. Instance 2 wants to update the same block. Figure 6-6 illustrates this scenario.

With respect to this figure, the following process occurs when instance 2 needs to modify a block that is currently in the process of being modified by instance 1:

1. A server process in instance 2 sends a request to a local LCK process to acquire the lock on the block.

2. The LCK process on node 2 then communicates with IDLM to acquire the lock.

3. IDLM determines that the lock is currently held by instance 1. IDLM communicates to the LCK process of node 1, requesting the release of the lock.

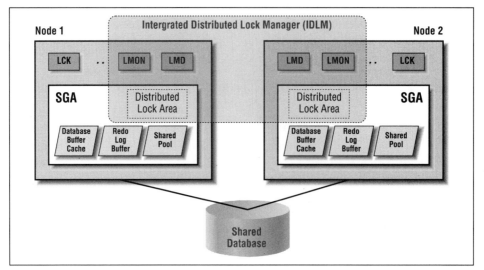

Figure 6-6. Interaction of IDLM with other Oracle components

4. Before instance 1 can release the lock, it must signal its DBWn process to write the block to disk.

5. After the block has been written to the disk, the LCK process on node 1 releases the lock and informs IDLM that the lock has been released.

6. IDLM then informs the LCK process on node 2 that the lock is available.

7. The LCK process on node 2 informs the requesting server process that it can acquire the lock.

8. The server process on node 2 acquires the lock, reads the block from disk, and modifies it.

Group Membership Service

Oracle Parallel Server runs in a multinode environment. In a multinode environment, operating systems typically provide a component called a cluster manager that manages inter-node communication and coordination. Cluster managers are hardware- and operating system-specific. Oracle8 provides a component known as the Group Membership Service (GMS) that communicates with the cluster manager and provides inter-instance initialization and coordination between multiple Oracle instances. A GMS daemon runs on each node. GMS keeps track of instance startup and shutdown in an OPS environment and is notified by the cluster manager of any instance failures. Figure 6-7 shows the relationship between the GMS daemon and the cluster manager on nodes of an OPS cluster.

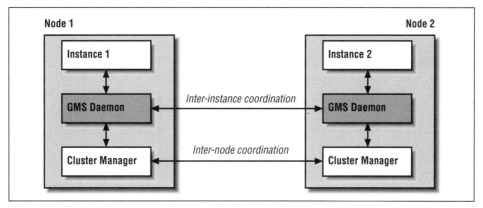

Figure 6-7. Group Membership Services

 When Oracle8*i* was released, the functionality provided by GMS was integrated into the Oracle kernel as the Cluster Group Service, and also into vendor-specific cluster managers. Consequently, in Oracle8*i*, the GMS daemon no longer exists.

Rollback Segments in OPS

All OPS instances need to use rollback segments to store undo information. The SYSTEM rollback segment is shared and is used by all instances for transactions involving system objects. In addition to the shared SYSTEM rollback segment, each instance needs at least one rollback segment of its own. You won't be able to successfully start an instance and open a database unless that instance can acquire at least one rollback segment. If an instance cannot acquire even a single rollback segment, the instance will start and the database will be mounted, but the database won't be opened. A rollback segment can be acquired by one instance only. Therefore, you must have at least as many rollback segments in your database as the number of concurrent instances that open that database.

A rollback segment acquired by an instance remains exclusive to that instance. No other instance can write undo information to this rollback segment. However, all instances can read from this rollback segment to maintain read consistency.

Public and Private Rollback Segments

Rollback segments can be public or private. A public rollback segment is created by using the PUBLIC clause with the CREATE ROLLBACK SEGMENT command. Any rollback segments created without using the PUBLIC clause are considered private. Public rollback segments can be acquired by any instance opening a database. A private rollback segment can be acquired by an instance only when the rollback segment's name has been listed in the ROLLBACK_SEGMENTS initialization parameter for the instance.

Private rollback segments are preferable for ease of administration. If your rollback segments are private, you will always know which rollback segment will be acquired by which instance. The same is not true for public rollback segments. Another advantage of private rollback segments is that you can place the rollback segments used by each instance into separate tablespaces. These tablespaces can then be spread across disks to avoid disk contention between two instances.

The ROLLBACK_SEGMENTS Parameter

The ROLLBACK_SEGMENTS parameter is an initialization parameter that lists the names of all the rollback segments that you want an instance to acquire and use. Whenever you start an instance, it will attempt to acquire all the rollback segments specified by this parameter. Failure to acquire even one of the specified rollback segments will prevent the instance from opening the database and will result in an error.

The default value for the ROLLBACK_SEGMENTS parameter is NULL. A NULL value causes an instance to attempt to acquire the available (not acquired by any other instance) public rollback segments when that instance starts.

As we said earlier, rather than allowing rollback segments to be randomly distributed among instances, it's generally preferable to create private rollback segments and to specifically assign those to the various instances operating on a database. Because one rollback segment can be acquired by only one instance, each instance must specify a different list of values for the ROLLBACK_SEGMENT parameter in the initialization file, as shown here:

```
ROLLBACK_SEGMENTS = (RBS01,RBS02)
```

In this example, the ROLLBACK_SEGMENTS parameter specifies a list of private rollback segments to be acquired at instance startup time. Note that the list is enclosed by parentheses, and the rollback segments are delimited by commas within the parentheses.

How Many Rollback Segments?

An instance needs at least one rollback segment (private or public) in order to open a database. However, it's often necessary or desirable for an instance to have more than one rollback segment. Two initialization parameters determine the number of rollback segments required by an instance—the TRANSACTIONS parameter and the TRANSACTIONS_PER_ROLLBACK parameter. Using these two parameters, Oracle applies the following mathematical formula to determine the number of rollback segments to acquire:

```
TRANSACTIONS / TRANSACTIONS_PER_ROLLBACK_SEGMENT
```

When you start an instance in which the ROLLBACK_SEGMENTS parameter is NULL, the instance will attempt to acquire the required number of rollback segments from the pool of available (not acquired by any other instance) public rollback segments for the database. If the ROLLBACK_SEGMENTS parameter contains a list, the instance first will attempt to acquire all the rollback segments specified in the list. Then it will acquire any additional rollback segments it needs from the pool of available public rollback segments. No error results if an instance cannot acquire the required number of rollback segments, but performance may be adversely affected.

The History of Oracle Parallel Server

Oracle first made its parallel server technology available in 1989. When OPS was first released, only DEC VAX clusters were supported. Since 1989, many new features have been added with each release of the Oracle software. Platform support has grown as well, and OPS is now available on a wide variety of platforms, including IBM, HP, Sun, and Windows NT. Here is a list showing some of the major milestones in the development of OPS:

1989

OPS introduced in Oracle Version 6 (release 6.2) on VAX/VMS.

1992

Redo log files made local to each instance in Oracle7.

1997

Distributed Lock Manager integrated with Oracle kernel in Oracle8.

1997

Global dynamic performance views (GV$) introduced in Oracle8.

1998

OPS supported under Windows NT.

1999

Cache fusion technique incorporated in Oracle8*i* to reduce OPS overhead.

7

In this chapter:
• *Creating an OPS Database*
• *Starting and Stopping an OPS Database*
• *Managing Instance Groups*
• *Backing Up an OPS Database*
• *Recovering an OPS Database*

Administering an OPS Database

In Chapter 6, *Oracle Parallel Server Architecture*, we introduced the fundamental concepts of Oracle Parallel Server (OPS) and its architecture. In this chapter we'll explain specifically how to administer an Oracle Parallel Server database. This discussion includes the process you go through to create the database.

Creating an OPS Database

An OPS database is created in much the same way as a standalone database. The actual startup of an instance and the execution of the CREATE DATABASE command are exactly the same for both types of databases. The differences involve how you manage initialization parameters and how you must convert the newly created database into an OPS database. Initially, an OPS database must be created by just one instance, as a standalone database. Only after the database has been created do you take steps to convert it into an OPS database, one that is open by multiple instances simultaneously.

Preparing to Create the Database

In preparation for creating an OPS database, you must do the following:

- Ensure that you have the proper hardware and software configuration. Refer to Chapter 6 and Chapter 2, *Architectures for Parallel Processing*, for more information on hardware and software configuration for Oracle Parallel Server.

- Organize your disk space to hold the Oracle software, the OPS database files, and other related files. On most platforms (including Unix and Windows NT) all datafiles, redo log files, and control files must be on raw devices. Refer to your operating system documentation for information on creating raw devices, and contact your system administrator for help in doing that.

- Install the Oracle server software, including the Oracle Parallel Server Option, on all the nodes that you are going to use. For detailed information on doing this, refer to the Oracle installation manuals for your platform.

- Create initialization parameter files for all instances. Create a common parameter file, accessible to all instances, to hold the global constant parameters. Recall from Chapter 6 that these parameters must be the same for all instances in an OPS environment.

- Write the CREATE DATABASE command, making sure that you properly specify the OPS-specific options.

The next few sections discuss the specifics of writing the initialization files and the CREATE DATABASE command for an OPS database. After that, we'll discuss the actual creation process, showing you how the database is first created as a stand-alone instance and how it is subsequently converted into an OPS database.

Managing Initialization Parameters

You will need to be concerned about three categories of initialization parameters in an OPS database:

- Some parameters *must be identical* across all instances. These are known as *global constant parameters*. To change a global constant parameter, you need to shut down all the instances, change the parameter for all the instances, and then restart the instances.

- Some other parameters *may be different* for each instance.

- A third set of parameters *must be different* for each instance.

You'll need to manage all these parameters in a way that will make them easy to modify.

Table 7-1 lists the global constant parameters, along with some other parameters that have OPS-specific considerations. This table does not cover all initialization parameters of Oracle, nor does it cover all the parameters required for OPS configuration; it shows only the parameters in the three categories just listed.

For a detailed discussion of the initialization parameters, please refer to the *Oracle Reference Manual*.

Some Oracle manuals refer to global constant parameters as GC_* parameters. GC_FILES_TO_LOCKS and GC_ROLLBACK_LOCKS are two good examples. However, not all GC_* parameters need to be identical across all instances. In addition, there are some parameters, without the GC_ prefix, that must be identical across all instances. In this book, we refer to all parameters that must be identical across instances as global constant parameters.

Table 7-1. The Impact of OPS on Initialization Parameters

Global Constant Parameters (Must Be Identical)	Recommended Identical (May Be Different)	Must Be Different
PARALLEL_SERVER	PARALLEL_MAX_SERVERS	ROLLBACK_SEGMENTS
PARALLEL_SERVER_ INSTANCES[a]	PARALLEL_DEFAULT_ MAX_INSTANCES[b]	THREAD
DB_BLOCK_SIZE	LM_LOCKS	INSTANCE_NUMBER
DB_NAME	LM_PROCS[c]	
CONTROL_FILES	LM_RESS	
GC_FILES_TO_LOCKS	LOG_ARCHIVE_FORMAT	
GC_LCK_PROCS[b]		
GC_ROLLBACK_LOCKS		
CACHE_SIZE_THRESHOLD[b]		
COMPATIBLE		
COMPATIBLE_NO_RECOVERY		
DB_DOMAIN		
DB_FILES		
DML_LOCKS[d]		
FREEZE_DB_FOR_FAST_ INSTANCE_RECOVERY[b]		
LOG_FILES[b]		
MAX_COMMIT_ PROPAGATION_DELAY		
ROW_LOCKING		

[a] New in Oracle8*i*.
[b] Obsolete in Oracle8*i*.
[c] Obsolete in Oracle8*i* (release 8.1.6).
[d] If one instance has this parameter set to zero, then all instances must have it set to zero. If the values are nonzero, they don't have to match.

Because the parameters for any one instance in an OPS configuration won't all match those used for the other instances, each instance must have its own initialization parameter file. It's best if you also have a separate common parameter file for the global constant parameters.

When you're using a common parameter file, make sure that each instance-specific parameter file uses the IFILE directive to include the common parameters. The IFILE directive tells Oracle to include the contents of another file. Also make sure that the common parameter file resides in a location that's accessible from each node in the parallel server environment.

For example, let's assume that you have an OPS database named TEST with two instances named TEST1 and TEST2. These two instances reside on two separate nodes. Each instance has its own specific parameter file, stored on its own node. The pathnames and filenames for these parameter files are *$ORACLE_HOME/dbs/ initTEST1.ora* and *$ORACLE_HOME/dbs/initTEST2.ora* respectively. In each case, *$ORACLE_HOME* refers to a node-specific directory. The global constant parameters, however, are all stored in a file named *init_common.ora* in a directory on a filesystem accessible to all nodes. Let's say that $COMMON points to this directory. To include the common parameter file, each instance-specific parameter file must contain the following line:

```
IFILE = $COMMON/init_common.ora
```

When you start each instance, Oracle reads the instance-specific parameter file, finds the IFILE directive, and then reads the common parameters from the specified include file. Figure 7-1 illustrates this arrangement.

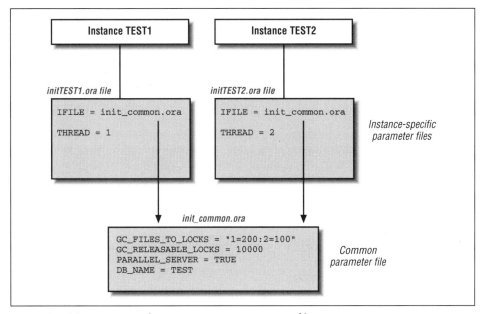

Figure 7-1. Two instances sharing a common parameter file

 If you do not have a common directory accessible from all nodes, you won't be able to create and use a common parameter file. Instead, the parameter file for each instance will have its own copy of the global constant parameters. In such a case, be careful when changing these individual files; make sure that you make identical changes in each file.

When changing a parameter in an OPS configuration, make sure to think about whether it is a global constant parameter. If you are changing a global constant parameter, then you must change it for each instance. If you are using a common parameter file for global constant parameters, this is easy because the change can be made in that one file. If you aren't using a common parameter file, you must edit each instance's parameter file, repeating the change for as many instances as you have. Using a common parameter file minimizes work and minimizes the chance of making a mistake.

Writing the OPS-Specific CREATE DATABASE Command

When writing the CREATE DATABASE command for a new OPS database, you will need to be aware of special considerations for the following command options:

    MAXINSTANCES
    MAXLOGFILES
    MAXLOGHISTORY
    MAXDATAFILES

If you don't specify these options properly during database creation, you will have to change the options by re-creating the database control file.

MAXINSTANCES

MAXINSTANCES sets the maximum number of instances that can access the database concurrently. The default value is 2 for most operating systems. Since the whole point of using OPS is to have many instances accessing a database at once, the default limit of 2 may be inadequate for your needs. It's best to specify this option explicitly rather than leaving it at the default.

Always set MAXINSTANCES to a value larger than the maximum number of instances expected on the database. This value allows for some growth, enabling you to later increase the number of instances without having to re-create the control file.

MAXLOGFILES

MAXLOGFILES sets the maximum number of redo log groups that can ever be created for the database. Each instance of an OPS environment has its own redo logs. Collectively, the redo log groups of an instance are referred to as a *thread*. Each instance has one thread of redo log. To set the MAXLOGFILES option, you should multiply the expected number of redo log threads by the expected number of redo log groups per thread.

MAXLOGHISTORY

MAXLOGHISTORY specifies the maximum number of archived redo log files that can be recorded in the log history of the control file for automatic media recovery. The default value for this option is 0, and this value disables the log history. When the log history exceeds the number specified by this option, old history entries are overwritten. Since OPS databases have many more redo log files than a standalone database has, we recommend that you set this option to a large value (approximately 1000).

MAXDATAFILES

MAXDATAFILES sets the maximum number of datafiles that can be created for a database. An OPS database generally has more datafiles than a standalone database. Give some thought to this fact, and make sure you set MAXDATAFILES to a high enough value.

Creating the Database as a Standalone Instance

An OPS database is created with the parallel server disabled. Only after the database is created do you enable OPS and open it as an OPS database. You need to do the following on one node to create the database:

1. Set PARALLEL_SERVER = FALSE in the initialization parameter file.

2. Start Group Membership Services (GMS) on the node being used to create the database. The process for starting GMS is discussed in the section "Using Group Membership Services" later in this chapter. The discussion about GMS applies only to Oracle8. There is no GMS in Oracle8*i*.

3. Start Server Manager and specify CONNECT INTERNAL.

4. Start up an instance with the NOMOUNT option.

5. Execute your CREATE DATABASE command.

Here is a sample CREATE DATABASE command:

```
CREATE DATABASE "TEST"
    MAXLOGFILES 200
    MAXLOGMEMBERS 4
    MAXDATAFILES 1000
    MAXINSTANCES 32
    MAXLOGHISTORY 1000
    CHARACTER SET "US7ASCII"
    DATAFILE
        '/dev/sys1_test1' size 200M
LOGFILE
  GROUP 1 (
    '/dev/redo1a_test1',
    '/dev/redo1b_test1'
```

```
  ) SIZE 270M,
  GROUP 2 (
    '/dev/redo2a_test1',
    '/dev/redo2b_test1'
  ) SIZE 270M,
  GROUP 3 (
    '/dev/redo3a_test1',
    '/dev/redo3b_test1'
  ) SIZE 270M
;
```

After the CREATE DATABASE command has successfully completed, the database will be left mounted and opened in exclusive mode by the instance that created it.

Converting the Database to OPS

To enable Oracle Parallel Server, you need to do the following:

1. Set PARALLEL_SERVER = TRUE in the initialization parameter file for all instances that will be opening the database.

2. Create additional rollback segments for each instance, and use the ROLLBACK_SEGMENTS parameter to associate rollback segments with each instance.

3. Create redo log threads for each instance.

4. Shut down the instance that created the database.

5. Start GMS on all of the nodes.

6. Start all the instances.

Most of these tasks are straightforward, and you should already know how to perform them. You'll change initialization parameters, start an instance, and stop an instance just as you would in a standalone configuration. There are, however, some considerations you need to take into account regarding rollback segments and redo log threads in an OPS configuration.

Additional rollback segments

You must create at least one rollback segment for each instance of a parallel server database. You may prefer to create more rollback segments for each instance, depending on the number of users and transactions that you expect that instance to handle.

In an OPS database, rollback segments can be private or public. You create a public rollback segment using the CREATE PUBLIC ROLLBACK SEGMENT command. You create a private rollback segment using the CREATE ROLLBACK SEGMENT command (omitting the PUBLIC keyword).

We recommend that each OPS instance use private rollback segments and that you assign them to each instance using the ROLLBACK_SEGMENTS initialization parameter. We also recommend that you place the rollback segments for each instance in separate tablespaces. Chapter 6 contains a more detailed discussion on managing rollback segments in an OPS environment and on the difference between private and public rollback segments.

Redo log threads

Redo logs (which we introduced in Chapter 6) are organized into threads. Each OPS instance needs a thread of redo log in order to open the database. Therefore, you must create online redo log threads for each instance. This section shows you how to create, enable, and disable redo log threads for the instances in an OPS database.

The redo log files specified in the CREATE DATABASE command comprise thread 1. Additional threads are created using the ALTER DATABASE ADD LOGFILE command. For example, the following command creates thread 2:

```
ALTER DATABASE ADD LOGFILE THREAD 2
    GROUP 4 ('/dev/redo4a_test2','/dev/redo4b_test2') SIZE 270M,
    GROUP 5 ('/dev/redo5a_test2','/dev/redo5b_test2') SIZE 270M,
    GROUP 6 ('/dev/redo6a_test2','/dev/redo6b_test2') SIZE 270M;
```

A thread must be enabled before an instance can use it. You can enable a thread as public or private. To enable a thread as public, use the command:

```
ALTER DATABASE ENABLE PUBLIC THREAD 2;
```

To enable a thread as private, use the command:

```
ALTER DATABASE ENABLE THREAD 2;
```

If a thread is enabled as a public thread, it can be used by any instance. If it is enabled as a private thread, then it must be explicitly acquired by an instance before it can be used. You can use the THREAD initialization parameter for that purpose. When an instance opens a database, it acquires the redo log thread specified by the THREAD parameter (if that parameter is set in the instance's initialization file). For example, the following *INIT.ORA* entry tells an instance to acquire redo log thread 3:

```
THREAD = 3      # This instance uses thread 3
```

Remember that a thread of redo log can be used by only one instance at a time. If you use the THREAD parameter to assign redo log threads to the instances of an OPS database, you must ensure that the setting is different for each instance.

In Oracle8*i*, you can also create an OPS database using the Database Configuration Assistant (DBCA). This utility is invoked at the end of the installation process when you first install the Oracle software. You can also invoke it any time using the command *dbassist*. The assistant asks questions about your OPS environment and the database that you want to create, prepares the necessary initialization files, and then runs the scripts necessary to create that database. You even have the option of using the assistant to generate scripts that you can later modify and run manually. Refer to Oracle Corporation's *Oracle8i Parallel Server Setup and Configuration Guide* for detailed information on the Database Creation Assistant.

Starting and Stopping an OPS Database

Starting up an OPS database is quite different from starting up a standalone database.

You can start an Oracle Parallel Server instance in either exclusive mode or shared mode. In exclusive mode, only one instance can mount and open the database. In shared mode, multiple instances can mount and open the database simultaneously. The initialization parameter PARALLEL_SERVER determines which mode is used when a database is started. Shared mode is the normal operating mode for an OPS database. Exclusive mode is required for certain administrative tasks such as switching ARCHIVELOG mode on or off. (See the "ARCHIVELOG Mode" section later in this chapter.)

If you are using Oracle8 (not Oracle8*i*), you must start Group Membership Services (GMS) before you can start an OPS instance. This is true regardless of whether you are starting the instance in shared or exclusive mode. The next few sections show you how to start up an OPS database in exclusive mode and shared mode and how to start GMS.

Starting an OPS Database in Exclusive Mode

To start up an instance in exclusive mode, you must choose an instance to use, and you must set the initialization parameter PARALLEL_SERVER to FALSE for that instance. Only one instance can open a database in exclusive mode. In order for that to happen, you must first shut down all the instances that normally open the database in shared mode.

While exclusive mode implies that only one instance has the database open, the reverse is not necessarily true. Suppose that you have a two-instance OPS database, with both instances running in shared mode. If you shut down instance 2, instance 1 is not automatically converted to exclusive mode. One instance in shared mode is not equivalent to one instance in exclusive mode.

Once you have PARALLEL_SERVER set to FALSE for the instance you want to start, you can use the STARTUP command from Server Manager to start the instance.

 The SHARED, PARALLEL, and EXCLUSIVE options of the STARTUP command are obsolete in Oracle8. You can issue the STARTUP EXCLUSIVE and STARTUP PARALLEL commands from Server Manager, but the result still will be controlled by the PARALLEL_SERVER initialization parameter. The EXCLUSIVE, SHARED, and PARALLEL options of the STARTUP command are ignored.

Starting an OPS Database in Shared Mode

To start up an instance in shared mode, set the initialization parameter PARALLEL_SERVER to TRUE. You can start multiple instances in shared mode at the same time. For an instance to start in shared mode, it must have the following:

- At least one rollback segment
- At least one thread of redo log having at least two redo log groups

Creating rollback segments and redo log threads is discussed earlier in this chapter. You can use the STARTUP command from Server Manager to start each instance separately, or you can use either the opsctl utility or Oracle Enterprise Manager (OEM) to start all the instances at once.

Using Group Membership Services

For Oracle8 (not Oracle 8*i*), the Group Membership Services (GMS) (described in Chapter 6) must be running on each node in which you want to start an OPS instance. Several OPS platforms provide a utility named ogmsctl that you can use to start and stop GMS. Refer to the Oracle installation manual for your platform to find out if your platform supports ogmsctl.

The ogmsctl Utility

The ogmsctl utility is installed on your server when you install Oracle with the OPS option. You can use ogmsctl to start, stop, and check the status of GMS. To start GMS on a node, issue the following command at the operating system prompt:

```
ogmsctl start
```

To stop GMS on a node, issue the following command at the operating system prompt:

```
ogmsctl stop
```

To check the status if GMS is running on a node, issue the following command at the operating system prompt:

```
ogmsctl status
```

The opsctl Utility

Several OPS platforms provide the opsctl utility, which can be used to start and stop an OPS instance. The opsctl utility is installed on your server when you install Oracle with the OPS option. To find out if your platform supports opsctl and for information on configuring opsctl, refer to your platform-specific Oracle installation manual.

The opsctl utility can start and stop three stages of an OPS instance: GMS, the instances, and the listener. These stages may be started and stopped individually or all together. You can use opsctl on one node to start or stop any of these three stages on all nodes of an OPS database.

To start GMS, the instances, and the listeners on all nodes, issue the following command at the operating system prompt:

```
opsctl start -s gms,inst,lsnr
```

If you are running a two-node OPS configuration, your output will look like this:

```
GMS successfully started on node# 1 ( 'n01' )
GMS successfully started on node# 2 ( 'n02' )
Instance successfully started on node# 1 ( 'n01' )
Instance successfully started on node# 2 ( 'n02' )
Listener successfully started on node# 1 ( 'n01' )
Listener successfully started on node# 2 ( 'n02' )
```

In the opsctl command shown here, "gms" stands for the GMS stage, "inst" stands for the instance stage, and "lsnr" stands for the listener stage. You need to use these keywords to start the respective stages. For example, to start GMS only, but on all nodes, you can issue the following command:

```
opsctl start -s gms
```

The output from this command will resemble this:

```
GMS successfully started on node# 1 ( 'n01' )
GMS successfully started on node# 2 ( 'n02' )
```

Starting an Oracle8i OPS Database

Starting an Oracle8i OPS database is a bit different from starting an Oracle8 OPS database; this is because GMS no longer exists in Oracle8i. Follow these steps to start an Oracle8i OPS database:

1. Start the cluster manager software on each node on which you want to run an OPS instance. The cluster manager software is platform-specific software supplied by the hardware vendor. For more details on cluster manager, refer to Oracle Corporation's *Oracle8i Parallel Server Concepts and Administration* manual and to your operating system–specific Oracle documentation.

2. Set the initialization parameter PARALLEL_SERVER to TRUE or FALSE, depending on whether you want to start in exclusive or shared mode.

3. Use Server Manager on each node to start each instance individually, or use the opsctl utility to start all instances at once.

Stopping an OPS Database

To stop an OPS database, you can use Server Manager on each node to stop each instance individually, or you can use the opsctl utility to stop all the instances at once. To stop GMS, all instances, and all the listeners, issue the following command at the operating system prompt:

```
opsctl stop -s gms,inst,lsnr
```

Here's what the output will look like in a two-node configuration:

```
Listener successfully shutdown on node# 1 ( 'n01' )
Listener successfully shutdown on node# 2 ( 'n02' )
Instance successfully shutdown on node# 1 ( 'n01' )
Instance successfully shutdown on node# 2 ( 'n02' )
GMS successfully shutdown on node# 1 ( 'n01' )
GMS successfully shutdown on node# 2 ( 'n02' )
```

There is no GMS in Oracle8i. To stop an Oracle8i OPS database, you can use Server Manager on each node to stop each instance individually, or you can use the opsctl command as shown here, but without the "gms" keyword, to stop all instances at once.

Managing Instance Groups

You can logically group instances of an OPS database into multiple instance groups. You do this by setting the INSTANCE_GROUPS parameter in the initialization parameter file. The INSTANCE_GROUPS parameter defines instance groups and assigns an instance to them. For example, when you specify the following *INIT.ORA* parameter for an instance, that instance will belong to groupA:

```
INSTANCE_GROUPS = groupA
```

One instance can belong to multiple instance groups at the same time. The INSTANCE_GROUPS parameter specifies the group names using a comma-separated list—for example:

```
INSTANCE_GROUPS = groupA, groupB
```

With this setting, the instance will be in groupA as well as in groupB.

The instances belonging to a particular instance group can be determined by referring to the *INIT.ORA* files of all the instances. Let's consider an OPS configuration with four instances having the settings shown in Table 7-2.

Table 7-2. INSTANCE_GROUPS Settings for a Four-Instance Configuration

Instance	INSTANCE_GROUPS Setting
1	g12, g14, g123
2	g12, g23, g123
3	g23, g123
4	g14

The settings shown in Table 7-2 define four instance groups—g12, g14, g123, and g23 in the system—and assign instances to groups as specified. Instance group g12 is specified in the initialization parameter files of instances 1 and 2. Therefore, instance group g12 consists of those two instances. Group names do not need to reflect the instance numbers. We could have used any arbitrary name in place of g12.

Instance groups can overlap each other, meaning that two groups can share one or more instances. The INSTANCE_GROUPS parameter is static and cannot be changed while the instances are running.

Instance groups are useful for two reasons:

- They allow you to summarize information returned by the GV$ views in a useful manner. The OPS_ADMIN_GROUP initialization parameter is used to facilitate this. Chapter 10, *Monitoring and Tuning OPS*, discusses this use of the GV$ views in more detail. Note that OPS_ADMIN_GROUP is obsolete in Oracle8*i*.

- They allow you to specify which group of instances gets used for parallel execution of SQL statements. The PARALLEL_INSTANCE_GROUP initialization parameter (discussed in Chapter 13, *Parallel Execution in OPS*) is used for this purpose.

Backing Up an OPS Database

Backing up an OPS database is much the same as backing up a standalone database. There are only a few differences to be aware of. This section presents a brief review of database backup concepts and points out the differences between backing up a standalone instance and backing up an OPS database. We'll briefly discuss ARCHIVELOG mode, cold and hot backups, and the use of standby databases and the Oracle8 Recovery Manager from an OPS.

ARCHIVELOG Mode

An Oracle database can run in either NOARCHIVELOG mode or ARCHIVELOG mode. In NOARCHIVELOG mode, the redo log files are recycled and overwritten without being saved offline. In ARCHIVELOG mode, the redo log files are archived before they are overwritten. Running in NOARCHIVELOG mode leaves open the possibility of data loss in the event of a failure. Complete and up-to-the-minute recovery from a failure is possible only when running in ARCHIVELOG mode. You must run the database in ARCHIVELOG mode if you want to do any of the following:

- Recover completely from a media failure
- Perform point-in-time recovery
- Perform a hot (online) backup

The following sections describe how to enable ARCHIVELOG mode and set the corresponding initialization parameters.

Setting initialization parameters for ARCHIVELOG mode

To run a parallel server database in ARCHIVELOG mode, set the following three initialization parameters on each instance:

LOG_ARCHIVE_START

Enables automatic archiving. When this parameter is set to TRUE, Oracle will start the ARCH background process to archive the online redo logs before they are overwritten.

LOG_ARCHIVE_FORMAT

Specifies the format to use when naming the archived log files. You can specify the thread number and the log sequence number in the format. The thread number specification is useful only for an OPS database. For non-OPS databases, the thread number is always 1. It is always best to specify the thread number in the LOG_ARCHIVE_FORMAT specification so that you can easily identify the archived log files associated with each thread. An example of a LOG_ARCHIVE_FORMAT specification is:

```
LOG_ARCHIVE_FORMAT = TEST_%t_%s.arc
```

While creating the archived redo log files, Oracle replaces the %t in the name by the thread number and the %s by the log sequence number. The preceding specification will result in filenames such as *TEST_1_23.arc, TEST_2_49. arc*, and so forth. You can use %T and %S in place of %t and %s to get left-zero-padded thread number and log sequence numbers.

LOG_ARCHIVE_DEST

Specifies the destination to which the archived log files will be written. The archive log destination can be one of the following:

— A separate filesystem for each instance local to each node

— A common directory for all instances in a filesystem that is NFS-mounted on all nodes

If you are having each instance write archived redo log files to a filesystem local to the node on which that instance is running, you can take either of two approaches to naming that location. One approach is to use the same name for all the archive log filesystems. While each node will have its own filesystem, the name will be uniform across all nodes. Doing this allows you to specify the archive log destination in the common initialization parameter file. The other approach is to use a different directory for each instance's archived log files. If your filesystem names are different on each node, you will have to specify the archived log destination in the instance-specific parameter files.

Another thing to be aware of when using local filesystems for archived log files is that the archived logs for each instance will be generated on the local node and will be accessible only to the instance that created them. During media recovery, you will have to collect the archived logs from all instances and put them in a location accessible to the instance that is actually performing the recovery.

Using an NFS-mounted directory allows all instances to archive to the same destination and also makes the archived logs of all instances accessible globally. The advantage of this approach is that, during a recovery, you don't have to perform the extra task of collecting all the archived logs and moving them to a location accessible from the instance performing the recovery. One drawback to this approach is the unreliability of NFS filesystems. If the filesystem goes down for some reason, all the instances will hang because the archiver processes won't be able to write to the archive log destination. The use of an NFS-mounted directory as an archive log destination requires a special setup. You should contact Oracle Support before using an NFS-mounted directory as your archive destination.

We recommend that you use a local filesystem as the archive log destination, even though you have to take extra care when performing media recovery to make the archive logs of all instances accessible from the instance performing the recovery. Do not use an NFS-mounted filesystem as the archive log destination.

Enabling ARCHIVELOG mode

Use the ALTER DATABASE command with the ARCHIVELOG option to put a database into ARCHIVELOG mode. You can do this only while the database is mounted, but not opened, by a single instance in exclusive mode. Follow these steps to enable ARCHIVELOG mode for an OPS database:

 Oracle recommends that you back up the database before changing its ARCHIVELOG mode.

---

1. Shut down all running instances.
2. Set the initialization parameters related to archiving for all instances.
3. Set the initialization parameter PARALLEL_SERVER to FALSE.
4. Start up an instance and mount the database. Do not open the database. Use a command such as this one:

   STARTUP MOUNT

5. Since the PARALLEL_SERVER parameter has been set to FALSE, the database is now mounted in exclusive mode.
6. Issue the following command from Server Manager to put the database into ARCHIVELOG mode:

   ALTER DATABASE ARCHIVELOG;

7. Shut down the instance.
8. Set the initialization parameter PARALLEL_SERVER back to TRUE.
9. Start up all instances in shared mode.

To reverse the process and put an OPS database into NOARCHIVELOG mode, follow steps 1, 3, and 4 as described earlier and then issue the following command from Server Manager:

   ALTER DATABASE NOARCHIVELOG;

Follow steps 7, 8, and 9 to complete the operation.

Archiving redo logs in Oracle8i

Oracle8*i* introduces some changes in database archiving. You can now have as many as 10 archiver processes. These will be named ARC0, ARC1, and so forth up to ARC9. A higher number of archiver processes helps in managing high archiving loads. Oracle8*i* also allows you to archive to more than one destination. This is accomplished using a new form of the LOG_ARCHIVE_DEST parameter that has a number on the end. For example, you can now use LOG_ARCHIVE_DEST_1, LOG_ARCHIVE_DEST_2, and so forth to set multiple archivelog destinations.

You can take advantage of the multiple archivelog destination feature in an OPS environment to improve the recoverability of the database. Using this feature, you can configure each instance to archive redo logs to the local disk, as well as to a remote destination. To archive to a remote destination, you can use NFS to mount a directory from another OPS node, and then specify this NFS-mounted directory as the second archivelog destination in your initialization parameter file.

If you have only locally archived redo logs, you have the potential of losing data in the event of a complete node failure. Having multiple copies of archive logs in local as well as remote destinations makes recovering your database easier in the event of a node failure.

Refer to Oracle Corporation's *Oracle8i Administrator's Guide* and *Oracle8i Parallel Server Setup and Configuration Guide* for more details.

Cold Backup

A cold backup of an OPS database is very similar to that of a standalone database. All the instances of the parallel server database must be shut down (with normal, immediate, or transactional priority). Once all instances have been shut down and the database closed, you can proceed to copy all the datafiles, control files, and redo log files to your backup media. If the database is running in ARCHIVELOG mode, you also should back up the archived log files from all the instances. Cold backups can be made regardless of whether the database is in ARCHIVELOG mode.

If the database is running in NOARCHIVELOG mode, the database is recoverable only to the time of the most recent cold backup. When ARCHIVELOG mode is enabled, you can use the last cold backup, together with the archived redo logs, to recover every committed change up to the point of failure.

Hot Backup

The procedure for taking a hot backup of an OPS database is the same as it is for a standalone database. The database must be running in ARCHIVELOG mode, and the hot backup is taken while the database is up and running. The database will be available to all the instances and all the users during the backup process.

Follow these steps to take a hot backup of a database:

1. Repeat these steps for each tablespace in the database:

    a. Issue the following command to place the tablespace into backup mode:

```
ALTER TABLESPACE tablespace_name BEGIN BACKUP;
```

   b. Back up the datafiles for the tablespace using an operating system utility.

   c. Issue the following command to take the tablespace out of backup mode:

   ```
   ALTER TABLESPACE tablespace_name END BACKUP;
   ```

You can take a hot backup of any tablespace from any instance.

2. Back up the control file using the following command:

   ```
   ALTER DATABASE BACKUP CONTROLFILE TO TRACE;
   ```

3. Issue the following command to archive redo log files on all threads and then back up the archived log files:

   ```
   ALTER SYSTEM ARCHIVELOG CURRENT;
   ```

 More redo information is generated during the time when tablespaces are put into backup mode. Therefore, we recommend that you take a hot backup during times when the load is light.

Standby Database for OPS

A standby database for an OPS database is similar to that of a standalone database. In an OPS environment, the archived log files from all the instances must be applied to the standby database. The following two items must be identical on the primary and the standby database systems:

- Operating system version and patch level
- Oracle version and patch level

The standby database need not be a parallel server database. If the standby is also a parallel server database, it need not have the same number of instances as that of the primary database.

Backup Using Recovery Manager

Oracle8 comes with a utility called Recovery Manager (RMAN) that may be used for backing up and recovering a database. You can use either operating system utilities or RMAN to back up and recover a database. When using RMAN with OPS, note the following:

- Recovery Manager needs a read-consistent view of the control file while performing a backup. To create this view, it generates a temporary backup of the control file. This file is called a *snapshot control file*. You can specify the name and location of the snapshot control file using RMAN's SET SNAPSHOT CONTROLFILE command.

For an OPS database, each node must be able to create a snapshot control file with the same name and location. You can create the snapshot control file on a raw device, which can be shared by all the nodes in the OPS environment. Alternatively, you can create a directory on each node to hold the snapshot control file. Use a command such as the following to specify the location of the snapshot control file:

```
SET SNAPSHOT CONTROLFILE TO '/u01/oracle/admin/snapshot/snap_test.cf';
```

- After you finish a hot backup of all tablespaces, you must issue the command ALTER SYSTEM ARCHIVE LOGFILE CURRENT to archive the redo log files on all threads; doing so ensures a consistent set of redo in the backup set.

- When performing recovery on multiple nodes, you must ensure that each node can access the LOG_ARCHIVE_DEST directory on all other nodes, or you must place the archive log files in a directory that's accessible to all instances involved in the recovery.

Recovering an OPS Database

In a parallel server environment, the following types of failures may occur:

- Node failure

- Instance failure

- Crash failure

- Integrated Distributed Lock Manager (IDLM) failure

- GMS failure

- Media failure

These types are described in the following sections.

Some of these failures—for example, an instance failure or a media failure—also can occur in a standalone instance environment. Other types of failures—for example, an IDLM failure or a GMS failure—are specific to an OPS environment. You may need to perform a database recovery as a result of any one of these failures.

Node Failure and Recovery

A node may fail because of a power outage, operating system crash, or any other event on the node that makes it nonfunctional. Failure of a node causes the instance, the IDLM processes, and the GMS process running on that node to fail. The recovery from a *node failure* consists of instance recovery, IDLM recovery, and GMS recovery. A surviving instance will perform instance and IDLM recovery. You will have to restart GMS and the instance manually after you have diagnosed and corrected the cause of the node failure.

Instance Failure and Recovery

When one or more of the Oracle background processes for an instance fails or dies or when the SGA for an instance is lost, the instance will stop running. This type of failure is called an *instance failure*. Issuing a SHUTDOWN ABORT command also causes instance failure.

The process of recovering from instance failure is called *instance recovery*. For a single-instance database, instance recovery is performed automatically by the SMON background process at the next database startup.

The failure of more than one instance is still referred to as instance failure. However, the failure of all instances is called a *crash*. (Crash recovery is discussed in the next section.) When an instance in an OPS environment fails, one of the surviving instances will perform online instance recovery automatically. This is possible as long as at least one instance is running. When one instance fails, other instances keep running without being affected.

The recovery of a failed instance is triggered when either of the following occurs:

- The SMON process of a surviving instance detects the failure. Each SMON process periodically wakes up to check the status of the other instances.

- A lock is requested on a data block being managed by the failed instance.

The SMON process of the instance that detected the failure performs the instance recovery. For one instance to be able to recover another, it must have access to the online redo log files of the failed instance. In an OPS environment, that's why all redo logs must be accessible to all instances.

Committed transactions are never lost as a result of an instance failure. During instance recovery, the SMON background process first rolls forward all the changes by reading from the redo logs and then rolls back any uncommitted changes using information from the database's rollback segments. Instance recovery releases locks held by the failed instance. After instance recovery is complete, the failed instance is not started automatically. You must detect, diagnose, and correct the cause of the instance failure and then start the instance manually.

You have some control over the behavior of the database during the instance recovery. You can set the initialization parameter FREEZE_DB_FOR_FAST_INSTANCE_RECOVERY to TRUE to freeze the entire database during recovery. Setting this parameter to TRUE avoids contention for the resources used in the recovery process. When this parameter is set to TRUE, all database activity, other than that generated by the recovery process, is stopped. As a result, instance recovery may take less time. The tradeoff is that the database is also unavailable until the recovery process completes. When this parameter is set to FALSE, the data needed for instance recovery (in other words, the data involved in the transactions being recovered) will be unavailable, but the rest of the database will be available for normal use.

FREEZE_DB_FOR_FAST_INSTANCE_RECOVERY   is   obsolete   in Oracle8*i*.

The default value for this parameter is determined by Oracle based on the Parallel Cache Management (PCM) locking mechanism that is being used. If any datafile uses fine-grained locks, the default is TRUE. If all datafiles use hash locking, the default is FALSE. Locking mechanisms such as fine-grained and hashed locks are discussed in Chapter 8, *Locking Mechanisms in OPS*.

All instances must have the same setting for this parameter. The sooner that instance recovery is completed, the better. Therefore, we recommend that you set this parameter to TRUE unless you can't afford to stop other database activities during those times when recovery takes place.

Crash Failure and Recovery

For a standalone database, instance failure and crash failure are the same. However, in an OPS environment, *crash failure* means the failure of all of the instances associated with the parallel server database.

Recovery of all the instances is performed automatically the next time an instance is started. When you start up an instance to open the database, it performs recovery for all the failed instances. However, as in instance recovery, crash recovery does not automatically start the failed instances. You have to start the instances manually.

IDLM Failure and Recovery

As we discussed in Chapter 6, the Integrated Distributed Lock Manager (IDLM) consists of the background processes LMON and LMD0, as well as a distributed lock area. Failure of any of these components results in an *IDLM failure*. When IDLM on one node fails, the LMON process on another node will detect it. The recovery from IDLM failure is reconfiguration of the IDLM. The LMON process that detected the failure will perform the recovery by remastering the locks managed by the failed node.

GMS Failure and Recovery

The Group Membership Services (GMS) may fail for any of the following reasons:

- Failure of the GMS daemon
- Failure of the interconnect between nodes
- Operating system crash

You have to detect and resolve the cause of a *GMS failure* before you can manually restart GMS. If the GMS failure has caused any instance to fail, you also will have to start the instance manually after starting the GMS.

Media Failure and Recovery

A *media failure* occurs when a database file becomes lost or corrupted, preventing Oracle from reading from or writing to that file. Media failure can be caused by damage to the disk or to the disk controller.

If the database is running in NOARCHIVELOG mode, the only possible recovery is to restore the complete database from the last cold (offline) backup, thereby losing all the transactions committed since then. If the database is running in ARCHIVELOG mode, it is possible to recover all committed changes up to the time of failure. That's done by using the most recent backup (hot or cold), together with information from the archived redo log files. You can perform media recovery using the Recovery Manager or by using Oracle's command-line utilities.

The database must be mounted, but not opened, by a single instance if you are recovering any of the following:

- The entire database
- The entire SYSTEM tablespace
- A datafile in the SYSTEM tablespace

To recover any other tablespace or datafile, the database must be opened by the instance that is performing recovery, and the respective tablespace or datafile must be offline.

Multiple instances can perform recovery at the same time. For example, if tablespaces TS1 and TS2 need media recovery, you can recover TS1 from instance 1 and TS2 from instance 2 simultaneously.

Media recovery requires archived log files and online redo log files. Each instance has its own online and archived redo log files. As discussed in Chapter 6, the redo log files for any one instance are accessible from all other instances. However, the archived redo logs may be residing in local destinations not accessible to all instances. Therefore, during recovery, you need to place the archived log files of all instances into one location that is accessible by the instance performing the recovery.

8

Locking Mechanisms in OPS

Synchronization among multiple instances is the single most crucial factor in achieving the benefits of Oracle Parallel Server. This chapter explains the various issues involved with synchronization and also explains the locking mechanisms and other techniques used by OPS to attain it.

In a standalone database system, locks play a crucial role in maintaining concurrency, thereby allowing multiple transactions to access the same data at the same time. In a parallel server environment, locks also play an important role in allowing multiple instances to access the same data at the same time. This chapter describes the many types of locks you'll need to be aware of as you administer an OPS system: transaction and instance locks, Parallel Cache Management (PCM) and non-PCM locks, hashed and fine-grained PCM locks, and fixed and releasable locks. We'll also discuss lock modes, conversion, and lock allocation.

Cache Coherency

In an OPS environment, multiple instances execute transactions at the same time. Each instance maintains a buffer cache in its System Global Area (SGA) to hold copies of database blocks read from the datafiles. It is possible that more than one instance may attempt to modify the same database block at the same time. An instance always modifies the copy of the block contained within its buffer cache. If multiple instances were to modify the same block concurrently, each instance would be modifying a different copy of that block. This would result in lost updates unless there was a mechanism in place to consistently propagate changes that one instance made to a data block to other instances that are about to modify that same block.

Data blocks aren't the only things subject to the lost update problem. Each Oracle instance maintains copies of frequently used data dictionary information in its data dictionary cache. Each instance also maintains copies of recently issued SQL statements in its shared SQL area. In an OPS environment, this information also needs to be coordinated among the various instances.

Because one instance may update data that is cached in the SGAs of one or more other instances, a mechanism is required to maintain consistency between the various cached copies of an object. This mechanism is called *cache coherency*. Oracle Parallel Server provides built-in mechanisms to maintain cache coherency, and these remain completely transparent to the end user. Whenever an instance accesses an object, it checks the validity of that object by coordinating with the other instances. To gain access to a database block, an instance has to acquire a lock on that data block. The mode of the lock obtained will depend on the type of access intended. For example, to read a data block, an instance would acquire the lock in shared mode, while to modify a data block, the instance would need to acquire the lock in exclusive mode. We'll describe various types of locks and the different lock modes in the remainder of this chapter.

Lock Types in OPS

Oracle Parallel Server uses different types of locks to control access to database resources by an instance. The following sections briefly describe the lock types used in a parallel server environment and contrast them with the types used in a standalone database.

Transaction Locks

An Oracle database (whether standalone or parallel server) allows multiple transactions to access the same data concurrently. Without proper control, this access would result in improper modifications and might destroy data consistency. Oracle maintains data concurrency and consistency using locks. Some locks prevent destructive interaction between simultaneous transactions that are accessing the same data. These locks are called *transaction locks*. Transaction locks are row-level locks, and they protect rows of data from being concurrently modified by more than one transaction. Row-level locking works identically in standalone Oracle (single-instance) and Oracle Parallel Server (multiple-instance) configurations.

Instance Locks

Parallel server environments have an additional need for locks to maintain cache coherency. However, the locks used to maintain cache coherency are entirely different from transaction locks and are known as *instance locks*. Because instance locks are managed globally across all instances, some people refer to them as *global locks*. As discussed in Chapter 6, *Oracle Parallel Server Architecture*, instance locks and inter-instance locking activities are coordinated by the Integrated Distributed Lock Manager (IDLM). Table 8-1 compares instance locks with transaction locks.

Table 8-1. Comparison of Instance Locks and Transaction Locks

Instance Locks	Transaction Locks
Specific to parallel server	Used in standalone as well as parallel server databases
Block-level locking	Row-level locking
Managed across multiple instances	Managed between multiple transactions
Maintain cache coherency	Maintain data concurrency and consistency
Protect data blocks, dictionary caches, etc., from modifications by more than one instance	Protect rows of data from concurrent modifications by more than one transaction
May be acquired and released many times during a transaction	Exist for the life of a transaction

Instance locks operate at the database block level and are used only when OPS is enabled. Row-level locking, achieved using transaction locks, is used regardless of whether OPS is enabled or disabled. Transaction locks and instance locks represent two different locking mechanisms that work independently of each other.

There are two types of instance locks: Parallel Cache Management (PCM) and non-Parallel Cache Management (non-PCM). PCM locks protect data blocks in an instance's buffer cache. Non-PCM locks protect the System Change Number (SCN), library cache, dictionary cache, and so on. These two types of locks are discussed in detail later in this chapter.

Latches

Latches protect the data structures in the SGA of each instance. Latches are local to each instance and do not require inter-instance synchronization. Latches are handled identically in standalone Oracle (single-instance) and Oracle Parallel Server (multiple-instance) configurations.

Enqueues

All locks, other than PCM locks, are grouped together as *enqueues*. Enqueues may be local or global. When OPS is disabled, all enqueues are local. Local enqueues comprise transaction locks, DML locks (table locks), SCN locks, and other types of locks. However, when parallel server is enabled, most of these become global and are managed across all instances. Most of these global enqueues are non-PCM locks.

For a detailed discussion on locks, latches, and enqueues, refer to *Oracle8i Internal Services for Waits, Latches, Locks, and Memory* by Steve Adams (O'Reilly & Associates, 1999).

Lock Modes

An OPS database may have various types of users. Some users (we'll call them readers) may be reading the data, and other users (we'll call them writers) may be modifying the data. Depending on the type of access required, instance locks are acquired in one of the following modes. Note that the null mode has the lowest level of access rights and that the exclusive mode has the highest level of access rights.

Null mode (NULL)

Locks generally are created in null mode and then converted to other modes as required. A lock in null mode indicates no access rights. Multiple instances can hold a lock in null mode.

Subshared (SS)

An SS lock allows an unprotected read on an object. When an instance is holding an SS lock on an object, it is allowed to read that object. However, other instances may be able to read as well as modify the object. Multiple instances can hold a lock in SS mode.

Shared exclusive (SX)

An SX lock allows an unprotected write on an object. When an instance is holding an SX lock on an object, it is allowed to modify (write) that object. However, other instances also may be able to read and modify (write) the same object. Multiple instances can hold a lock in SX mode.

Shared mode (S)

Shared locks are needed for read operations. Multiple instances can own an instance lock in shared mode and simultaneously can read the associated block(s). Writes are not allowed on a block when it is locked in shared mode.

Subshared exclusive (SSX)

When an instance is holding an SSX lock on an object, that instance is the only one allowed to modify (write) the object. However, other instances may be able to perform unprotected reads on the object. Only one instance can hold a lock in SSX mode; locks on rollback segment blocks normally are acquired in this mode.

Exclusive mode (X)

Exclusive mode allows the protected write of a data block. As the name conveys, only one instance can hold a lock in exclusive mode at any given moment. When an instance holds a lock in X mode, no other instance can read or modify the associated block(s).

SS, SX, and SSX lock modes allow unprotected read or write. User operations do not directly involve any unprotected reads or writes. These three lock modes are used as intermediate lock modes. The null, S, and X lock modes directly correspond to user operations. In Table 8-2, we describe the compatibility of the null, S, and X lock modes. The table shows the results that you'll see when one instance attempts to lock an object that's already locked by another instance. A result of Success indicates that the lock modes are compatible and that no lock conversion is necessary. More than one instance can own a lock when the modes are compatible. For example, two instances can own a lock in shared mode when both the instances are reading the data. A result of Failure indicates that two lock modes are incompatible, and therefore the instance owning the current lock must release that lock before the requesting instance can acquire the lock that it needs.

Whenever the requesting instance requests a lock in a mode that is incompatible with the lock mode held by the holding instance, *lock mode conversion* takes place. The instance holding the lock must downgrade its lock mode. Only then can the requesting instance acquire the lock in the desired mode. The examples of lock mode conversion are noted as footnotes e, f, and g to Table 8-2.

Table 8-2. Lock Modes

Lock Mode Requested	Lock Mode of the Holding Instance		
	NULL	S (reader)	X (writer)
NULL	Success[a]	Success[b]	Success[b]
S (reader)	Success[c]	Success[d]	Fail[e]
X (writer)	Success[c]	Fail[f]	Fail[g]

a Multiple instances can hold a lock in null mode.

b The requesting instance can acquire the lock in null mode regardless of the lock mode of the holding instance. That's because the null mode does not convey any access rights.

c When one instance holds a lock in null mode, another instance can acquire it in any desired mode without requiring lock mode conversion in the owning instance.

d Multiple instances can own an instance lock in shared mode and simultaneously can read the associated block(s).

a, b, c, d Do not cause any cache coherency conflicts.

e When an instance holds a lock in X mode, no other instance can even read the associated block(s) because doing so would result in an inconsistent read. This is a reader/writer conflict. If the second instance requests the lock in S mode, the request fails and initiates a lock mode conversion in the owning instance. The owning instance then must downgrade its lock mode to null or release the lock before the requesting instance can acquire it.

f If one instance is reading a block by holding an S lock on it, another instance cannot write on that block. This is a writer/reader conflict. If the second instance requests the lock in X mode, the request fails and initiates a lock mode conversion in the owning instance. The owning instance then must downgrade its lock mode to null or release the lock before the requesting instance can acquire it.

g When an instance holds a lock in X mode, no other instance can write the associated block(s) because doing so would result in a lost update. This is a writer/writer conflict. If the second instance requests the lock in X mode, the request fails and initiates a lock mode conversion in the owning instance. The owning instance then must downgrade its lock mode to null or release the lock before the requesting instance can acquire it in X mode.

The LCK processes do the work of acquiring and converting instance locks.

Parallel Cache Management

The instance locks that manage consistency among copies of objects in the buffer caches of multiple instances are called PCM (Parallel Cache Management) locks. Parallel Cache Management ensures that an instance reads from, or writes to, only the latest copy of a block. PCM locks protect blocks in datafiles. These blocks include data blocks, index blocks, rollback segment blocks, and segment headers.

An instance must acquire a PCM lock on a block before reading or modifying it. Acquiring a PCM lock may result in a lock mode conversion as shown in Table 8-2. One PCM lock can protect one or more database blocks. However, only one lock is needed to protect a data block.

Pinging

When there is contention for the same block by multiple instances, one instance has to write the block to disk so that the other instances can read or modify it. This process is referred to as *pinging*. The concept of pinging in OPS is best explained through an example. Let's look at what happens in a two-instance OPS configuration in which instance 1 is updating row 1 of a table that resides in block 1. Let's assume that block 1 is protected by PCM lock L1. Instance 1 acquires lock L1 in exclusive mode. Then instance 1 reads block 1 from the datafile on disk, places that block in its buffer cache, and modifies it. For the other instance, instance 2, the mode of lock L1 is NULL, indicating that it does not have access rights to block 1 at this time.

Now, if instance 2 needs to modify row 5, also in block 1, it needs to acquire lock L1 as well. Because instance 2 needs to modify the block, the lock must be acquired in exclusive mode. However, because instance 1 already holds lock L1 in exclusive mode, the request by instance 2 to acquire it will fail. Figure 8-1 illustrates this situation.

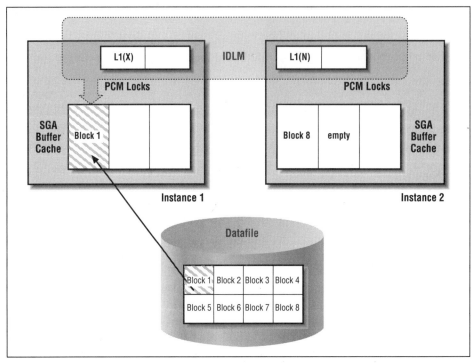

Figure 8-1. Instance 1 holds an exclusive lock on block 1

To allow instance 2 to acquire lock L1 in exclusive mode, instance 1 must write block 1 back to disk. That way, instance 2 sees the most current version of the block, and none of the changes are lost. Instance 1 then must downgrade its lock mode for lock L1 from X to NULL. After that, instance 2 can acquire lock L1 in exclusive mode (via a NULL-to-X conversion), read block 1 into its buffer cache, and modify it. Figure 8-2 shows the resulting situation.

 If instance 2 needs to update row 1 (the same row that instance 1 has updated), then it needs the row lock on row 1. In that case, instance 2 has to wait until instance 1 completes the transaction.

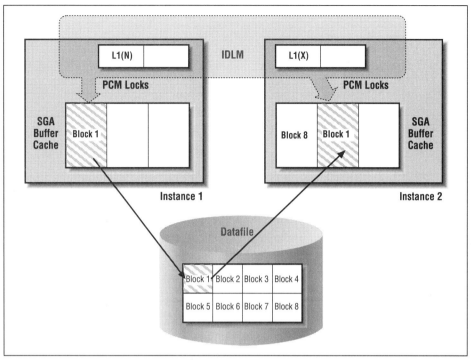

Figure 8-2. Instance 2 has acquired an exclusive lock on block 1

This entire sequence of events is referred to as a *ping*. A ping occurs when a block has to be written to disk by one instance so that it can be read or modified by another instance. Pinging occurs when there is contention for the same data block by two or more instances. Like the Ping-Pong ball shown in Figure 8-3, database blocks are bounced back and forth between SGAs when multiple instances need to access the same blocks.

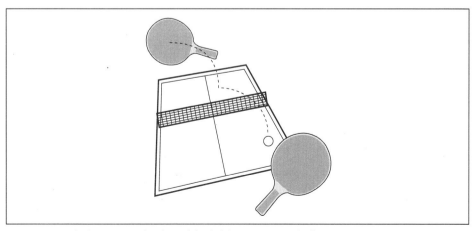

Figure 8-3. Blocks are sent back and forth like Ping-Pong balls

Because of the disk I/O and lock mode conversion involved, frequent pinging can hurt the performance of an OPS database.

False Pinging

When there is contention for the same lock by multiple instances, one instance may have to write blocks protected by that particular lock to disk so that another instance can acquire it. It may be that the acquiring instance does not even need the particular blocks that were written. This process is referred to as *false pinging* and can occur when one lock protects more than one data block. Let's look at an example in which one PCM lock protects two data blocks, and let's further assume that lock L1 protects blocks 1 and 8. This situation is shown in Figure 8-4.

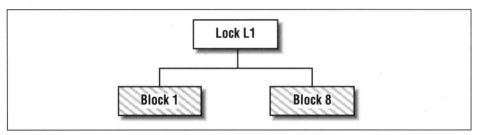

Figure 8-4. One PCM lock protecting multiple databases blocks

Continuing with our example, let's say that instance 1 is modifying block 1 and consequently acquires lock L1 in exclusive mode. Let's also say that instance 2 needs to modify block 8. Block 8 also is protected by lock L1. Thus, instance 2 also needs to acquire lock L1 in exclusive mode. Even though both instances are modifying different blocks, there still is contention for lock L1. To resolve that conflict, instance 1 must release lock L1 (via a lock downgrade from X to NULL). To do that, it must write block 1 to disk. After block 1 has been written to disk and the lock has been released, instance 2 can acquire lock L1 in exclusive mode (via a lock upgrade from NULL to X) and modify block 8. This is referred to as a false ping (as shown in Figure 8-5), because the block that was written was not actually the block required by the other instance.

A false ping occurs when one or more blocks protected by a lock are written to disk by one instance because another instance needs to modify another block protected by the same lock. While pinging occurs due to block contention, false pinging occurs due to lock contention. As Figure 8-6 shows, if block 1 and block 8 had been protected by separate locks, then no false ping would have occurred.

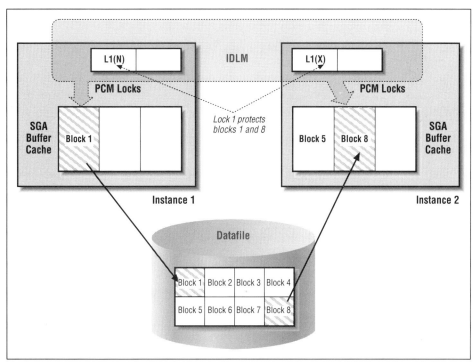

Figure 8-5. A false ping occurs when a block is written only to enable a lock to be released

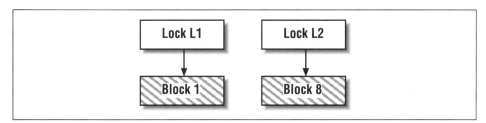

Figure 8-6. No false pinging occurs when one lock protects one block

 Often the term *ping* is used for both a ping and a false ping. In order to differentiate, we'll use the term *true ping* in this book when what we say specifically applies only to a ping and not to a false ping. We'll use the word *ping* as a generic term when referring to both true pings and false pings.

Lock Mode Conversion in Pinging

When two instances need to modify a data block, there is a writer/writer conflict. The lock mode in the holding instance is downgraded from X to NULL, while the lock mode in the requesting instance is upgraded from NULL to X.

When a reading instance needs data blocks that have been modified by another instance, there is a reader/writer conflict. In this case, the holding instance writes data to disk, and the lock mode in the holding instance is downgraded from X to S. Then, the lock mode in the requesting instance is converted from NULL to S. Table 8-3 shows lock mode conversion in the holding and requesting instances for different types of lock mode conflicts. This table also shows the cases in which a write to disk is needed, thus resulting in pings.

Table 8-3. Lock Mode Conversions with Ping

Requesting Instance	Holding Instance	Lock Mode Conversion in Requesting Instance	Lock Mode Conversion in Holding Instance
Writer (X)	Writer (X)	NULL → X	X → NULL (ping)
Reader (S)	Writer (X)	NULL → S	X → S (ping)
Writer (X)	Reader (S)	NULL → X or S → X	S → NULL
Reader (S)	Reader (S)	NULL → S	None

The Overhead of Pinging

As you've seen, maintaining buffer cache coherency across multiple instances requires ping operations. A ping involves both lock conversion and disk I/O to write data blocks. The following steps are performed whenever a ping occurs:

1. The holding instance writes blocks to disk.

2. The holding instance downgrades its lock mode on those blocks.

3. The requesting instance acquires the lock that it needs.

4. The requesting instance reads the blocks that it needs. In the case of a true ping, these will be the blocks that the holding instance wrote.

These lock operations involve coordination between OPS instances through the IDLM. The IDLM overhead, coupled with the disk I/O required for pinging, can decrease the response time of an OPS database as compared to a standalone database.

When a required data block is found in the buffer cache of an instance, disk access is avoided, and access time is quite fast as compared to the time required to read the block from disk. This is, of course, the reason that data blocks are buffered in the SGA of an Oracle instance. However, in an OPS environment, this buffering can be a liability. When data blocks are in the buffer cache of remote instances, ping operations are required. Because of this pinging, accessing data blocks from a remote instance's buffer cache is even more expensive than accessing them from the disk. Figure 8-7 illustrates this. If an OPS environment is not properly tuned, too many pings will occur, and the resulting overhead can degrade the performance of an OPS database to a point at which it's worse than that of a standalone database.

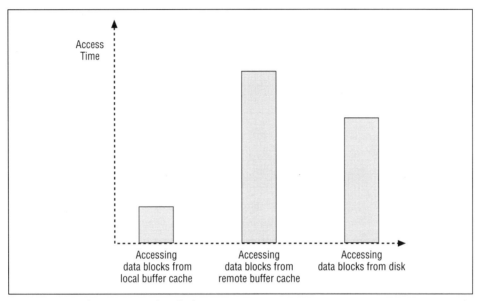

Figure 8-7. Performance overhead of pinging

Soft Pings

You saw in Table 8-3 that when the mode of a lock in a holding instance is converted from exclusive (X) to null or from exclusive (X) to shared (S), the holding instance has to write the blocks covered by that lock to disk. The requesting instance then can acquire those locks in whatever mode is necessary. This situation describes pinging. However, in some situations, it is not necessary for the holding instance to write the blocks to disk because the blocks in question already have been written to disk as a result of the normal checkpoint operation of the instance. This may occur for true pings as well as for false pings. In such cases, neither true pinging nor false pinging involves any disk writes. Only the lock mode conversion takes place. Such a ping is referred to as a *soft ping*, or an *I/O-less ping*. The overhead of a soft ping obviously is less that it would be for other pings since it doesn't involve any actual disk I/O.

Reducing the Number of Pings

Since false pinging is caused by lock contention, it can be reduced by allocating more PCM locks. However, true pings are caused by block contention and cannot be reduced by allocating even an infinite number of PCM locks. The only way to reduce true pinging is by proper application partitioning. Table 8-4 contrasts the causes and solutions for the two types of pinging.

Table 8-4. Contrasting True Pinging and False Pinging

Ping Type	Cause	Tuning Method
True pinging	Contention for the same block across multiple instances	Application partitioning
False pinging	Contention for the same lock across multiple instances	Proper PCM lock allocation

The goal of application partitioning, which is performed when you first design your applications and your database, is to reduce pings. During your design process, you must perform an analysis of table access by your applications, and you must design your applications so that different nodes run different applications and access a disjoint set of tables. For example, one instance could be used for a payroll application, while another instance could be used for an inventory application. Since each of these applications is likely to access a completely different set of tables, any one block is not likely to end up in the buffer cache of more than one instance. As a consequence, pings are minimized. However, if one application (e.g., the payroll application) runs on more than one instance, then pings still could occur between those. Chapter 11, *Partitioning for OPS*, talks about this subject in more detail.

Cache Fusion in Oracle8i

With Oracle8*i*, a new technique called *cache fusion* has been introduced to reduce the performance overhead of ping in OPS. With this new technique, data is transferred directly from the SGA of one instance to the SGA of another instance without the need to write the blocks to disk. Figure 8-8 illustrates this transfer.

We have seen in Table 8-3 that pinging occurs when there is writer/writer and reader/writer conflict. Cache fusion has been implemented only for the subset of conflicts that results in pings and applies only to reader/writer conflicts. A cache fusion solution for writer/writer conflicts is planned for a future release of OPS. Writer/writer conflicts are currently handled through ping operations. Table 8-5 illustrates the scenarios in which cache fusion is applied and shows how cache coherency is maintained in other cases.

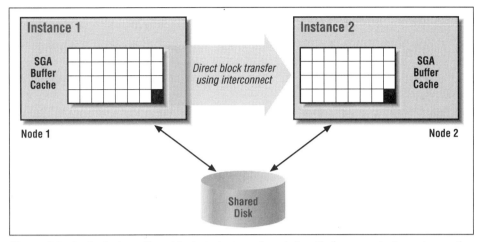

Figure 8-8. Cache fusion allows blocks to be transferred directly from one instance to another

Table 8-5. Methods Used in Maintaining Cache Coherency

Requesting Instance	Holding Instance	Modified Block Exists in Buffer Cache of Holding Instance?	Cache Coherency Method
Reader (S)	Writer (X)	Yes	Cache fusion
Reader (S)	Writer (X)	No	Read from disk (soft ping)
Writer (X)	Writer (X)	Doesn't matter	Ping

Oracle has introduced a new server process called the Block Server Process (BSP) to facilitate cache fusion. The Block Server Process is responsible for transferring the required blocks directly from the buffer cache of the holding instance to the buffer cache of the requesting instance. When there is a reader/writer conflict, the IDLM communicates the request to the BSP of the holding instance. If the requested buffer already has been written to disk in the holding instance, the requesting instance is permitted to read the blocks from the disk. Otherwise (if the modified block is in the buffer of the holding instance), the BSP on the holding instance prepares a consistent read (CR) image of the data block. The BSP uses rollback information if required to prepare that CR copy. It then sends a message with the CR copy of the block to the requesting node. The blocks are sent over a fast interconnect that doesn't involve costly disk I/O.

Fast interconnects are communication links between OPS nodes. These links use Ethernet, FDDI, or other proprietary communication protocols. Communication links between OPS nodes are designed for reliability and for transparent recovery from hardware and software failures. High bandwidth and low latency also are highly desirable. The characteristics of a specific interconnect depend on the hardware platform being used.

Cache Fusion Benefits

Cache fusion is a much less expensive operation than pinging, because with cache fusion, expensive disk I/O and lock mode conversion is no longer necessary. With cache fusion, you'll notice fewer X-to-S lock conversions than you would otherwise. Figure 8-9 illustrates the significant reduction in access time for blocks held in a remote cache when Oracle8*i*'s cache fusion feature is used as opposed to the access time required in prior releases that do not support the feature. Oracle Corporation reports that the access time can be reduced by as much as a factor of 100.

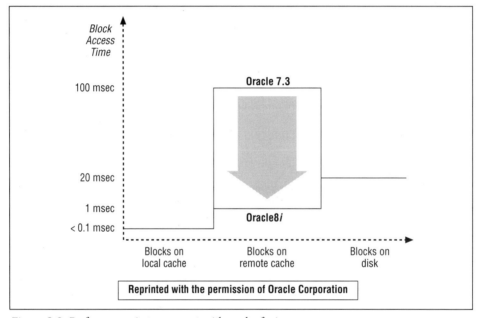

Figure 8-9. Performance improvement with cache fusion

OPS implementation requires that applications be well partitioned when they are designed. With the introduction of cache fusion in Oracle8*i*, OPS can be implemented with some OLTP applications that already have been designed without application partitioning in mind (see Chapter 11 for details on application partitioning). If those applications have numerous reader/writer conflicts, cache fusion results in a substantial performance gain, thus making OPS implementation possible.

PCM Lock Types

PCM locks are classified based on the following two criteria: lock granularity and a combination of lock acquisition and retention. *Lock granularity* refers to the number of data blocks protected by one PCM lock. *Lock acquisition and retention* refers to the method by which an instance acquires the locks. Locks may be acquired only once, at the time of instance startup, or they may be acquired and released as needed.

Lock Granularity

One PCM lock can protect one or more data blocks. The number of blocks covered by a PCM lock is referred to as the lock's *granularity*. The greater the number of blocks covered by one lock, the coarser the granularity. The lesser the number of blocks covered by one lock, the finer the granularity. Based on granularity, PCM locking approaches may be classified as either hashed locking or fine-grained locking. With hashed locking, one PCM lock protects more than one block, whereas with fine-grained locking, one PCM lock protects only one block.

Hashed locking

Coarse granularity in locking increases the likelihood of lock contention because each lock protects many blocks. For a large transaction that's accessing many blocks, the lock overhead may be less with coarse granularity locking because fewer locks may need to be acquired or converted. With coarse granularity locking, a hash function is used to associate locks to blocks. Therefore, this type of locking is referred to as *hashed locking*.

As you will see later in this chapter, PCM locks are assigned on a per-datafile basis. When assigning locks to a datafile, you specify the number of PCM locks that protect the blocks in that datafile. Oracle uses a hash function to assign PCM locks to data blocks. The intent of using a hash function is to achieve a uniform distribution of data blocks to PCM locks. Along with specifying the number of locks for a datafile, you also can specify a blocking factor that determines the sequence of data blocks protected by a PCM lock.

For example, let's assume that file 1 has 20 data blocks and is assigned 4 PCM locks. The number of data blocks protected by each lock is computed as follows:

```
20 data blocks / 4 locks = 5 blocks per lock
```

In this case, each lock will protect five data blocks in file 1. The data blocks protected by each lock may or may not be contiguous. The sequence of data blocks protected by a lock is determined by the blocking factor, which can be specified along with the number of locks for each file. If the blocking factor is not specified, the default value is taken as 1. The default blocking factor of 1 results in the mapping of locks to blocks shown in Figure 8-10.

Locks	L1	L2	L3	L4	L1	L2	L3	L4	L1	L2	L3	L4	L1	L2	L3	L4	L1	L2	L3	L4
Data blocks	1	2	3	4	5	6	7	8	9	10	11	12	13	14	15	16	17	18	19	20

Figure 8-10. PCM lock allocation to data blocks using the default blocking factor of 1

In Figure 8-10, the squares in the second row represent data blocks, and the squares in the first row represent locks protecting those data blocks. The labels inside the squares in the first row are the lock numbers. Lock L1 protects data blocks 1, 5, 9, 13, and 17. Lock L2 protects data blocks 2, 6, 10, 14, and 18.

If a blocking factor other than 1 is specified for the locks assigned to file 1, the assignment of locks to data blocks will be different from that shown in Figure 8-10. Figure 8-11 represents the same lock assignment as shown in Figure 8-10, but with a blocking factor of 2. A blocking factor of 2 means that each lock will protect two contiguous data blocks. Thus, lock L1 protects data blocks 1, 2, 9, 10, 17, and 18. Lock L2 protects data blocks 3, 4, 11, 12, 19, and 20.

Locks	L1	L1	L2	L2	L3	L3	L4	L4	L1	L1	L2	L2	L3	L3	L4	L4	L1	L1	L2	L2
Data blocks	1	2	3	4	5	6	7	8	9	10	11	12	13	14	15	16	17	18	19	20

Figure 8-11. PCM lock allocation to data blocks using a blocking factor of 2

Note that with the blocking factor illustrated in Figure 8-11, the number of blocks protected by each lock is different. Locks L1 and L2 each protect six blocks, whereas locks L3 and L4 each protect four blocks. In this case, the number of data blocks protected by the various locks varies by 2, and that variation probably is not significant. However, in some situations this variation can be significant. If we use a blocking factor of 16 in this example, lock L1 will protect 16 blocks, lock L2 will protect 4 blocks, and locks L3 and L4 will protect none at all. Such an uneven distribution of data blocks to locks can harm performance. Therefore, you should choose your blocking factor carefully and with respect to the total number of locks and data blocks that you are dealing with. Try to keep the distribution as even as possible.

 Refer to the "PCM Lock Allocation Parameters and Verification" section later in this chapter for detailed information on the mechanics of assigning PCM locks to datafiles.

Fine-grained locking

When one lock protects only one block, you are using what is referred to as *fine-grained locking*. With fine-grained locking, lock contention is eliminated completely. This is good. However, the use of fine-grained locking requires more system resources than hashed locking in order to maintain the increased number of locks. For a transaction accessing many blocks, the lock overhead is higher with fine-grained locking because more locks need to be acquired or converted.

Lock Acquisition and Retention

Oracle provides two types of lock acquisition and retention mechanisms:

Fixed locking

Fixed locking is a proactive method. Locks are acquired at instance startup time and retained throughout the life of the instance. Fixed locking reduces lock acquisition overhead but increases instance startup time.

Releasable locking

Releasable locking represents an as-needed method. Locks are not acquired when an instance starts. Instead, locks are acquired and released as needed. Releasable locking reduces instance startup time but increases lock acquisition overhead while the instance is running.

Fixed locks are not released after a read or write operation on the protected blocks is complete. Once acquired in a specific mode, fixed locks continue in that mode until they are required by another instance in a conflicting mode. For example, if an instance is holding a lock in shared mode, it will continue to do so even after the read operation that initiated the acquisition of that mode is complete. The lock mode is preserved until another instance asks to acquire the same lock in a conflicting mode. Fixed locks continually use system memory and increase the size of the SGA.

Releasable locks are released when they are no longer required. If a read or write operation results in the acquisition of a releasable lock, that lock is held only for the duration of the operation that initiated its acquisition. Once that read or write operation is complete, the lock is released. Memory is released as well, so the use of releasable locks reduces overall memory consumption.

Table 8-6 compares the consequences of using the various types of PCM locks that we've discussed.

Table 8-6. Effects of Different Types of PCM Locks

Fixed Hashed Locks	Fixed Fine-Grained Locks	Releasable Hashed Locks	Releasable Fine-Grained Locks
Increased likelihood of lock contention. False pings may occur.	No lock contention. False pings eliminated.	Reduced likelihood of lock contention. False pings may occur.	No lock contention. False pings are eliminated.
Reduced lock acquisition overhead.	Reduced lock acquisition overhead.	Increased lock overhead for both acquisition and release.	Increased lock overhead for both acquisition and release
Increased instance startup time.	Increased instance startup time.	Reduced instance startup time.	Reduced instance startup time.

Table 8-6. Effects of Different Types of PCM Locks (continued)

Fixed Hashed Locks	Fixed Fine-Grained Locks	Releasable Hashed Locks	Releasable Fine-Grained Locks
Lock mode preserved in a steady state.	Lock mode preserved in a steady state.	Lock mode not preserved.	Lock mode not preserved.
Reduced memory consumption as compared to fixed fine-grained locking.	Increased memory consumption as compared to fixed hashed locks and releasable fine-grained locks.	Reduced memory consumption as compared to fixed fine-grained locking.	Reduced memory consumption as compared to fixed fine-grained locking.

See the section later in this chapter titled "What Kind of Locks to Use?" for some tips on choosing the right lock types to use in your environment.

> With the release of Oracle8*i*, Oracle has changed the nomenclature used to identify types of locks based on granularity. Hashed locks are renamed as 1:*n* locks, and fine-grained locks are renamed as 1:1 locks. 1:*n* represents one lock protecting multiple (*n*) blocks. 1:1 represents one lock protecting one block. Throughout this book, we have used the words "hashed" and "fine-grained." All the discussion also applies to 1:*n* and 1:1 locks, respectively.

PCM Lock Allocation Parameters and Verification

There are three initialization parameters that control the allocation of PCM locks in an OPS environment:

GC_FILES_TO_LOCKS
> Controls PCM lock allocation to datafiles. The value of this parameter must be the same for all instances of an OPS database.

GC_RELEASABLE_LOCKS
> Allocates releasable locks. The value of this parameter may be different for each instance of an OPS database.

GC_ROLLBACK_LOCKS
> Specifies the number of locks available for each rollback segment that is being modified concurrently. The value of this parameter must be the same for all instances of an OPS database.

The following sections describe these parameters, how you can use them to best advantage, and how you can verify lock allocation.

The GC_FILES_TO_LOCKS Parameter

This parameter specifies the manner in which PCM locks are allocated to different datafiles. It specifies the number of locks allocated to a specific file, and/or to a set of datafiles, except for those files that contain rollback segments. The GC_ROLLBACK_LOCKS parameter is used to allocate locks to files with rollback segments.

GC_FILES_TO_LOCKS syntax

The syntax for the GC_FILES_TO_LOCKS parameter is rather complex and looks like this:

```
GC_FILES_TO_LOCKS = "LOCK_ALLOCATION[:LOCK_ALLOCATION...]"

LOCK_ALLOCATION := FILE_LIST=num_locks[!blocking][R][EACH]

FILE_LIST := fileid[-fileid][,fileid[-fileid]...]
```

LOCK_ALLOCATION

Allocates a specific number of locks to one or more files. Multiple LOCK_ALLOCATION entries are permissible and should be separated by colons.

FILE_LIST

Can be a single file ID number or a range of file ID numbers (*fileid*). The ID numbers of your datafiles can be obtained from the DBA_DATA_FILES data dictionary view. Multiple ranges of file IDs may be specified, but one file ID cannot be referenced more than once. Use commas to separate ranges of file IDs.

num_locks

Specifies the number of locks to be allocated to the files specified in FILE_LIST.

blocking

Specifies the blocking factor that determines the number of contiguous data blocks that each PCM lock protects. The default blocking factor is 1.

R Specifies that the locks are releasable and are to be included in the number specified by the GC_RELEASABLE_LOCKS parameter. Otherwise, the locks will be fixed.

EACH

Specifies that the number of locks is for each file in the file list. If EACH is not specified, then the locks are allocated collectively to all the files in the list. Allocating locks collectively results in each lock's protecting one or more blocks in each of the datafiles listed.

Sample GC_FILES_TO_LOCKS settings

This section shows several sample GC_FILES_TO_LOCKS settings. Each of the following examples assumes the use of a hypothetical database with seven files. Table 8-7 shows the file ID numbers, the number of blocks, and the tablespace name for each of those seven files.

Table 8-7. FILE_ID and Block Count for the Files in the Example Database

FILE_ID	Blocks	Tablespace Name
1	1000	SYSTEM
2	1000	TOOLS
3	2000	USERS
4	2000	APP1
5	1000	APP2
6	2000	RBS (for rollback segments)
7	1000	TEMP

Don't include the datafiles containing rollback segments in the GC_FILES_TO_LOCKS parameter, because locks for rollback segments are allocated using the GC_ROLLBACK_LOCKS parameter. In addition, don't include the datafiles comprising temporary tablespaces in GC_FILES_TO_LOCKS, because temporary segments are not shared. Thus, none of our examples include file IDs 6 or 7 in the GC_FILES_TO_LOCKS specification.

The following examples show various permutations of the syntax for the GC_FILES_TO_LOCKS parameter. Most of these examples aren't complete, because they don't illustrate lock allocation for all the files. They just illustrate various features of the parameter specification syntax. Example 8, however, which happens to be the last example, is complete. Example 8 illustrates lock allocation to each of the files listed in Table 8-7.

1. `GC_FILES_TO_LOCKS = "1=10:2-3=20:4-5:20EACH"`

    File 1 has been allocated 10 hashed locks. There are 1000 blocks in the file, so each lock covers 100 blocks.

    Files 2 and 3 together have been allocated 20 locks. Each lock covers blocks from both files. For file 2, each lock covers 50 blocks. For file 3, each lock covers 100 blocks. In total, each lock covers 150 blocks.

    Files 4 and 5 each have been allocated 20 locks. For file 4, each lock covers 100 blocks. For file 5, each lock covers 50 blocks.

    All of the locks allocated in this example are *fixed hashed locks*. If the number of blocks in the file is not evenly divisible by the number of locks requested, then the number of blocks covered by each PCM lock may vary by one. For example, if file 1 with 1000 blocks is protected by six PCM locks, then four PCM locks will cover 167 blocks each, and the other two PCM locks will cover 166 blocks each.

2. `GC_FILES_TO_LOCKS = "2=20R:3-5=20REACH"`

   Because R has been used in the specification, file 2 has been allocated 20 *releasable hashed locks*. Files 3, 4, and 5 each have been allocated 20 *releasable hashed locks*. As illustrated in the syntax diagram, REACH is valid when you want to combine R and EACH. You cannot, however, use EACHR.

3. `GC_FILES_TO_LOCKS = "0=200:1=100"`

   In this example, 200 locks are allocated to file ID 0. Note that 0 is not a real file ID. You allocate locks to file ID 0 in order to reserve a pool of locks to use for files that are not explicitly mentioned in the GC_FILES_TO_LOCKS parameter.

   100 locks are allocated for file 1. All remaining files use locks from the pool of 200 locks that was allocated using a file ID of 0. All the locks, both those in the pool and those for file ID 1, are *fixed locks*.

4. `GC_FILES_TO_LOCKS = "1=100"`

   File 1 is allocated 100 fixed locks. Unlike the previous example, no locks have been set aside in a pool using a file ID of 0, so there is no default bucket of hashed locks available. Thus, by default, *releasable fine-grained locks* are allocated to all remaining files. These locks are included in the number of locks specified by the GC_RELEASABLE_LOCKS parameter.

5. `GC_FILES_TO_LOCKS = "1-3=20EACH:4=0"`

   The GC_FILES_TO_LOCKS parameter also can specify the use of releasable fine-grained locking for a file by explicitly allocating zero locks to that particular file. For file ID 4, the number of locks allocated is zero. This indicates that *releasable fine-grained locks* should be used for this file. These locks are allocated from the pool of releasable locks specified using the GC_RELEASABLE_ LOCKS parameter.

6. `GC_FILES_TO_LOCKS = "1=1000"`

   File 1 has 1000 blocks, and we have allocated 1000 locks to it. This results in *fixed fine-grained locks* (one lock per block) for file 1.

7. `GC_FILES_TO_LOCKS = "1=100!5"`

   Locks allocated to file 1 are set with a blocking factor of 5. In this case, the granularity is 10 blocks per lock. However, each lock protects five contiguous blocks in one location and another five contiguous blocks in another location. A blocking factor like this would be useful for an application in which contiguous blocks are often referenced together. In such a case, specifying the proper blocking factor may result in fewer lock operations.

The GC_FILES_TO_LOCKS parameter setting *must* be the same for all OPS instances accessing a database. This parameter cannot be changed in one instance at a time, because the changed instance can't be restarted with a setting that doesn't match the others. Thus, if you want to change GC_FILES_TO_LOCKS, you must stop and restart all OPS instances. This makes it a difficult parameter to tune in OPS implementations that also have high availability requirements.

8. GC_FILES_TO_LOCKS = "1=100:2=0:4=100R:5=1000:0=500"
   GC_RELEASABLE_LOCKS = 5000

This example summarizes various lock allocation types and granularities for our hypothetical database. It's a complete example that illustrates lock allocation to all the files listed in Table 8-7 (except for the files for the temporary tablespace and rollback tablespace), and both the GC_FILES_TO_LOCKS and GC_RELEASABLE_LOCKS parameters have been included. The next several paragraphs cover each piece of this scenario in detail. The results then are summarized in Table 8-8.

File 1 is allocated 100 locks to cover 1000 blocks. These are *fixed hashed locks*.

No hashed locks are allocated to file 2. Thus, *releasable fine-grained locks* are used. These count against the 5000 locks specified by the GC_RELEASABLE_LOCKS parameter.

File 4 is allocated 100 hashed locks. The R after the 100 makes them releasable locks.

File 5 is allocated 1000 hashed locks covering 1000 blocks. This results in fine-grained locking being used, since there is one lock for every block.

There is no specific allocation for file 3. The entry 0=500 results in 500 fixed locks being placed into the default bucket. Some of these will end up being allocated to file 3.

Table 8-8. Lock Allocation for Example 8

File Number	File Size in Blocks	Value Specified in GC_FILES_TO_LOCKS	Lock Type	Granularity
1	1000	100	Fixed hashed	1 lock per 10 blocks
2	1000	0	Releasable fine-grained	1 lock per block

Table 8-8. Lock Allocation for Example 8 (continued)

File Number	File Size in Blocks	Value Specified in GC_FILES_TO_LOCKS	Lock Type	Granularity
3	2000	NONE	Fixed hashed lock from default bucket of 500 locks	1 lock per 4 blocks
4	2000	100R	Releasable hashed	1 lock per 20 blocks
5	1000	1000	Fixed fine-grained	1 lock per block

The GC_RELEASABLE_LOCKS Parameter

This parameter specifies the number of releasable locks that are allocated. The default value for this parameter is equal to the number of DB_BLOCK_BUFFERS. Files are protected by releasable locks when the GC_FILES_TO_LOCKS specification has these characteristics:

1. The file ID is specified in the GC_FILES_TO_LOCKS parameter with an R indicator. Those files use releasable locks.

2. The file ID is specified in the GC_FILES_TO_LOCKS parameter with a value of 0 for the number of locks. For example, a GC_FILES_TO_LOCKS = "2=0" specification means that file 2 is protected by releasable locks.

3. The file ID is *not* specified in the GC_FILES_TO_LOCKS parameter, and a default bucket has not been allocated using a file ID of 0.

The GC_ROLLBACK_LOCKS Parameter

The GC_ROLLBACK_LOCKS parameter controls the number of locks used to protect rollback segment blocks. The format of the GC_ROLLBACK_LOCKS parameter specification is similar to that of the GC_FILES_TO_LOCKS parameter. However, unlike datafiles, rollback segments do not share locks. Let's assume that, in addition to the SYSTEM rollback segment, our hypothetical database has four rollback segments named R1, R2, R3, and R4. The following specification then allocates 40 locks to each rollback segment, including the SYSTEM rollback segment, for a total allocation of 200 fixed locks.

```
GC_ROLLBACK_LOCKS = "0-5=40EACH"
```

Rollback segments are identified in the GC_ROLLBACK_LOCKS parameter by their rollback segment ID. You can get that from the SEGMENT_ID column in the DBA_ROLLBACK_SEGS data dictionary view.

Verifying Lock Allocation

The data dictionary view FILE_LOCK displays the allocation of locks to datafiles. This display will match what was specified in the GC_LOCKS_TO_FILES parameter setting and can be used to verify lock allocation. The following example shows a sample GC_FILES_TO_LOCKS setting together with the results that you would get from querying the FILE_LOCK view with that parameter setting in effect:

```
GC_FILES_TO_LOCKS = "1=100:2=0:3=400!5:4-5=200R"

SQL> SELECT file_id, ts_name, start_lk, nlocks, blocking
  2  FROM file_lock
  3  ORDER BY file_id;

   FILE_ID   TS_NAME             START_LK      NLOCKS   BLOCKING
---------- ----------------  ----------  ----------  ----------
         1 SYSTEM                     0         100           1
         2 TOOLS                      0           0           1
         3 USER                     100         400           5
         4 APP1                     500         200           1
         5 APP2                     500         200           1
         6 RBS                        0           0           1
         7 TEMP                       0           0           1
```

Column START_LK shows the starting lock number for each file, while NLOCKS shows the total number of locks allocated to that file. The total number of locks allocated overall is determined by summing the NLOCKS column for all rows with a different START_LK value. If two rows have the same START_LK value, then the files represented by those rows share the same locks. Notice that in our example, files 4 and 5 have the same START_LK value. That indicates that they share the same locks. Each lock beginning with number 500 and extending through number 699 protects one or more blocks in both file 4 and file 5.

PCM Lock Allocation Guidelines

So far in this chapter we've discussed various types of PCM locks, their characteristics, and the initialization parameters used to allocate the locks. This section discusses key criteria that you should consider when deciding on PCM lock allocation in your environment and guides you in deciding what types of locks to use in different situations.

Strategy for PCM Lock Allocation

There are a number of strategies that you should keep in mind when deciding on PCM lock allocation. These include:

- Allocating PCM locks based on blocks in cache, not on disk
- Planning for more datafiles

- Treating each datafile separately

- Giving special treatment to the SYSTEM tablespace

- Separating read-only and modifiable data

- Separating indexes from tables

- Adding locks when you add a datafile

The following sections discuss each of these strategies.

Allocate PCM locks based on blocks in cache, not on disk

Data on the disk does not contribute to the problem of maintaining cache coherency. Data in the cache does. In addition, however, clean data (data that has not been modified) in the cache and locally accessed data in the cache also do not impact cache coherency. Consequently, you should base the number of instance locks on the amount of data in the cache that is being modified globally, not the total amount on disk.

For example, let's assume that an OPS database has one billion data blocks distributed among several datafiles. Allocating PCM locks for all of these blocks may not be practical. You might not have the memory to allocate one billion locks. You can maximize the efficiency of your locking scheme by analyzing your data and allocating locks accordingly.

You need to know the usage patterns of your data. You can segregate data into separate datafiles based on their usage patterns. Then you will be able to allocate different types and numbers of locks to each datafile based on the usage pattern of the blocks in that particular datafile. Allocate very few locks to the blocks accessed only locally, since these blocks will not be required by other instances. Similarly, read-only data can be protected by only a single PCM lock. This single PCM lock can be owned by multiple instances in shared mode simultaneously to read the data. Data modified only occasionally can be protected by a few locks. However, frequently modified data blocks need better protection and should have more locks allocated in order to avoid false pings. Try to allocate fine-grained locks to datafiles containing frequently modified blocks if you have sufficient memory to do so. The system memory and startup time may set practical limits for the actual number of locks that you can allocate. Refer to the section "How Many Locks to Allocate?" later in this chapter for more details.

Plan for more datafiles

PCM locks are allocated on a per-file basis. Thus, the granularity of lock allocation (the number of blocks per lock) can be varied from one file to the next. If you plan for more tables, and you place tables having different usage characteristics in separate datafiles, then you can vary the granularity of lock allocation based on the particular access pattern of the file. Thus, it is better to plan for more datafiles (and hence tablespaces) in an OPS environment than in a standalone database.

Treat each datafile separately

The purpose of lock allocation is to protect data blocks that remain in the database buffers. Thus you should allocate more locks to files that have more blocks in the cache. Also, allocate more locks to files that have higher write activity.

Give special treatment to the SYSTEM tablespace

The SYSTEM tablespace contains the data dictionary tables that are read and modified by all instances. Therefore, be generous in allocating locks to the datafile(s) of the SYSTEM tablespace. If practicable, use fine-grained locking for the SYSTEM tablespace.

Separate read-only and modifiable data

Separate read-only and modifiable objects into different tablespaces. This will help you to control lock allocation better. Read-only data is protected by locks in shared mode, and the same lock can be held in shared mode by multiple instances. Thus, you should allocate only a few locks (one is good enough) to datafiles containing read-only data and allocate more locks to datafiles containing modifiable data.

Separate indexes from tables

Place indexes in datafiles separate from those used for tables, so that separate PCM locks can be allocated for index blocks. Allocate fewer locks to index datafiles when those indexes are modified infrequently.

Add locks when you add a datafile

When new datafiles are added, allocate additional locks for them. This is something you don't need to worry about in a standalone instance environment but which you should worry about in an OPS environment. Remember to revisit your GC_FILES_TO_LOCKS parameter setting each time you add a datafile.

Fine-Tuning Lock Allocation

All of the discussion so far has pertained to the initial lock allocation for a new OPS database. As the database grows in size and as the number of users increases, you must periodically reevaluate your allocation of locks. You may need to redistribute locks as a result of changing usage patterns or add new locks as a result of growth. Several data dictionary views are available to help you identify blocks that have high ping activity and also provide information as to the nature of the contention causing that pinging. You can fine-tune your lock allocation based on the results of monitoring these data dictionary views. Refer to Chapter 10, *Monitoring and Tuning OPS*, for details on how to monitor locks and lock activities.

What Kind of Locks to Use?

As we've explained, there are four different types of PCM locks. Not all types are suitable for all environments. Each type of lock is suitable for a different type of application. You may see all four types of locking in one database, but a single datafile can have only one type of locking associated with it. The following sections describe the strong points of each type of lock and provide examples of situations for which they're best suited.

Hashed locks

One hashed lock protects multiple blocks. The blocks protected by a hashed lock can belong to one or more datafiles depending on the specifications in the GC_FILES_TO_LOCKS initialization parameter. When you share locks between datafiles, make sure that these datafiles belong to the same tablespace. An exception to that rule is when the files contain read-only data. All read-only data can be protected by just one lock.

Hashed locks are beneficial when there is no false pinging involved. Read-only data and data accessed by only a single instance both fall into this category.

Take advantage of the read-only tablespace feature of Oracle in this situation. A datafile of a read-only tablespace can be protected by a single hashed lock because every instance can own that lock in shared mode.

Why do you need to allocate even a single PCM lock to the read-only tablespace? If no PCM locks are specifically assigned to the datafile for the read-only tablespace, then either fixed locks from the default bucket or releasable fine-grained locks are going to be allocated to the datafile based on the GC_FILES_TO_LOCK parameter specification. Fixed locks that are allocated from the default bucket could have been better used for protecting another tablespace. If releasable locks are used, then there is the overhead of acquiring and releasing the locks.

In contrast, if only one PCM lock is allocated to the read-only tablespace, then each instance acquiring the single PCM lock in share mode retains the lock with much less overhead.

If a certain set of tables is accessed by one instance only, put them in a separate datafile. Since the blocks in that datafile will always be accessed by one instance, they will never undergo pinging. All of the blocks in that datafile then can be protected by a single hashed lock.

If a table is accessed by multiple instances but is partitioned in such a way that each partition is accessed by only one instance, you can place each partition in a separate datafile and then allocate one hashed lock for each of those.

Fine-grained locks

Fine-grained locks are recommended for datafiles containing blocks that are accessed by multiple instances and blocks that undergo an appreciable amount of false pinging. By allocating one PCM lock for each block, you can avoid false pings entirely.

Fixed locks

Once a fixed lock has been acquired by an instance, it is not released unless it's requested by another instance. Fixed locks are recommended for datafiles containing blocks accessed primarily by one instance, so that locks remain allocated throughout the life of that instance.

Fixed locks also are beneficial for read-only data. In such cases, each instance acquires the lock in shared mode and keeps it for the lifetime of the instance.

Releasable locks

If a database is very large, allocating the number of fixed locks sufficient to avoid false pings won't be practical because of the amount of memory required. In such a situation, releasable fine-grained locks are useful. You can assign releasable fine-grained locks to datafiles that contain globally modified data. Releasable fine-grained locks help to eliminate false pings, and because they are acquired and released as required, they do not require too much memory.

How Many Locks to Allocate?

You've seen that by allocating additional PCM locks to datafiles you can reduce false pings. If you allocate one lock per block, then you can totally eliminate false pings. However, locks consume memory in the SGA, and allocating large numbers of locks requires extra time during database startup and recovery. Proper lock allocation is a tradeoff. It isn't practical to allocate one lock for each block in a large database. Thus, design your tablespaces and allocate your locks prudently, so that the available locks will reduce false pings as much as possible.

The maximum number of PCM locks that can be allocated depends on the memory available on the database server. PCM locks are allocated within the SGA, and allocating more locks increases the size of the SGA.

You can find out how much memory is consumed by a single PCM lock on your platform by performing a small experiment. Increase the locks allocated for a particular file by changing the GC_FILES_ TO_LOCKS parameter. Shut down and restart the instance, and then record the size of the SGA. Make certain that you don't change any other parameters. You can compute the number or bytes consumed by each lock by making a few such changes in succession and each time dividing the difference in the resulting SGA size by the difference in the number of locks allocated. Results may vary by platform. Under IBM's AIX operating system, for example, PCM locks take 64 bytes each.

Please note that GC_FILES_TO_LOCKS is a global constant parameter and must be identical across all instances. Therefore, when you conduct this experiment in one instance, you must shut down all other instances.

Non-PCM Locks

In an Oracle Parallel Server environment, several database resources are shared across multiple instances. As we've discussed previously, data blocks are protected by PCM locks. All other shared resources are protected by non-PCM locks. When parallel server is enabled, local enqueues become global. These are included in the non-PCM locks. The most important non-PCM lock types are the following:

Transaction locks

These locks are row-level locks acquired by transactions during the execution of INSERT, UPDATE, DELETE, and SELECT FOR UPDATE statements. These locks are acquired in exclusive mode and are held for the life of the transaction. Transaction locks are released when the transaction is committed or rolled back.

DML locks

These locks protect an entire table during a DML or DDL operation. The number of DML locks is controlled by the DML_LOCKS initialization parameter. If this parameter is set to zero in one instance, then it must be set to zero in all of the instances. Setting DML_LOCKS to zero disables table locking for the whole database. The advantage of setting this parameter to zero is that doing so eliminates contention and overhead for these locks. However, the disadvantage is that you cannot perform any DDL operations such as DROP TABLE, CREATE INDEX, LOCK TABLE, and so forth.

System Change Number lock

Oracle uses a number called the System Change Number (SCN) to record the proper sequencing of changes to the database. The SCN is global to all instances in a parallel server database. To reduce communication overhead, a cached copy of the SCN is kept in the memory of each instance. Each instance may increment the SCN as a result of a change. Oracle uses a lock known as the SCN lock to protect the global SCN. To increment the global SCN, a process must acquire this lock in exclusive mode.

Library cache locks

The library cache resides in the SGA of each instance and holds the parse trees and execution plans for SQL statements and compiled PL/SQL program units. This facilitates reuse of identical SQL statements executed by multiple users. When a process parses a DML or DDL statement, it acquires a library cache lock on the objects referenced in the statement. Similarly, when a PL/SQL program unit is compiled, library cache locks are acquired on the objects referenced. These locks are released after completion of parsing or compilation.

Dictionary cache locks

A data dictionary cache is maintained in the SGA of each instance in a parallel server database to hold information from the data dictionary. This information includes the definition of database objects, integrity constraints, user security, and so on. Since this information is replicated in the SGA of each instance, there is a danger of its getting out of sync when one instance drops a table or grants a privilege to a user. Dictionary cache locks are used to synchronize between the dictionary caches of multiple instances.

Database mount lock

In Oracle Parallel Server, multiple instances mount the database in shared mode. An instance acquires the mount lock in shared mode before mounting the database. If an instance acquires the mount lock in exclusive mode, it mounts the database in exclusive mode and no other instance can mount the database.

Non-PCM locks constitute 5 to 10 percent of total locks. You do not have much control over non-PCM locks, but you must take them into account when you're performing capacity planning.

Storage Management in OPS

Storage management is an important aspect of database tuning. Oracle manages storage space using several storage management parameters. You can use some of these storage management parameters—in particular, FREELISTS, FREELIST GROUP, and PCTFREE—to improve the performance of Oracle Parallel Server. This chapter explains the concepts behind these parameters and describes how to set them in an OPS environment.

In this chapter we also discuss Oracle's reverse key index feature, which you can use to spread the index entries in an index tree more evenly when the indexes are based on sequential keys. Use of reverse key indexes can reduce contention for index leaf blocks during index updates when many instances are inserting rows into the same table.

Using Free Lists and Free List Groups

Free lists and *free list groups* are structures that Oracle uses to keep track of the free space within a segment such as a table, index, or cluster. If you have a large number of processes updating or inserting data into a segment, they will all need access to the segment's free list. Too much contention for a segment's free list can cause performance to suffer. The FREELISTS and FREELIST GROUP space management parameters are used to reduce contention for a segment's free list as follows:

FREELISTS

You can set this parameter in both OPS and non-OPS environments. Use it to reduce contention for free lists when multiple-user processes are inserting or updating the same table.

FREELIST GROUP

Unlike FREELISTS, this parameter is useful only in OPS environments. Use it to reduce contention when processes from multiple OPS instances are inserting or updating the same table.

Both of these storage parameters apply to clusters and indexes, as well as to tables. These parameters are not useful for read-only tables.

The Master Free List

Whenever you create a table, cluster, or index, Oracle creates at least one segment to hold the data for that object. Each segment consists of one or more extents, and each extent consists of a set of contiguous database blocks. Within the first block of each segment is a segment header. The segment header contains, among other things, a list of blocks allocated to the segment that still have free space available. This list of free blocks is maintained in a linked list known as the *master free list.*

The *high-water mark* (HWM) represents the upper limit of blocks that have been used in a segment. Any blocks above the HWM have never been used. When a table, index, or cluster needs additional space, the HWM for that segment is increased, and free blocks above the HWM are made available for use. Oracle automatically allocates new extents when the HWM cannot be increased any further, and those new extents are added above the HWM. Whenever the HWM is increased, five new blocks are added to the master free list. Blocks are removed from the master free list when the free space in those blocks becomes less than that specified by the PCTFREE storage parameter. (See the discussion of this parameter in the "The PCTFREE Parameter: Reserving Free Space" section later in this chapter.) Blocks are added back to the master free list when their used space falls below the threshold specified by the PCTUSED parameter.

All processes use the master free list during insert and update operations to locate blocks with space for new data. These processes also update the master free list, removing blocks when their free space falls below PCTFREE and adding them back when their used space falls below PCTUSED. All updates to the master free list involve writes to the segment header. When multiple processes in an Oracle instance perform concurrent insert and update operations on a single table, the result is contention for the master free list. Figure 9-1 illustrates this contention.

The FREELISTS Parameter: Creating Process Free Lists

In order to avoid contention for the master free list, you can organize a segment's free space into several *process free lists.* A process free list is another level of free

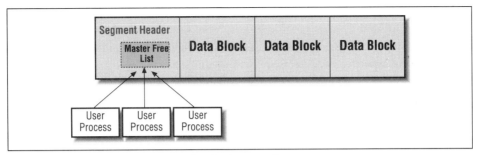

Figure 9-1. Contention for a master free list by several user processes

list that is used by specific processes. You create process free lists, sometimes just called free lists, by specifying the FREELIST storage parameter when you first create an object. Each time the high-water mark for the segment is increased, 5 * (number of free lists + 1) free blocks are transferred. For example, if you have a table with 10 free lists, a total of 55 free blocks will be moved. Each free list will get 5 blocks, and another 5 will go into the master free list.

Each user process updating an object is assigned to one process free list and is not allowed to access any of the others. When a user process needs to find a block with free space, it scans its assigned process free list first, before looking in the master free list. The result is that update activity is spread out over several process free lists instead of being concentrated in the master free list. Oracle processes are mapped to specific process free lists using the following modulo function:

```
Specific process free list used =
    (process_id modulo number_of_freelists) + 1
```

The master free list and process free lists are located in the segment header, as illustrated in Figure 9-2. Having multiple process free lists improves performance in OLTP applications in which several processes are concurrently inserting or updating the same object. Ideally, make sure that the value for the FREELISTS parameter is equal to the number of concurrent insert operations.

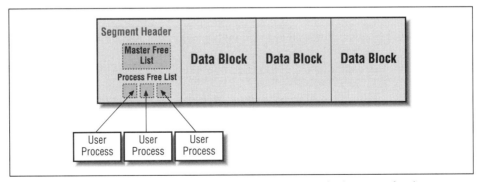

Figure 9-2. Contention for master free list reduced by using multiple process free lists

There is one drawback to using process free lists—you may end up with more disk space allocated to a segment than you would otherwise. This is because each user process takes free blocks from a specific process free list or from the master free list. If the specific process free list and the master free list are both empty, additional extents will be allocated to the segment even though other free lists may have free blocks available. However, free blocks that are available in those other process free lists eventually will be used up as new user processes are assigned to those process free lists.

The FREELIST GROUP Parameter: Creating Groups of Free Lists

In an OPS environment, multiple instances may concurrently perform insert or update operations against a table. This can lead to contention for the master free list—not between processes, but between instances. The solution to this problem is similar to the solution for the problem of contention between processes. Instead of creating free lists for individual processes, you create groups of free lists for use by the individual instances.

Segment header contention

In an OPS environment, processes from multiple instances refer to the master free list of a segment in order to locate free blocks. These processes also update the master free list to remove any blocks that are no longer free. Because updates to the master free list involve writes to the segment header, concurrent access from multiple instances can result in unwanted ping activity as the instances all contend for the same segment header block. This pinging occurs even if you have used the FREELISTS parameter to specify multiple process free lists for the segment, because the segment header also contains those process free lists. If the number of concurrent insert and update operations is high, the segment header will experience heavy ping activity, resulting in a loss in performance. Figure 9-3 illustrates this situation.

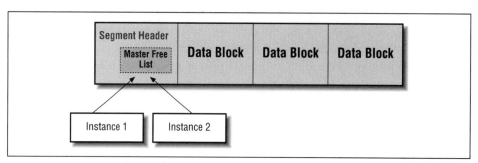

Figure 9-3. Contention for a segment header by OPS instances

To resolve the contention shown in this figure, you can create a free list group for each of the instances. A free list group is a combination of a group-specific master free list with group-specific process free lists. Each free list group is stored in its own block. Instances are assigned to different free list groups, thus reducing contention between instances for the same segment header block.

Creating a free list group for each instance

The FREELIST GROUP storage parameter is used to create multiple free list groups, each with its own master free list and each in its own block. These blocks are referred to as *free list blocks* and are always created in the first extent of a segment, immediately after the segment header. The segment header block contains a special free list called the *central master free list*, or the *segment master free list*. When multiple instances insert into or update the segment concurrently, each instance will access a different free list group to find free blocks. Pinging is reduced or eliminated because each free list group is in its own block, and different instances are assigned to different free list groups. If you can manage to have one free list group for each instance, you'll never have two instances contending for a free list block. This scenario is illustrated in Figure 9-4.

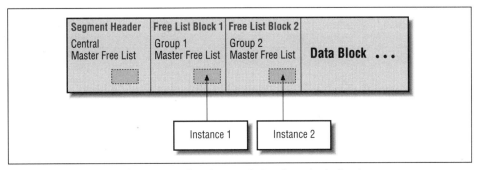

Figure 9-4. Contention for segment header avoided with multiple free list groups

Combining free lists and free list groups

The FREELISTS and FREELIST GROUP parameters can be specified together in an OPS environment in which each OPS instance also has several processes that perform concurrent inserts or updates. In such a configuration, each free list block stores a master free list together with the number of process free lists specified by the FREELISTS parameter. For example, the following SQL statement creates a table named emp with two free list groups and three process free lists in each group:

```
CREATE TABLE emp
(
emp_id   NUMBER(5),
emp_name VARCHAR2(20),
```

```
dob       DATE
)
STORAGE
        (INITIAL 10K NEXT 10K MAXEXTENTS 10
        PCTCREE 20  PCTUSED 60 PCTINCREASE 0
        FREELIST GROUP 2 FREELISTS 3);
```

Figure 9-5 illustrates how each instance in a two-instance OPS environment can then access separate free list blocks, each with its own master free list and its own set of process free lists. If multiple processes in an instance are accessing the same segment, those processes will be distributed among the available process free lists within the free list group allocated to the instance.

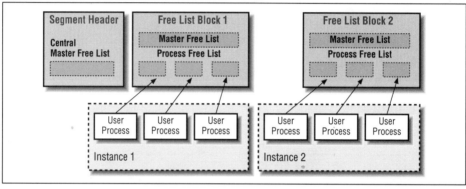

Figure 9-5. Multiple free lists in a free list group

Both the FREELISTS and FREELIST GROUP parameters can be specified only at the time of object creation. The default value for FREELISTS and FREELIST GROUP is 0. The ALTER TABLE statement cannot change these parameters. To apply new values for these parameters, you have to re-create the database object in question.

The MAXINSTANCES Parameter: Mapping Free List Groups to Instances

The MAXINSTANCES parameter specifies the maximum number of OPS instances that can access a database; you set it when the database is created. If you're using multiple free list groups, it's generally best to use a FREELIST GROUP value equal to the MAXINSTANCES value. If both values are the same, each instance will map to a different free list group. However, in an environment with a very large number of OPS instances, space limitations may prevent you from setting FREELIST GROUP to such a high value. When the number of free list groups is less than the number of instances, you'll have multiple instances assigned to some free list groups. OPS instances are mapped to specific free list groups during instance start-up using the following modulo function:

```
Free list group allocated to instance i =
    (instance number modulo number of free list groups) + 1
```

When the number of free list groups is larger than the number of OPS instances, free list groups are divided among the instances. For example, if there are four free list groups for two OPS instances, the first instance will use the first two free list groups, and the second instance will use the remaining two free list groups. In this case, the particular free list group used by an Oracle process in an instance is determined by applying a hashing function to the process ID of that particular process.

Free Lists for Indexes and Clusters

You can specify the FREELISTS and FREELIST GROUP parameters for indexes and clusters in the same way you specify them for tables. With clusters, you have one STORAGE clause that applies to a group of tables. Consequently, all tables in a cluster share the same FREELISTS and FREELIST GROUP settings. The following example shows how you would create an index with two free list groups, and with three free lists in each group:

```
CREATE INDEX emp_index ON emp (emp_id)
STORAGE (FREELIST GROUP 2 FREELISTS 3);
```

Preallocating Extents

If you're using multiple free list groups to minimize pinging on the segment header blocks, you can further reduce the potential for pinging by preallocating extents to your instances. To preallocate an extent, you use the ALLOCATE EXTENT clause of the ALTER TABLE, ALTER CLUSTER, or ALTER INDEX commands. It only makes sense to preallocate extents if you use multiple free list groups, and you must first number each of your instances so that you have a way to identify them when you create new extents.

Instance numbers

To give each instance a number, use the INSTANCE_NUMBER parameter in your instance-specific parameter files. Give each instance a unique number, starting sequentially from 1, for example:

```
INSTANCE_NUMBER = 1
```

These instance number values will be read at instance startup and can then be used to uniquely identify each instance when you preallocate extents.

ALLOCATE EXTENT clause

The ALLOCATE EXTENT clause is used with the ALTER TABLE, ALTER CLUSTER, and ALTER INDEX commands to manually create and allocate an extent for a table,

PCM Lock Blocking Factors and the High-Water Mark

In a standalone Oracle instance, the high-water mark moves five blocks at a time as more rows are inserted into a table. Under OPS, the blocking factor that you specify for a datafile using the GC_FILES_TO_LOCKS parameter has an effect on how the high-water mark moves as a table grows.

The blocking factor represents the number of contiguous data blocks covered by one lock. It's what you specify using the *!block* notation in your GC_FILES_TO_LOCKS initialization parameter setting. For example, the following setting allocates 1000 locks to datafile #5 and uses a blocking factor of 10 to specify that each lock protects 10 contiguous blocks:

```
GC_FILES_TO_LOCKS = "5=1000!10"
```

Beginning with OPS release 7.2, the blocking factor controls the movement of the high-water mark as an object grows. Instead of moving five blocks at a time, the high-water mark will move the same number of blocks as specified by the blocking factor. With respect to this example, as a table uses space in datafile #5, the high-water mark will move in 10-block increments. As a DBA, you need to be aware of this, because the location of the high-water mark affects the performance of full table scans. Under OPS, you may find that the blocks below the high-water mark actually include a significant number of unused blocks. This is not bad; it's just something that you need to be aware of.

The good part about the way in which the blocking factor affects the movement of the high-water mark is that it provides you with another mechanism for moving blocks to an instance's free list group. When new blocks are allocated automatically, the instance that caused that allocation to occur gets ownership of those blocks.

cluster, or index. When you manually allocate an extent for an object, you have the option of associating that extent with a specific instance. The following example shows an ALTER TABLE statement that allocates a 20K extent to instance 1:

```
ALTER TABLE emp
    ALLOCATE EXTENT (SIZE 20K INSTANCE 1);
```

This form of the statement leaves the choice of datafile up to Oracle. If the tablespace containing the object in question is spread across multiple datafiles, you can go even further by specifying the datafile from which the new extent is to be allocated. For example:

```
ALTER TABLE emp
    ALLOCATE EXTENT (SIZE 20K
                DATAFILE 'emp_data_1'
                INSTANCE 1);
```

When you do allocate an extent to a specific instance in this way, the free blocks from that extent are assigned to the free list group associated with the instance. Assuming that you assign separate datafiles to preallocated extents belonging to the separate instances, and that you allocate separate PCM locks to these datafiles, pinging will be minimized during insert operations. Pinging also will be greatly reduced on those operations if the instance that inserts data is also the same instance that subsequently executes DML statements on the data or is the same instance that queries the data.

If you don't specify an instance when you preallocate an extent, or an extent is automatically allocated because no more space is available in the segment, the space in that extent is not allocated to any particular free list group. Instead, it is assigned to the central master free list. Space from the segment master free list can be used by any instance when no space is available in that instance's free list group.

ALTER SESSION SET INSTANCE command

Normally, when you allocate an extent to an instance, other instances will not use the blocks that make up that extent. You can override that behavior, however, using the ALTER SESSION SET INSTANCE command. This command allows you to associate your session with the extents allocated to an instance other than the one to which you are connected. Suppose, for example, that you issue the following command:

```
ALTER SESSION SET INSTANCE 3;
```

After executing this command, your session will now go to the free list group normally assigned to instance 3 whenever it needs to find a data block with free space. This occurs regardless of which instance you are really connected to.

> The ALTER SESSION SET INSTANCE command does not actually connect you to the instance that you specify. It only causes your session to use that instance's free list group.

Guidelines for Managing Free List Groups

In general, every object that is likely to sustain concurrent insert activity from multiple instances should be created with enough free list groups so that each instance can have its own. For example, if you have two OPS instances, then you should set the FREELIST GROUP parameter to 2 for all the tables, indexes, and clusters that will encounter concurrent insert or update activity from both of those instances. If you expect additional OPS nodes to be configured, then you may want to create enough extra free list groups to accommodate the anticipated growth without needing to re-create all those objects. That will save you the effort of re-creating those objects after the new instances are added.

Through careful application partitioning, you can limit insert and update activity on an object to a single instance. Multiple free list groups are not required in such cases nor are they beneficial. However, if you've partitioned your application, and you still have a few objects that sustain concurrent inserts and updates from multiple instances, you should create free list groups for just those objects.

If you partition objects using the partitioning features introduced in Oracle8, be aware that each partition is stored in its own segment. If each instance in an OPS environment is inserting into or updating a separate partition, then you don't need to worry about creating free list groups. Similarly, with process free lists, if multiple processes are updating a table but each is updating a different partition, then multiple process free lists are not necessary.

The PCTFREE Parameter: Reserving Free Space

The PCTFREE storage parameter specifies the percentage of each data block that is to be kept free for future updates that might expand the rows stored in that block. This parameter also can be used to control the number of rows that reside in a block. By reducing the number of rows in each block, you may be able to reduce pings on tables that are frequently accessed from many instances.

Let's use for an example a table that takes up 20 blocks and that is accessed randomly by multiple OPS instances. By increasing the value of the PCTFREE parameter and re-creating the table, you can cause that same data to be spread out over 80 blocks—four times as many as the original number. This reduces the probability of block contention to one-fourth of what it used to be. In essence, you are trading space for performance. This concept is practical for relatively small tables. In an extreme case, for a very "hot" table that cannot be partitioned, you can adjust PCTFREE high enough so that only one row is assigned per block. As long as no two instances are contending for the same row, no pinging will occur.

Assume that your database block size is 16K and that one row of our particular table takes up 200 bytes. You can specify the following STORAGE clause to ensure that each row is written to a block of its own:

```
STORAGE (INITIAL 128K NEXT 64K PCTINCREASE 0 PCTFREE 98 PCTUSED 2)
```

As you can see, the PCTFREE parameter in this example requests that each block be kept 98% free. That leaves only 2% of the data block for data. Then, 2% of 16K is 320 bytes, which is just a bit more than one of our 200-byte rows. In this case, we are leaving 120 bytes for overhead purposes. *Overhead* in this case refers to the data structures that Oracle uses within a block to keep track of your table data. Note that block overhead factors into the PCTFREE equation.

Using Reverse Key Indexes

Reverse key indexes are a new feature of Oracle8. With reverse key indexes, the byte string for each column in an index is reversed. Consider a two-column index on last name and first name. The following two lines illustrate the difference between a normal index and a reverse key index:

```
Mahapatra,Tushar      (normal index)
artapahaM,rahsuT      (reverse key index)
```

This key reversal results in an improved distribution of data across the leaf nodes of the index tree as compared to what you get using the standard indexing method. That's the upside. The downside is that you can't perform range scans using reverse key indexes.

Reverse key indexes can improve OPS performance by reducing the occurrence of pinging on index blocks. This is especially true when records are inserted with sequentially increasing key values. Order records, with sequentially increasing order numbers, provide an example of when this might occur. When the key values of inserted records increase sequentially, all of the index inserts take place in the rightmost block of the index tree. If the inserts are performed from more than one OPS instance, that index block becomes a "hot" block and will experience a large amount of pinging. When the bytes of a sequentially increasing index column are reversed, the updates will be spread over a number of index blocks. That's because the leading digit will no longer always be the same.

Specify the REVERSE keyword in the CREATE INDEX command to create a reverse key index. The following index generates a reverse key index on the ord_id column of the orders table:

```
CREATE INDEX ord_idx ON orders (ord_id) REVERSE;
```

Now, as new orders are added, the order ID numbers will be reversed before being indexed. For example, the sequential order numbers 831, 832, and 833 will be reversed to 138, 238, and 338, respectively. These reversed values will be spread out in the index tree and are likely to reside in different blocks. Because more than one block is involved, the odds that pinging will occur are reduced.

A standard index cannot be rebuilt as a reverse key index. To convert a standard index to a reverse key index, you will need to drop the index and re-create it using the REVERSE keyword.

10

Monitoring and Tuning OPS

Monitoring and tuning are important activities in any Oracle server environment, and all of the tuning activities required in a standalone Oracle server environment also are applicable in Oracle Parallel Server environment. With Oracle Parallel Server, you'll need to perform additional tuning activities to reduce PCM lock contention and pinging. OPS monitoring and tuning activities have added significance because OPS performance can degrade to a point at which it's worse than that of a single-instance server if PCM locks are not properly tuned. In this chapter we focus on the essentials of tuning and monitoring for OPS, covering the following topics:

- Monitoring PCM lock activity

- Monitoring overall system statistics

- Monitoring Integrated Distributed Lock Manager statistics

 The last section in this chapter, "Oracle Performance Manager," describes an Oracle tool that automates some of the monitoring operations described in this chapter. You must have a license for this software.

OPS Performance Views

One of the major goals of OPS tuning is to properly allocate PCM locks in order to reduce pinging. When you first create an OPS environment, you typically use guidelines such as those provided in Chapter 8, *Locking Mechanisms in OPS*, to help make your initial PCM lock allocation. After your OPS instances are started, you can use dynamic performance views to monitor lock activity, pinging, and other OPS-related statistics. You should analyze these statistics to identify the particular files, objects, and blocks that are pinged the most. Then, modify your PCM lock allocation and restructure tablespaces as necessary in order to reduce the amount of pinging that occurs.

Tuning is an iterative activity, and you may need to repeat the monitoring and adjustment process several times before you are satisfied with your OPS response times. After you've achieved an acceptable performance level, further tuning may not be required even if you do observe some pinging, unless you expect a large increase in database size or in the number of transactions. Figure 10-1 illustrates the OPS tuning process.

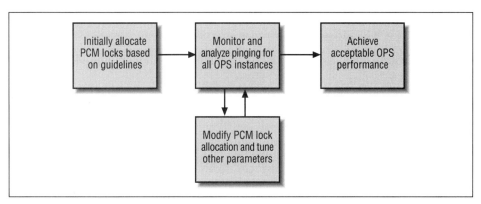

Figure 10-1. The OPS tuning process

Dynamic Performance Views

Oracle's dynamic performance views are available to monitor OPS-related activities and are referred to as *V$ views*. These views display Oracle server performance data from internal data structures of the Oracle instance and are continuously updated. Each OPS instance has its own set of performance data and hence has its own set of V$ views. Some of these views are OPS-specific. To create the OPS-specific views, you have to run the SQL script *catparr.sql* while you are logged in as the user SYS. Normally, you would do this when you first create an OPS database, but you can run *catparr.sql* at any time. In Unix environments, the *catparr.sql* script is located in the *$ORACLE_HOME/rdbms/admin* directory.

Global dynamic performance views, referred to as *GV$ views*, have been available since the release of Oracle8. The GV$ views have the same columns as the V$ views, plus an additional instance identifier (INST_ID) column. These views return performance information for all instances opening an OPS database and allow an administrator to monitor most OPS performance statistics centrally. No matter which instance you are connected to, you can use the GV$ views to retrieve statistics for any other instance, for example:

```
SELECT *
FROM gv$ping
WHERE inst_id = 2;
```

Monitoring PCM Locking

Several dynamic views are available to monitor PCM locking activity. Some of these views provide ping statistics at the instance level, while other views provide information about ping activity at the block level. Table 10-1 lists all the V$ views that provide PCM locking statistics and tells you the level at which each view is useful. Statistics for some of the views (e.g., V$PING, V$FALSE_PING, and V$CACHE) are derived from the V$BH view. They contain the same columns as V$BH but provide additional database object information.

Table 10-1. Views with PCM Lock Contention Statistics

Dynamic View	Description
V$LOCK_ACTIVITY GV$LOCK_ACTIVITY	*Instance-level lock activity* Return the cumulative number of lock conversions performed by the instance. One row is returned for each type of conversion such as X to NULL, X to S, NULL to X, and so forth.
V$FILE_PING GV$FILE_PING	*Lock activity by datafile* Return the number of lock conversions for each datafile. One row is returned for each datafile. This view can be used to identify datafiles with a high amount of ping activity.
V$BH GV$BH	*Block-level statistics* Buffer header views. Return one row for each block in the buffer cache and show buffer status, forced reads, forced writes, and so forth.
V$CACHE GV$CACHE	*Block- and object-level lock activity* Like V$BH, return one row for each block in the buffer cache. The view provides the name and owner of the database object that contains the block.
V$CACHE_LOCK	*Block- and object-level lock activity* Like V$CACHE but with two operating system-specific columns.
V$PING GV$PING	*Block- and object-level lock activity* Same as V$CACHE but return a list of only those blocks that have been pinged at least once.

Table 10-1. Views with PCM Lock Contention Statistics (continued)

Dynamic View	Description
V$CLASS_PING GV$CLASS_PING	*Lock activity by block class* Show the number of lock conversions for each block class. Block classes include data blocks, undo blocks, segment headers, and so forth. One row is returned for each block class. Can be used to identify block classes having a high amount of ping activity.
V$FALSE_PING GV$FALSE_PING	*False ping activity* Return one row for each buffer in the buffer cache that is likely experiencing false pings.
V$LOCKS_WITH_COLLISIONS GV$LOCKS_WITH_COLLISIONS	*Locks with high collisions* Return one row on each lock that protects multiple buffers, each of which has been pinged at least 10 times.
V$LOCK_ELEMENT GV$LOCK_ELEMENT	*Information on PCM locks* Return information on each PCM lock that is protecting a buffer in the buffer cache.

One approach to monitoring OPS ping activity is to determine at the instance level and at the datafile level if a lot of pinging is taking place. After you determine this fact, you can identify the specific objects and blocks that are causing the most pings. You also can investigate false pinging. After identifying the objects responsible for most of the pings, you should focus on tuning PCM lock allocation, restructuring tablespaces, and repartitioning the application as required.

Important V$ View Columns

Some of the columns in the dynamic performance views are found in many of the views. This section explains the meaning of the common columns and their significance, along with values of the column where appropriate.

The XNC column

The XNC column is present in the VBH, VCACHE, V$PING, and V$FALSE_PING dynamic performance views, as well as in the corresponding GV$ views. The XNC column shows the number of X-to-NULL lock conversations for the block. Each X-to-NULL lock conversion represents a ping. However, this statistic captures only part of the pinging activity for a block. Pinging also is caused by other lock conversions, such as X-to-S changeovers.

This column is now obsolete. It is present in Oracle7 and has been retained in Oracle8 to provide backward compatibility. We recommend that you use the FORCED_READS and FORCED_WRITES statistics to measure ping activity.

The FORCED_WRITES column

The FORCED_WRITES column is present in the VBH, VCACHE, V$PING, and V$FALSE_PING dynamic performance views. It's also present in the corresponding global dynamic (GV$) performance views. FORCED_WRITES shows the number of times a block has been written to disk because another instance needed the lock on that block in a conflicting mode. Forced writes entail the following lock conversions:

> X to NULL
> X to S
> X to SSX

The FORCED_READS column

The FORCED_READS column is present in the same views as the FORCED_WRITES column. It shows the number of times a block has to be *reread* from disk because of a previous forced write. Together, the FORCED_WRITES and FORCED_READS values represent *extra* I/O that is performed by an OPS instance as a result of PCM lock conflicts. This extra I/O would not be necessary in a standalone instance configuration.

The STATUS column

The STATUS column shows the status of the blocks in the database buffer cache. This column is present in the VBH, VCACHE, V$PING, and V$FALSE_PING dynamic performance views. Buffer status also is referred to as the *buffer state,* and it corresponds to the lock modes. For example, when an instance acquires an exclusive lock on a block, the buffer state changes to XCUR. Table 10-2 shows the buffer state codes along with any applicable corresponding lock modes.

Table 10-2. Buffer States

Buffer State	Description	PCM Lock Mode
XCUR	Instance has an exclusive lock on the buffer.	X
SCUR	Instance has a shared lock on the buffer.	S
CR	Instance has a NULL lock on the buffer.	N
READ	Instance is reading from disk to the buffer.	N/A
MREC	Buffer is in media recovery mode.	N/A
IREC	Buffer is in instance recovery mode.	N/A
FREE	Buffer is currently not used.	N/A

The KIND column

The KIND column tells you the type of database object represented by the data in a particular block. KIND is present in the VBH, VCACHE, V$PING, and

V$FALSE_PING views, as well as in the corresponding global dynamic performance views. Table 10-3 shows the possible values for this column.

Table 10-3. Object Type Codes for the KIND Column

Value	Object Type
1	INDEX
2	TABLE
3	CLUSTER
4	VIEW
5	SYNONYM
6	SEQUENCE
7	PROCEDURE
8	FUNCTION
9	PACKAGE
10	NON-EXISTENT
11	PACKAGE BODY
12	TRIGGER
13	TYPE
14	TYPE BODY
19	TABLE PARTITION
20	INDEX PARTITION
21	LOB
22	LIBRARY

The V$LOCK_ACTIVITY View

The V$LOCK_ACTIVITY view provides statistics on the number of overall lock mode conversions in an instance. These statistics are cumulative from the time that the instance was started. The query in the following example reports on the lock conversions in instance 1:

```
SQL> SELECT *
  2  FROM gv$lock_activity
  3  WHERE inst_id = 1;


FROM_VAL TO_VAL ACTION_V                                 COUNTER
-------- ------ --------------------------------------- --------
NULL     S      Lock buffers for read                      45595
NULL     X      Lock buffers for write                    139115
S        NULL   Make buffers CR (no write)                 50625
S        X      Upgrade read lock to write                 87555
X        NULL   Make buffers CR (write dirty buffers)     108366
X        S      Downgrade write lock to read               94261
                (write dirty buffers)
```

```
X        SSX    Write transaction table/undo blocks     11142
SSX      X      Rearm transaction table write mechanism  11142
```

8 rows selected.

Rate of change

When you look at V$LOCK_ACTIVITY, you can't just query the view once and look at the raw numbers. The statistics are cumulative, and if you're looking at the statistics a few weeks after you start your instance, the numbers may indeed look high. The point to focus on is the rate at which the lock conversions are taking place. To determine the rate, you need to query V$LOCK_ACTIVITY twice and note the difference in the COUNTER values between the two queries.

As an example, assume that in instance 1 the count of X-to-NULL conversions increases from 108,400 to 120,400 between two queries against V$LOCK_ACTIV-ITY. The net number of X-to-NULL lock conversions during the time period is then 12,000. This indicates that instance 1 is forced to write many modified blocks to disk because another instance needs the corresponding locks in exclusive mode. This represents pinging. If you run the same query while connected to the other instance, you would notice a large number of lock conversions from NULL to X, as the second instance is acquiring those same locks in exclusive mode.

Lock-related disk writes

Lock downgrades from exclusive (X) modes to other modes such as NULL, shared (S), or subshared exclusive (SSX) involve disk writes. The following list describes the implications of these downgrades:

X to NULL

An instance is modifying a block and is holding the corresponding lock in exclusive mode. Another instance needs the same lock in exclusive mode in order to modify a block covered by the same lock. The instance holding the lock has to write the data to disk and then downgrade the lock from X to NULL. The other instance then upgrades its lock from NULL to X.

X to S

An instance is modifying a block and is holding the corresponding lock in exclusive mode. Another instance needs the same lock in shared mode in order to read a block covered by the lock. The instance holding the lock has to write the data to disk and then downgrade the lock mode from X to S. The other instance then upgrades its lock from NULL to S.

X to SSX

SSX locks are used for undo blocks in the rollback segment. One instance is modifying blocks and is holding the corresponding locks in exclusive mode. The instance also acquires exclusive locks on the undo blocks as these blocks also are modified when recording the rollback entries. Another instance is running a query that needs data from undo blocks. The first instance has to write the undo blocks to disk. The locks covering the undo blocks then are downgraded from X to SSX. After the consistent read operation is performed by the second instance, the lock mode changes back from SSX to X. In any instance, the number of X-to-SSX conversions will be the same as the number of SSX-to-X conversions.

As an example of how to look at lock-related disk writes, say that we queried the V$LOCK_ACTIVITY view and found the following lock mode conversion numbers:

```
X   to  NULL    108366
X   to  S       94261
X   to  SSX     11142
```

Adding the number of all X-to-NULL, X-to-S, and X-to-SSX conversions together, we get a total of 213,769 lock conversions. These lock mode conversions result in disk writes. Now, let's find the total number of blocks that are written to disk because of these lock conversions. The "DBWR cross instance writes" statistic in the V$SYSSTAT view provides the total number of blocks written to disk because of lock mode conversions. You can query for that information as shown in this example:

```
SQL> SELECT * FROM v$sysstat
     WHERE statistic# = 'DBWR cross instance writes';

STATISTIC# NAME                                   CLASS     VALUE
---------- ---------------------------- ---------- ----------
        77 DBWR cross instance writes              40    417,143
```

The ping rate shows the average number of blocks written to disk for each lock downgrade. The ping rate is computed as follows:

```
Ping rate = DBWR cross instance writes
            /Lock operations resulting in disk writes
          = 417,143/213,769
          = 1.95
```

The ping rate provides an indication as to whether false pings are occurring. The following paragraphs explain how to interpret the ping rate:

Ping rate < 1

A ping rate of less than 1 indicates a high degree of soft ping activity. Typically, each X-to-NULL, X-to-S, and X-to-SSX lock conversion causes at least one block write to disk. However, in some situations, no disk write occurs if the blocks covered by the lock have already been written to disk as a result of a normal checkpoint operation. This scenario is referred to as a *soft ping*. In this case, a lot of soft ping activity in the instance is bringing down the overall ping rate to less than 1.

Ping rate > 1

A ping rate of greater than 1 indicates a high degree of false ping activity. In other words, on average, each lock operation is causing more than one block to be written to disk. In this chapter's example, the ping rate is 1.95. This number indicates that false pings are definitely occurring. The goal is to bring down the ping rate to 1 by reducing the occurrence of false pings. You can compute the percentage of disk writes due to false pings using the following formulas and query:

```
Percentage of disk writes due to false pings
    = ((DBWR cross instance writes - Lock operations resulting in disk write)
            /DBWR cross instance writes) * 100
    = (417,143-213,769) / 417,143
    = 48.754024
```

```
SQL> SELECT ((s.value - ( a.counter + b.counter + c.counter)) / s.value )* 100
  2  "PERCENTAGE FALSE PING"
  3  FROM  v$sysstat s, v$lock_activity a, v$lock_activity b, v$lock_activity
  4  WHERE a.from_val ='X' AND a.to_val ='NULL'
  5  AND · b.from_val ='X' AND b.to_val ='S' and
  6  AND   c.from_val ='X' AND c.to_val ='SSX'
  7* AND   s.name = 'DBWR cross instance writes'

PERCENTAGE FALSE PING
---------------------
          48.754024
```

In this example, more than 48% of the blocks written to disk are due to false pings. False pings occur when one lock covers more than one block, and you can allocate additional PCM locks to reduce the occurrence of false pings.

Ping rate = 1

A ping rate of 1 indicates that, on average, each lock operation is causing one block to be written to disk. Either soft pings and false pings are not occurring, or they are occurring together in a way that masks each other's effects on the ping rate statistic. Unfortunately, it isn't possible to reach any definite conclusion.

You also should monitor lock activity in all OPS instances using the GV$LOCK_ACTIVITY view. Once you know that in general there is high ping activity in the instance, you then should monitor the V$FILE_PING view to find out which specific datafiles have high ping activity.

The V$FILE_PING View

The V$FILE_PING view tells you the amount of lock activity for each file in your database. This view returns one row for each datafile and is very useful in identifying files that incur a high number of pings. Once you identify files with high ping rates, you can further investigate to find out which specific objects and blocks in those files are being pinged the most. You also can investigate to find out which instances are contending for those resources. Here's an example of a query against the GV$FILE_PING view:

```
SQL> SELECT file_number, x_2_null, X_2_S, S_2_NULL
  2* FROM v$file_ping

FILE_NUMBER   X_2_NULL       X_2_S   S_2_NULL
----------- ---------- ---------- ----------
          1     134198      187545     165542
          2       3094        2700       4838
          3        512       17858       4202
          4      40569          65        175
```

This report indicates that datafile 1 has the greatest amount of lock activity. Because these statistics are cumulative since instance startup, you should run this query repeatedly in order to determine the rate of lock activity for each file. If a table has high lock activity, particularly X_2_NULL and X_2_S lock mode conversions, this fact also implies high ping activity. Further monitor V$FALSE_PING and other views to find out if the pings are false pings or true pings.

The V$BH and V$CACHE Views

The V$BH view returns buffer header information. For every buffer in the database buffer cache, it returns the buffer status and the number of X-to-NULL lock conversions, forced reads, and forced writes. It also provides the block number and the file number for the block that is in the buffer. V$BH does not contain any information on the database object associated with the block that is in the buffer. However, you can join this view with the OBJ$ view in order to identify the objects corresponding to V$BH's blocks. The V$BH view is defined internally in the server, and other views such as V$CACHE and V$PING are based on the V$BH view.

The V$CACHE view returns one row for each block in the buffer cache, except for those blocks that do not have a lock element associated with them. Temporary blocks, for example, do not have locks. V$CACHE contains many of the same columns as the V$BH view, including XNC, FORCED_READS, and FORCED_WRITES. In addition, this view maps blocks to their respective database objects and also indicates the type and owner of those objects.

The V$PING View

The V$PING view contains a subset of rows from the V$CACHE view. It shows only those blocks in the buffer cache that have experienced at least one forced read or one forced write. Query V$PING to find out which blocks and objects have a high number of forced reads and forced writes. You may limit the query to a particular datafile that you have identified as a result of querying V$FILE_PING. Run the same query on other instances to identify all the instances involved in pinging the objects in question, for example:

```
SQL> SELECT name, block#, kind, forced_writes,
  2          forced_reads, lock_element_addr
  3  FROM v$ping
  4  WHERE forced_writes > 10 AND forced_reads > 10
  5  AND file# = 4
  6* ORDER BY name
```

NAME	BLOCK#	KIND	FORCED_WRITES	FORCED_READS	LOCK_ELE
CUST_INFO	13631	TABLE	3170	2180	34E054CC
CUST_INFO	13643	TABLE	150	268	34E0578C
CUST_INFO	13633	TABLE	170	180	34E0550C
.	.	.	.	.	.
.	.	.	.	.	.
.	.	.	.	.	.
PK_CUST_INFO	53691	INDEX	1176	200	64E0638C
PK_CUST_INFO	53759	INDEX	756	636	64E0748C
PK_CUST_INFO	53758	INDEX	756	636	64E0744C

This sample report shows the tables and indexes that have encountered high forced read and forced write activity. In this example, CUST_INFO is a "hot" object. Note the block number for each hot object. Then query the GV$BH view to find out if the same block numbers also show up in other OPS instances. Query GV$BH instead of V$BH, because you want to see this information for all instances. With respect to the example shown here, we need to query GV$BH for block number #13631, because the number of forced writes and forced reads is high for that block. If the same block number does not show up in other instances, there is contention for locks, implying false pings. If you see the same block number in other instances, then there is contention for the block, and true pings are occurring.

If the lock activity is due to true pings, check to see whether access to this object can be localized to only one instance. Investigate the various application partitioning strategies described in Chapter 11, *Partitioning for OPS*. If the object is a small object, consider using a high PCTFREE value for the object so that the data is spread out among more blocks. This reduces the likelihood of block contention.

If identifying the specific blocks of an object that are experiencing high amounts of ping activity isn't enough to help you reduce that activity, you can further drill down to find out which rows are in those blocks. To identify the rows contained in a hot block, start by converting the block number to hexadecimal. Once you've done that, you can take advantage of the fact that the first part of the database rowid is the block number. In Oracle7, you can issue a query such as the following to identify the rows contained in a hot block:

```
SELECT *
FROM trans_log
WHERE ROWID LIKE '%372A%'
```

This query will return all rows in which the ROWID contains the block number of interest. Note that Oracle8 and Oracle8*i* use a new ROWID format. You still can use this technique under Oracle8 and Oracle8*i*, but you need to use a conversion function in your query in order to convert the new ROWIDs back into the old format, for example:

```
SELECT *
FROM trans_log
WHERE DBMS_ROWID.ROWID_TO_RESTRICTED(rowid,1) like '%372A%'
```

Drilling down to the row level and identifying the rows in a "hot" block may provide some insight as to the data for which multiple instances may be contending.

The V$LOCKS_WITH_COLLISIONS and V$FALSE_PING Views

There is always the possibility that false pings will occur whenever a single PCM lock covers more than one block. Even when two instances are modifying different blocks, pinging still can occur because of lock conflicts.

The V$LOCKS_WITH_COLLISIONS view identifies locks that protect more than one block in cases in which the number of forced reads and forced writes for each block exceeds 10. Since each such lock is protecting more than one block with a high degree of ping activity, it is likely that false pings are occurring. The locks are identified by their address, which is returned by the LOCK_ELEMENT_ADDR column. LOCK_ELEMENT_ADDR is the only column returned by the view.

The V$FALSE_PING view shows the blocks that are protected by the locks identified by the V$LOCKS_WITH_COLLISIONS view. These are the blocks most likely to be experiencing false pings. The following query retrieves a list of these blocks that includes their respective object names and file numbers:

```
SELECT name, kind, file#, block, forced_reads, forced_writes
FROM v$false_ping
ORDER BY name, file#;
```

If a query of the V$FALSE_PING view returns a large number of blocks, then note the file IDs for those blocks and consider allocating additional hashed PCM locks to those datafiles. Doing so will reduce the granularity (the number of blocks covered by a lock) for all objects in the datafile, consequently reducing the number of false pings. If the file is very large and contains many other objects, it may not be possible to allocate enough locks to significantly reduce the granularity for the object you are interested in. In that case, consider placing the object in a separate tablespace and hence in its own datafile. The new datafile will contain fewer blocks than the original datafile, so the same incremental allocation of locks to the new datafile will greatly reduce granularity, which will more effectively reduce false pings. Alternatively, you also might consider using releasable fine-grained locks for those datafiles.

The V$CLASS_PING View

The V$CLASS_PING view summarizes ping activity by block class for the blocks in the database buffer cache. Here's an example of the output that you'll get when querying this view:

```
SQL> SELECT class, X_2_NULL, X_2_S, X_2_SSX, SSX_2_X,  S_2_NULL, S_2_X
  2  FROM v$class_ping;

CLASS               X_2_NULL   X_2_S X_2_SSX SSX_2_X S_2_NULL  S_2_X
------------------- -------- ------- ------- ------- -------- ------
                           0       0       0       0        0      0
data block            570139 1017442       0       0   238738 356407
sort block                 0       0       0       0        0      0
save undo block            0       0       0       0        0      0
segment header         27842     393       0       0      258    439
save undo header           0       0       0       0        0      0
free list                  0       0       0       0        0      0
extent map                 0       0       0       0        0      0
bitmap block               0       0       0       0        0      0
bitmap index block         0       0       0       0        0      0
unused                     0       0       0       0        0      0
undo header                0    2183   24705   24705     2531   2197
undo block                 0       0    5335    5335        0      0

13 rows selected.
```

The data in this report shows that most of the lock conversion takes place for data blocks and segment headers. Segment headers contain information on free data blocks. Segment header contention occurs when more than one instance is inserting data into an object at the same time. Chapter 9, *Storage Management in OPS*, describes some techniques that you can use to reduce segment header contention.

Also notice the values for the X_2_SSX and SSX_2_X columns in this example. These represent X-to-SSX and SSX-to-X conversions, respectively. These conversions occur only for undo headers and undo blocks. The counts for X-to-SSX and SSX-to-X conversions will always be the same because each X-to-SSX conversion is followed by a corresponding SSX-to-X conversion.

The V$LOCK_ELEMENT View

A *lock element* is a data structure in an Oracle instance that stores information on a PCM lock. There is one lock element for each PCM lock allocated. The V$LOCK_ELEMENT view contains one row for each lock element and has information such as the lock element name, the lock element address, the number of blocks protected by the lock, and so forth. Using this view, you can get an idea of how many blocks are protected by locks and the average number of blocks protected by one lock. The following two queries provide this information:

```
SELECT block_count, COUNT(*)
FROM v$lock_element
GROUP BY block_count;

SELECT AVG(block_count)
FROM v$lock_element;
```

Using this view, you also can confirm that the number of PCM locks allocated matches what you think you asked for using the GC_ initialization parameters. For example, with the following GC_FILES_TO_LOCKS and GC_RELEASABLE_LOCKS parameter settings, the total number of PCM locks in the instance will be 11,000:

```
GC_FILES_TO_LOCKS = "1=2000:2-5=1000EACH"
GC_RELEASABLE LOCKS = 5000
```

You can query V$LOCK_ELEMENT to find out the overall number of PCM locks that have been allocated. You also can query for the number of fixed and releasable PCM locks that have been allocated. The following query, for example, returns the total number of PCM locks allocated to each instance. This total includes both fixed and releasable PCM locks:

```
SQL> SELECT COUNT(*) FROM v$lock_element;

Count(*)
---------
11,0000
```

To count up the number of fixed PCM locks that have been allocated, use the FLAGS column in the WHERE clause as follows:

```
SQL> SELECT COUNT(*) FROM v$lock_element
     WHERE BITAND(flags,4) != 0;

Count(*)
--------
6,000
```

You can use a similar query to count up the number of releasable PCM locks. You only need to change the WHERE clause so that the query counts lock elements where BITAND(flags,4) = 0. Once you have the values returned by these queries, you then can verify that they correspond to your GC_ parameter settings.

Monitoring Overall Statistics

There are several dynamic performance views in Oracle that contain server statistics such as events, wait times, and so forth. While these views are not used exclusively for OPS, they do contain many OPS-related statistics. Table 10-4 summarizes these views.

Table 10-4. Views with OPS-Related Statistics

Dynamic View	Description
V$SYSSTAT GV$SYSSTAT	Provide several statistics on OPS related to database resource contention and global lock operations
V$SYSTEM_EVENT GV$SYSTEM_EVENT	Provide wait statistics for various system events, including events related to global lock operations
V$WAITSTAT GV$WAITSTAT	Provide statistics for the number of waits for each class of blocks
V$FILESTAT GV$FILESTAT	Provide statistics on file reads and writes

The V$SYSSTAT View

This view contains several performance statistics. Statistics are grouped into various statistics classes. For example, statistics related to the operating system are stored with a class value of 16. Statistics specific to Oracle Parallel Server are stored with class values of 32 and 40. This section discusses some of the statistics available in this view that are related to OPS and explains how they can be used.

The following example shows V$SYSSTAT being queried for all the OPS-related statistics:

```
SQL> SELECT *
  2  FROM v$sysstat
  3  WHERE class IN (32,40)
  4  ORDER BY name;

STATISTIC# NAME                                          CLASS      VALUE
---------- --------------------------------------------- ---------- ----------
        77 DBWR cross instance writes                        40     839727
       169 DDL statements parallelized                       32          0
       168 DML statements parallelized                       32          0
       171 PX local messages recv'd                          32     103968
       170 PX local messages sent                            32     102989
       173 PX remote messages recv'd                         32       1821
       172 PX remote messages sent                           32         42
        91 Unnecesary process cleanup for SCN batching       32          0
        92 calls to get snapshot scn: kcmgss                  32   28876985
        81 cross instance CR read                            40          0
       116 global cache convert time                         40          0
       115 global cache converts                             40    1073863
       111 global cache defers                               40       5999
       110 global cache freelist waits                       40          0
       114 global cache get time                             40          0
       113 global cache gets                                 40     236035
       112 global cache queued converts                      40        960
        32 global lock async converts                        32    1618504
        29 global lock async gets                            32     303083
        33 global lock convert time                          32          0
        30 global lock get time                              32          0
```

```
 34 global lock releases                          32    7375572
 31 global lock sync converts                     32    2210896
 28 global lock sync gets                         32    7188009
117 instance recovery database freeze count       32          0
 95 kcmccs called get current scn                 32          0
 94 kcmgss read scn without going to DLM          32          0
 93 kcmgss waited for batching                    32          0
 90 next scns gotten without going to DLM         32          0
167 queries parallelized                          32         21
 78 remote instance undo block writes             40       4707
 79 remote instance undo header writes            40       5122
 80 remote instance undo requests                 40       5066
```

In addition to the statistics for classes 32 and 40, there are a few other statistics that are helpful in tuning OPS. You can obtain them using the following query:

```
SQL> SELECT *
  2  FROM v$sysstat
  3  WHERE name IN ('db block gets', 'consistent gets',
                    'physical writes', 'DBWR undo block writes');

STATISTIC# NAME                                       CLASS      VALUE
---------- ------------------------------------- ---------- ----------
        38 db block gets                                  8   78576050
        39 consistent gets                                8  920284235
        41 physical writes                                8    4304306
        64 DBWR undo block writes                         8     739797
```

Table 10-5 summarizes the most useful of the statistics returned by the previous two queries.

Table 10-5. V$SYSTAT Statistics

Statistic Name	Description
DBWR cross-instance writes	The number of blocks written to disk by one instance so that other OPS instances can access those blocks in a consistent manner
physical writes	The number of blocks written to the disk by Oracle processes
global cache gets	A count of new PCM locks acquired
global cache get time	Elapsed time for acquiring new PCM locks
global cache converts	A count of PCM locks that are converted
global cache convert time	The elapsed time required to convert PCM locks
global lock get time	The elapsed time for acquiring new instance locks (PCM and non-PCM locks)
global lock sync gets	A count of synchronous instance lock acquisitions
global lock async gets	A count of asynchronous instance lock acquisitions
global lock convert time	The elapsed time required to convert instance locks
global lock sync converts	A count of synchronous instance lock conversions

Table 10-5. V$SYSTAT Statistics (continued)

Statistic Name	Description
global lock async converts	A count of asynchronous instance lock conversions
remote instance undo writes	The number of times undo blocks are written by the instance at the request of a remote instance
remote instance undo requests	The number of times the instance requested undo blocks from a remote instance's rollback segment in order to create consistent read data

Using the statistics described in Table 10-5, you can compute a number of other statistics useful for tuning OPS configurations. These other statistics are summarized in Table 10-6, which also shows the formulas used to derive them.

Table 10-6. Derivable V$SYSTAT Statistics

Statistic Name	Derivation Formula	Recommendations
Percentage of disk writes due to OPS ping activity	(DBWR cross-instance writes / physical writes) * 100	If greater than 10, continue tuning in order to reduce pings.
Average time taken to allocate a new PCM lock	global cache get time / global cache gets	Should be between 20–30 milliseconds.
Average time taken for PCM lock mode conversion	global cache convert time / global cache converts	Should be between 10–20 milliseconds.
Average time required to acquire a global lock	global lock get time / (global lock sync gets + global lock async gets)	Should be between 20–30 milliseconds.
Average time required to convert a global lock	global lock convert time / (global lock sync converts + global lock async converts)	Should be between 10–20 milliseconds.
Percentage of remote instance undo writes	(remote instance undo writes / DBWR undo block writes) * 100	A high value indicates both rollback segment contention and rollback segment pinging activity.

The V$SYSTEM_EVENT View

The V$SYSTEM_EVENT view returns information about events for which Oracle processes have had to wait. The query shown in the following example returns the number of waits due to different types of global lock operations in an OPS instance. The TOTAL_WAITS and TIME_TIMEOUTS columns provide the number of waits and the cumulative wait times for each of these global cache lock events. A high value of waits for global cache lock operations compared to other waits indicates a high amount of contention for PCM locks.

```
SQL> SELECT event,total_waits_timeouts
  2  FROM v$system_event
  3* WHERE event like '%global%';
```

```
EVENT                        TOTAL_WAITS TOTAL_TIMEOUTS
---------------------------- ----------- --------------
buffer busy due to global cache    32406            181
global cache lock open s             166              0
global cache lock open x           33378              1
global cache lock open ss           5490            304
global cache lock null to s       102362             43
global cache lock null to x       269541             52
global cache lock s to x          223473             16
global cache multiple locks         8716              1
global cache lock busy              1690             13
global cache bg acks                   2              1
```

The V$WAITSTAT View

The V$WAITSTAT view provides statistics on the number of waits for each class of blocks. These statistics are cumulative from when the instance first started. The following example shows some results returned as the result of a query to V$WAITSTAT:

```
SQL> SELECT * FROM v$waitstat;
```

```
CLASS                  COUNT       TIME
------------------ ---------- ----------
data block              5899          0
sort block                 0          0
save undo block            9          0
segment header           168          0
save undo header           0          0
free list                 36          0
extent map                 0          0
bitmap block               0          0
bitmap index block         0          0
unused                     0          0
system undo header        65          0
system undo block        124          0
undo header             3100          0
undo block               123          0
```

```
14 rows selected.
```

Table 10-7 summarizes the more important V$WAITSTAT statistics.

Table 10-7. Important V$WAITSTAT Statistics

Statistic Name	Description
data block	Number of waits for data blocks.
segment header	Number of waits for blocks containing segment headers.

Table 10-7. Important V$WAITSTAT Statistics (continued)

Statistic Name	Description
system undo header	Number of waits for blocks containing system rollback segment headers.
system undo block	Number of waits for blocks containing system rollback segment blocks. This does not include rollback segment header blocks.
undo header	Number of waits for blocks containing rollback segment headers for rollback segments other than the system rollback segment.
undo block	Number of waits for blocks containing rollback segment blocks. This does not include system rollback segment blocks.
free list	Number of waits for free list blocks in the free list.

To reduce contention for undo header blocks, add more rollback segments. To reduce contention for undo blocks, use larger rollback segments. Compare the number of waits for rollback segment blocks to the total number of blocks that were requested. If the ratio of waits to requests is greater than 0.01, then you should create additional rollback segments for the instance. To compute the total number of blocks requested, query V$SYSTAT for the "db block gets" and "consistent gets" statistics, and add those two values together.

To reduce waits on data blocks, change the PCTFREE and PCTUSED settings so that you have fewer rows per block. Use reverse key indexes too. Waits on segment header blocks indicate contention for free lists in the segment header. Use free list groups. A high number of "free list" waits implies high contention for the free list blocks. To remedy this, you can increase the value of your FREELIST GROUP storage parameters. Refer to Chapter 9 for an in-depth discussion of tuning these parameters.

The V$FILESTAT View

This view provides I/O statistics for different datafiles. The PHYRDS and PHYWRTS columns provide information on the number of reads and the number of writes to each datafile. Run the query shown in the following example, and analyze the results to determine if a particular disk is overburdened with I/O activities. Redistribute files on different disks as necessary in order to balance the I/O load.

```
SQL> SELECT name, phyrds, phywrts
     FROM v$datafile, v$filestat
     WHERE v$datafile.file# = v$filestat.file#;


NAME                                          PHYRDS       PHYWRTS
------------------------------------------ ---------- ----------
/dev/rifassys1                                 497215        544468
/dev/rifassystemp1                               4789          6663
/dev/rifasrbs1                                   3877        423011
```

```
/dev/rifastools1                    1435        588
/dev/rifasusers1                     384        383
/dev/rifasrbs2                       4960     308014
/dev/rifasdata                   42928399     255236
/dev/rifasindex                   1353862    2299197
/dev/rifaslog                     1773110     134947
/dev/rifastemp1                      384        383
```

Monitoring and Tuning IDLM

The Integrated Distributed Lock Manager is responsible for maintaining a list of database resources and for allocating locks on those resources. IDLM coordinates lock requests from different OPS instances. In some cases, lock requests are granted immediately, while in other cases lock requests are queued up until the remote instance that holds the lock in a conflicting mode releases the lock. The views that return information about IDLM performance are summarized in Table 10-8.

Table 10-8. Views with IDLM Statistics

Dynamic View	Description
V$DLM_CONVERT_LOCAL GV$DLM_CONVERT_LOCAL	Returns the counts for different types of local lock mode conversions, as well as the time taken for those conversions
V$DLM_CONVERT_REMOTE GV$DLM_CONVERT_REMOTE	Returns the counts for different types of lock mode conversions in a remote node, as well as the time taken for those conversions
V$DLM_LATCH GV$DLM_LATCH	Returns IDLM latch statistics
V$DLM_MISC GV$DLM_MISC	Returns some miscellaneous IDLM statistics
V$DLM_RESS GV$DLM_RESS	New in Oracle8*i*; returns information on all resources known to IDLM
V$DLM_ALL_LOCKS GV$DLM_ALL_LOCKS	New in Oracle8*i*; returns information on all locks known to IDLM
V$DLM_LOCKS GV$DLM_LOCKS	New in Oracle8*i*; returns a subset of results of the V$DLM_ALL_LOCKS view and return information on all locks that are either blocked or blocking others

Tuning IDLM

IDLM has internal data structures that contain lists of all database resources. IDLM also tracks the status of both PCM and non-PCM locks on all instances. The IDLM internal data structures that contain these types of information are referred to as *IDLM resources* and *IDLM locks*. The LM_RESS and LM_LOCK initialization parameters determine how many of these data structures are allocated. These parameters are used to configure the capacity of the IDLM:

LM_RESS

Specifies the number of resources that can be locked by each Lock Manager instance

LM_LOCKS

Specifies the number of locks to configure for the Lock Manager

Consider, for example, an OPS environment with two instances, where data block B1 is protected by PCM lock L1. Also assume that instance 2 is updating the block. Since instance 2 is updating block B1, it will hold lock L1 in exclusive mode. The other instance then has lock L1 in null mode. In this case, you need one LM_RESS data structure to keep information about the resource, and you need two LM_ LOCKS data structures to maintain the lock status on both the instances, as shown in Figure 10-2.

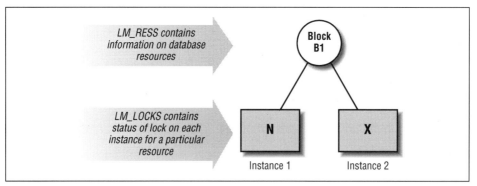

Figure 10-2. Lock Manager parameters

The value of the LM_RESS parameter must take into consideration all of the database resources that are protected by PCM as well as non-PCM locks. The value of LM_LOCKS depends on the number of instances in the OPS environment. One "bottom-up" approach to setting up LM_RESS and LM_LOCKS is to compute the total number of PCM resources, non-PCM resources, and locks required in your OPS environment. A detailed discussion and worksheet are provided in Oracle Corporation's *OPS Concepts and Administration* manual in the chapter titled "Ensuring IDLM Capacity for all Resources and Locks." See also the related discussions in other chapters of the same manual.

A "top-down" approach that we suggest is to initially set up a high value for these parameters based on the available memory that can be allocated to the SGA. Then monitor the V$RESOURCE_LIMIT dynamic performance view, and adjust these parameters based on utilization. In order to do this, you have to first determine how much memory each IDLM lock and IDLM resource data structure take up. The exact amount of memory consumed by each IDLM lock and IDLM resource for each additional increment of the LM_RESS and LM_LOCKS parameter settings is platform-dependent. On an IBM RS/6000 platform, each additional increment of the LM_RESS and LM_LOCKS parameter settings requires 220 bytes of memory. You can do a test on your own platform to determine the memory requirements for these parameters. Successively increase the value of each initialization parameter (one at a time), and note the size of the SGA after restarting the OPS instance after each increase. After a few such changes, you should be able to compute the memory required for allocating IDLM data structures in accordance with these parameter settings.

Once you know the memory requirements for each of these parameters, you can initially set up high values for LM_RESS and LM_LOCKS based on the most memory that can be allocated to the SGA. This is only a starting point for the tuning activity. You then can check the usage of LM_RESS and LM_LOCKS periodically by executing the query shown in the following example. Note that using higher values beyond the utilization limits shown in the V$RESOURCE_LIMIT view results in unnecessary overhead. Tune your LM_RESS and LM_LOCKS values based on the CURRENT_UTILIZATION and MAX_UTILIZATION values:

```
SQL> SELECT *
  2 FROM v$resource_limit
  3 WHERE resource_name like 'lm%';

RESOURCE_NAME   CURRENT_UTILIZATION MAX_UTILIZATION INITIAL_AL LIMIT_VALU
--------------- ------------------- --------------- ---------- ----------
lm_procs                        228             268       1200       1200
lm_ress                       29702           29828      31024  UNLIMITED
lm_locks                      34206           34231      35000  UNLIMITED
```

If the number of LM_RESS and LM_LOCKS specified by the initialization parameters is not adequate, then additional IDLM locks and resources are allocated dynamically. Memory for dynamically allocated LM_RESS and LM_LOCKS is taken from the shared pool in the SGA. Each time there is a dynamic allocation, one of the following messages will be written to the alert log:

DYNAMIC LOCKS ALLOCATED
DYNAMIC RESOURCES ALLOCATED

Dynamic allocation has an adverse impact on performance and also reduces the memory that is allocated to the shared pool in the SGA. So make sure you provide adequate initial values for these parameters. If you see these messages frequently in your alert log, you should increase your LM_RESS and LM_LOCKS parameter values. In Oracle8*i* (Version 8.1.6) these parameters values are automatically set by Oracle.

Oracle Performance Manager

A component of Oracle Enterprise Manager (OEM), referred to as the Oracle Performance Manager, allows you to monitor Oracle Parallel Server. Using this monitoring tool, you can graphically view several OPS statistics through charts and graphs. You can drill down from some charts to get further detailed statistics. This provides a convenient way to monitor key OPS performance statistics. Refer to the *Oracle Enterprise Manager Configuration Guide* for information on how to set up Oracle Performance Manager for your Oracle Parallel Server environment. Figure 10-3 shows the available charts for Oracle Parallel Server.

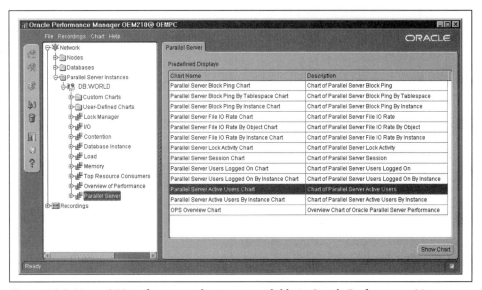

Figure 10-3. Many OPS performance charts are available in Oracle Performance Manager

The graphical views provided by this tool are based on data from dynamic performance views such as V$PING and V$LOCK_ACTIVITY. For example, Figure 10-4 shows the Parallel Server Block Ping by Tablespace Chart. This view shows statistics from the V$PING view and shows the number of blocks pinged for each tablespace by a given OPS database instance. From this graph, you can drill down to get object-level ping information. You can either use the drilldown menu or right-click a specific tablespace and select one of the drilldown options from the fly-out menu.

Figure 10-5 shows some sample output of the Parallel Server Lock Activity Chart. This chart is based on the V$LOCK_ACTIVITY dynamic performance view and shows the counts for various types of lock conversions.

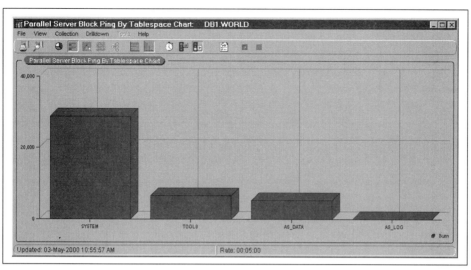

Figure 10-4. Parallel Server Block Ping By Tablespace Chart

Oracle Server Instance	From	To	Sum
X:NULL	X	NULL	94187.0
X:S	X	S	801751.0
X:SSX	X	SSX	10488.0
SSX:X	SSX	X	10488.0
S:NULL	S	NULL	703445.0
S:X	S	X	781179.0
NULL:S	NULL	S	697532.0
NULL:X	NULL	X	894696.0

Figure 10-5. Parallel Server Lock Activity Chart

Oracle Performance Manager gets its data from the same V$ and GV$ views that we've discussed in this chapter. It just places an easy-to-use GUI interface between you and those views. If you have a license for the Oracle Performance Manager software, you may find it more convenient to use the GUI than to query the V$ and GV$ views directly.

11

In this chapter:
- *When Is Partitioning Needed?*
- *Partitioning Techniques*
- *Changing Your Partitioning Scheme*

Partitioning for OPS

Partitioning is the process of designing database applications in such a way that OPS instances running on different nodes access mutually exclusive sets of data. This reduces contention for the same data blocks by multiple instances. The end result is that pinging is reduced, and the OPS system will run more efficiently.

Partitioning must be done when a database application or set of database applications is designed. You have to analyze the data access requirements of each application that you are designing and assign applications to OPS nodes so that contention for data from multiple nodes is minimized. This chapter describes three common approaches to partitioning in an OPS environment.

When Is Partitioning Needed?

In an OPS environment, several nodes access a shared database. If multiple database instances access the same set of data objects, these data objects end up in the buffer cache of each of those instances. The system will then need to synchronize the buffer caches in the different instances using Parallel Cache Management (PCM) locks. The use of these locks results in *pinging*, a process (introduced in Chapter 8, *Locking Mechanisms in OPS*) that has a high amount of overhead associated with it. The result is a decrease in overall database performance.

Chapter 8 described two types of pings: false pings and true pings. *False pings* result when multiple OPS instances are contending for the same PCM locks but not the same database blocks. You can reduce false pings by allocating additional PCM locks and by using an appropriate PCM lock allocation strategy.

True pings occur when multiple OPS instances contend for the same block in the database. This happens when one or more applications running on different nodes need read/write access to the same set of data blocks. Because true pings represent conflicts for a database block, allocating additional PCM locks won't help. The only way to reduce the occurrence of true pings is to partition your database and applications in a way that reduces the need for two instances to access the same database block.

Partitioning works well for certain types of database applications and is quite difficult for others. Application partitioning may not be possible for an OLTP database in which many users use one large application with read/write access to all the tables. Using multiple OPS instances in an environment like that will result in a large number of pings due to conflicts between the instances. This situation may degrade OPS performance to the point at which it's worse than that of a standalone database. An OPS database is not suitable for such an environment, and you should consider other options, such as an Oracle database on SMP hardware.

Partitioning makes a lot of sense for many types of departmental and DSS applications. It's easy to partition departmental applications in which the data overlap is minimal. An example might be two applications in which the sales department and the accounts department each has its own set of tables. Since these applications have few overlap tables, each set of tables can be placed in its own tablespace, and pings will not occur. Figure 11-1 illustrates such an arrangement.

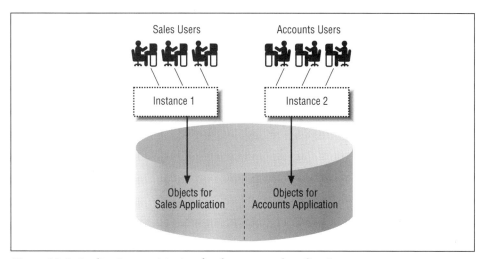

Figure 11-1. Application partitioning for departmental applications

Partitioning Techniques

You need to start planning for partitioning during the database analysis and design. In addition to dealing with the usual database analysis and design issues, you need to analyze every application and transaction with respect to the data that it accesses. Then you need to formulate an appropriate partitioning technique for each application.

There are three partitioning techniques that you can use in an OPS environment in order to reduce contention between instances:

Application partitioning
    Aligns applications and nodes in a manner that avoids inter-nodal conflicts.

Data partitioning
    Makes each node responsible for a different subset of the data within a table.

Transaction partitioning
    Makes each node responsible for a different set of tables. Transactions are then routed to the most appropriate node by a transaction monitor or by the applications themselves.

Application Partitioning

Application partitioning is the process of separating database applications in such a way that each OPS node accesses a disjoint set of tables. Figure 11-2 shows two applications that are neatly partitioned between two nodes. Instance 1 runs the sales application, which has its own set of tables. Instance 2 runs the accounts application, which uses a different set of tables.

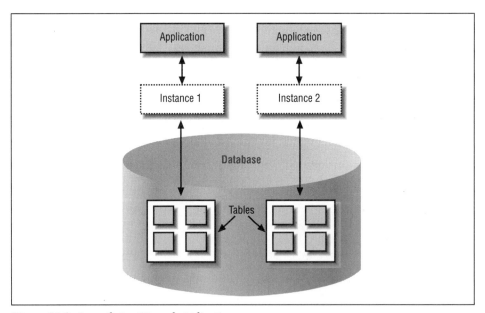

Figure 11-2. A neatly partitioned application

Tables used by multiple applications are referred to as *overlap tables*. There are no overlap tables in Figure 11-2. Each application is completely independent of the other. Because of this, the two instances will never contend for the same database block, and true pings will never occur.

Eliminating overlap tables from applications that are run from different OPS nodes is not sufficient to reduce or eliminate the occurrence of false pings. To reduce false pings, you must reduce the amount of PCM lock contention that occurs. A god way to do this is to place the tables and indexes used by each application in a separate tablespace and allocate separate PCM locks for the datafiles in each of those tablespaces. You want to ensure that the PCM locks protecting the data for one application are not also used to protect data used by another application. If one PCM lock covers data accessed from two different instances, you run the risk of false pings as a result of contention for that lock.

Even though OPS runs on a shared disk architecture, OPS performance is better when application partitioning makes the architecture function as if it's a shared nothing architecture. In the scenario illustrated in Figure 11-2, for example, the instance on each node functions independently of the other—as if each node had its own disk, as would be the case with a shared nothing architecture.

Application partitioning must be performed when you first design the database and the applications that access it. If you don't partition applications properly when you design them, your tuning of PCM lock allocation at later stages won't be enough to reduce true pings. Tuning cannot substitute for proper application partitioning.

The process of application partitioning can be broken down into the following steps:

1. Identify database applications.

2. Identify overlap application tables.

3. Identify operations on overlap tables.

4. Configure tablespaces and deploy applications to nodes.

As an example, let's consider three applications developed by the ABC Sales Company. One application is used by Product Sales clerks, another is used by Inventory clerks, and the third is used by Human Resource (HR) clerks. The Product Sales clerks of the ABC Sales Company use the Product Sales application to enter customer information into the database and to record sales transactions. Inventory clerks use the Inventory application to update the stock status and record the receipt of products from vendors. The HR clerks use the Human Resource application and are responsible for handling employee information, benefits, timesheets, and payroll. The company is planning to use a two-node OPS database to run these applications, and it's your job to set up the database and applications to run as efficiently as possible. With that in mind, you can work through each of the four steps in the application partitioning process.

Identify database applications

The first step is to identify all applications that will run on the OPS database. Identify the various types and numbers of users who will run each application. Table 11-1 shows this information for our example of the ABC Sales Company.

Table 11-1. Database Applications and Database Users

Application	Users	Number of Users
Product Sales	Sales clerks	400
Inventory	Inventory clerks	100
Human resource	HR clerks	50

Identify overlap application tables

After identifying the applications, your next step is to identify the tables that will be accessed by each of those applications. Table 11-2 shows each of the tables accessed by the Product Sales, Inventory, and Human Resource applications, along with the type of table access (R=read, W=write, RW=read/write) by each application. Since this is a hypothetical example, we've shown only a few tables from each application. Using this information, you next will identify the tables that are used by two or more applications.

Table 11-2. Database Tables Used by the Product Sales, Inventory, and Human Resource Applications

Tables	Product Sales	Inventory	Human Resource
CUSTOMERS	RW		
SALES	RW		
SALES_DETAIL	RW		
PRODUCTS	R	RW	
STOCK	RW	RW	
VENDORS		RW	
RECEIPT		RW	
EMPLOYEE			RW
BENEFITS			RW
APPRAISALS			RW

In our example, the PRODUCTS and STOCK tables are overlap tables. They are accessed by both the Product Sales application and the Inventory application. Figure 11-3 shows the overlap tables between Product Sales and Inventory applications.

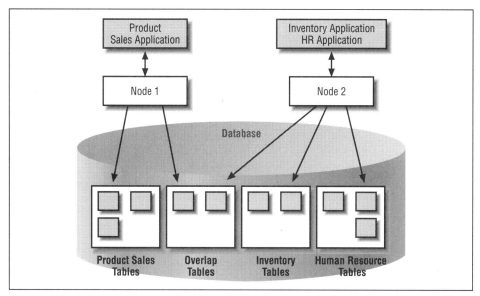

Figure 11-3. Overlap tables

Identify operations on overlap tables

Once you've identified the overlap tables, you can focus your attention on them. Tables that are used by only a single application do not cause true pings, unless you run that one application from multiple nodes. For the overlap tables, you need to perform a detailed analysis and determine both the type of data access and the volume of operations.

For each overlap table, identify the operation (INSERT, DELETE, UPDATE, or SELECT) performed by each application. In addition, estimate the daily volume of those operations. Let's assume that the ABC Sales Company maintains a stock of 200,000 distinct products. Let's further assume that in a one-hour period there are 20,000 inquiries by customers, each resulting in a SELECT operation on the PRODUCTS and STOCK tables. In addition, 10,000 items are sold to customers within the same time frame. The Product Sales application thus needs to update the stock status for 10,000 products per hour. Changing the stock status involves an update to the STOCK table. Once an item is created in the STOCK table, it is not deleted, so there will be no DELETEs. Finally, let's assume that the Inventory clerks make 5,000 selects and 2,000 updates per hour and that the STOCK table is not used at all by the Human Resource application. Given these assumptions, Table 11-3 summarizes the hourly operations against the STOCK table for the three applications.

Table 11-3. Database Operations on the STOCK Table

Operation	Product Sales	Inventory	Human Resource
INSERT	None	None	None
UPDATE	10,000	2,000	None
DELETE	None	None	None
SELECT	20,000	5,000	None

The PRODUCT table is also an overlap table, and you would need to look at database operations on that table in the same manner as we just did for the STOCK table.

Configure tablespaces and deploy applications to nodes

After you've analyzed your database applications with respect to the tables they access, the types of operations performed by the applications on those tables, and the rate at which those operations occur, you can design tablespaces based on those access characteristics. The following sections give some general guidelines to follow for the different table types that you might encounter.

Non-overlap tables. For each application, identify tables that are not shared by any other application. These are the non-overlap tables. Put the non-overlap tables for each application in their own tablespace. The non-overlap tables of large applications may require more than one tablespace. It's OK to use multiple tablespaces, but do not place non-overlap tables from two different applications in the same tablespace.

 If you allow the non-overlap tables from different applications to share a single tablespace, they would also share the PCM locks allocated to the datafile. This situation increases the chance of false pings occurring as the result of lock contention.

In our example, the CUSTOMERS, SALES, and SALES_DETAIL tables are the non-overlap tables used by the Product Sales application and should be placed in a tablespace or tablespaces separate from all other tables. For the Inventory application, the VENDOR and RECEIPTS tables are non-overlapping and should be placed in their own separate tablespace. All of the HR tables are non-overlapping, and they should be stored separately as well.

Read-only tables. Combine all tables that have only SELECT operations on them, and place them into a separate tablespace of their own. These are your read-only tables. For example, in many applications reference tables are read-only. Also, data warehouse and data mart applications consist of mostly read-only tables. Use multiple tablespaces if necessary, but keep read-only tables separate from any others. Read-only data can be accessed by many instances in shared mode, but does not cause pinging. You can declare tablespaces containing read-only tables as read-only and allocate a single PCM lock to cover the file(s) containing the read-only tablespaces.

Concurrent insert or update tables. Concurrent INSERT and UPDATE operations from multiple instances cause contention for the segment header of the tables involved. Specify a FREELIST GROUP parameter for these tables to reduce segment header contention. In addition, preallocate extents for these tables, specifically to each instance and in the datafiles reserved for each instance. These datafiles would require separate but few PCM locks. The key factor is ensuring that the instance that initially inserts data is the same instance that also accesses the data for later DML or query operations. Chapter 9, *Storage Management in OPS*, discusses the use of FREELIST GROUP and allocation of extents to specific instances.

Read/write tables. Overlap tables that will undergo query and DML operations by *many* OLTP applications will cause particularly difficult contention problems. You will need to analyze each of these tables very carefully with respect to the size of the table, the type of transactions, and the transaction volume from each application. In our example, the PRODUCTS and STOCK tables are overlap tables—they are accessed by both the Product Sales and Inventory applications. Analyze these types of tables in detail, and allocate PCM locks very carefully. We recommend that you do the following:

- For small tables, allocate a few rows per data block by assigning a high value for the PCTFREE parameter.
- For very large tables that are accessed randomly, allocate releasable locks.
- Consider using the data partitioning or transaction partitioning schemes discussed later in this chapter.

If the frequency of overlap operations is relatively small (up to 100 accesses per second), then pinging may occur, but it may not occur often enough to noticeably degrade performance. However, the threshold at which pinging becomes a problem is a factor of your specific OPS hardware and network characteristics.

If there is reader/writer conflict on overlap tables between OPS nodes, and you are using Oracle8*i*, you'll find that the cache fusion architecture of Oracle8*i* reduces the performance penalty associated with this type of conflict. For example, transaction processing applications running on one node may be performing write operations on the overlap tables at the same time that reporting applications running on some other node are reading the tables. Oracle8*i*'s cache fusion architecture results in consistent read blocks being shipped directly from the cache of the "writer" node to the cache of the "reader" node. This transfer is done over the interconnect between the two nodes. Shipping the required blocks over the interconect is much faster than a disk-based ping operation would be. Chapter 8, *Locking Mechanisms in OPS*, discusses the benefits of cache fusion in more detail.

If many concurrent users from multiple nodes access a small OLTP application (small in this case refers to a small set of tables) and the suggestions provided in these sections are not practical, then an OPS configuration is *not* suitable for the application.

 In an upcoming release of the Oracle database software, Oracle plans to enhance cache fusion to also handle writer/writer conflicts. Newer interconnects (such as Intel's VI architecture) provide low latency and high bandwidth (over 1 GB). Combine these faster interconnects with the planned writer/writer implementation of cache fusion, and you'll probably be able to implement new classes of database applications, even applications that can't be partitioned very well, in an OPS environment while still maintaining an acceptable level of performance.

In our hypothetical example, we have two OPS nodes. The Product Sales application has more users than the Inventory and Human Resource applications combined. Therefore, we'll assign the Product Sales application to node 1 and the Inventory and Human Resource applications to node 2. As we've seen during analysis, this is not a case of clean partitioning. Some overlap tables exist between the Product Sales and Inventory applications, so true pings can't be avoided. We also will use separate tablespaces for overlap and non-overlap tables. The PRODUCTS table is one of the overlap tables and contains product codes, product descriptions, and product characteristics. This table is read only by the Product Sales application. The Inventory application, on the other hand, updates this table randomly but not very frequently. A few hashed PCM locks may be allocated to protect this tablespace because the frequency of update and hence the frequency of writer/reader conflict is less.

The STOCK table is the other overlap table. Because the stock status of various products changes as materials are received from vendors and as they are sold to customers, the STOCK table is updated frequently by both the Inventory and Product Sales applications. You should place this high-activity table in a tablespace of its own and allocate a large number of fixed hashed PCM locks to this tablespace. This will reduce the granularity of hashed PCM locks and will reduce false pings. Releasable fine-grained locks also may be used to protect this table. Releasable fine-grained locks will eliminate false pings but will have a higher overhead compared to fixed hashed locks.

Data Partitioning

With *data /partitioning*, also referred to as *horizontal partitioning*, data objects—for example, tables—are partitioned, and each OPS node accesses a set of partitions distinct from those accessed by the other nodes. In order to implement this partitioning scheme, you must do the following:

- Partition application tables based on the value of a key column
- Route the application to an appropriate node based on the value of the key used to partition the tables

For example, you might partition the data of a table based on a REGION column. If valid regions for our Product Sales application are East and West, then transactions from East can be routed to node 1, and transactions from West can be routed to node 2. Even though the nodes are accessing the same table, they will be accessing different partitions of that table, eliminating any contention for the same database block. You can perform data partitioning using the Oracle8 partitioning features.

Oracle8 partitioned tables

If you specify a partitioning key at the time you create a table in Oracle8, you will be able to automatically partition a table so that data in the table is stored in multiple partitions. Each partition then can be stored in its own tablespace. This feature is commonly used in data warehouse applications to manage large tables. For example, the following CREATE TABLE statement creates the SALES table with two partitions using the region_code column as the partitioning key:

```
CREATE TABLE sales
     (
     sale_no              NUMBER(9) NOT NULL,
     region_code          NUMBER(1) NOT NULL,
     cust_id              NUMBER(6) NOT NULL,
     sales_rep_id         NUMBER(6) NOT NULL,
     sale_date            DATE      NOT NULL,
     CONSTRAINT pk_sales  PRIMARY KEY (sale_no)
)
     PARTITION BY RANGE (region_code)
     (
         PARTITION s_east VALUES LESS THAN (2) TABLESPACE s_east,
         PARTITION s_west VALUES LESS THAN (3) TABLESPACE s_west
     );
```

Figure 11-4 shows the resulting partitioned SALES table with East and West partitions based on region code.

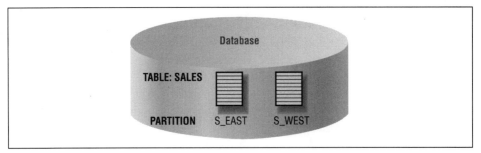

Figure 11-4. The sales table partitioned by region

Data-dependent routing

Routing a transaction to an appropriate node based on the value of the data in a table requires extra application logic. Using a three-tier architecture is very helpful in implementing data-dependent routing (i.e., routing based on the value of data). In a three-tier architecture, the middle layer is responsible for routing transactions to the appropriate backend server and can be configured to route database transactions to specific nodes based on the data value of a specific column. The front-end application need not know which OPS instance is being used for any given transaction. This approach makes the design of your frontend applications independent of database location logic. You might use a product like the Tuxedo TP monitor to implement this type of data-dependent routing, as shown in Figure 11-5.

Transaction Partitioning

With *transaction partitioning*, individual transactions are routed to the most appropriate node based on the tables accessed by the transaction. This is different from data partitioning. Data partitioning is based on the value of a specific partition key, whereas transaction partitioning is based on the tables involved in a transaction. For example, an order entry transaction may be routed to a node that is primarily responsible for the subset of data required by order entry transactions. Stock status transactions may be routed to a different node, which is responsible for the subset of data required by those transactions. When application partitioning or data partitioning is not possible, you might choose to use transaction partitioning. Transaction partitioning is more complex. This type of partitioning, with its precise routing of transactions to appropriate nodes, is possible only in a three-tier architecture.

Transaction partitioning provides some advantages over other partitioning methods. If the data access characteristics of an application change, then individual transactions can be routed to the appropriate OPS node by changing the configuration in the middle layer. If new OPS nodes are added, then also changing the configuration in the middle layer can reroute transactions to the most appropriate node.

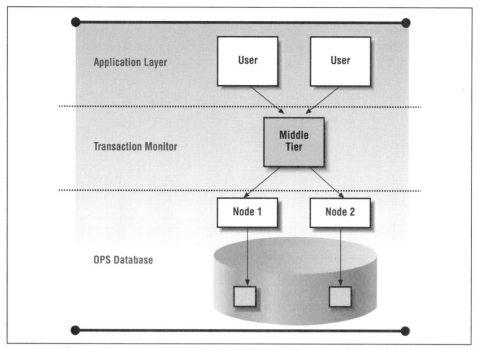

Figure 11-5. Data-dependent routing in a three-tier architecture

One way to do transaction partitioning is to route transactions to different OPS nodes during different hours of operation. For example, in a two-node OPS setup, let's assume that transactions T1 and T2 access the common data set D1. Let's also assume that transactions T3 and T4 access data sets D3 and D4, respectively. During the day, when the frequency of transactions T1 and T2 is high, these transactions are routed to one specific node in order to minimize contention. Transactions T3 and T4 are processed through a completely different node. At night, when the volume of T1 and T2 transactions is significantly less, and the volume of T3 and T4 transactions is quite high, T3 and T4 can be routed to different nodes. Running high-frequency transactions T3 and T4 through different nodes during the night achieves load balancing but does not cause any conflicts because these transactions access different data sets. If required, transactions T1 and T2 may be processed through different nodes at night without any problem because of the low frequency of these transactions at that time. This time-based partitioning helps to balance the overall load and also minimize concurrent access to the same data objects from different nodes.

Changing Your Partitioning Scheme

You may need to review the partitioning scheme you've selected if you add a new OPS instance to your environment or if you add new database functionality.

When you add a new instance to your OPS environment, you need to look at how that instance operates on existing database tables. If the new instance performs queries on data that is in read-only tables or if it runs an application that has its own set of tables, it won't impact your existing partitioning design. However, you will need to revisit your partitioning strategy if the new instance does either of the following:

- Runs an application that is already used by another instance
- Updates data that is read-only by all other instances

You also will need to reevaluate your partitioning scheme if new application functionality is added to an application and that new functionality changes the read/write access patterns of that application. If the new functions access only read-only tables or new tables, then you won't need to change your partitioning scheme. However, if the new application functionality causes an OPS instance to access tables that are used in a read/write mode by another instance, then you will have to start over with your application analysis. Once again, you will need to determine the overlap tables and decide upon the appropriate partitioning strategy for them.

12

Application Failover

For many applications, the cost of having a database be unavailable is enormous. For applications used in the banking and brokerage industry, for example, the cost of database downtime can exceed a million dollars per hour. Consequently, backup databases often are used to provide protection against the failure of a primary database.

When a primary database instance fails, applications connected to the instance will receive an error indicating a lost connection. Not only do those user connections to the database get lost, but their uncommitted transactions also get lost. Users then are forced to reestablish a connection to the backup database and resubmit their transactions. This creates a lot of work disruption. The process of automatically switching an application from the primary database to a backup database is referred to as *application failover*. The objective of application failover is to minimize work disruptions as much as possible by transparently reconnecting to the backup database.

Often, an Oracle Parallel Server database is used to support application failover. In an OPS environment, when one or more Oracle instances fails, applications still can access the shared database through one of the surviving instances. Other approaches to failover include the use of standby databases and replicated databases. Although the focus in this chapter is on application failover in an OPS environment, we'll talk briefly about these other approaches as well.

In this chapter, we'll discuss the factors you need to consider when an OPS database is used to support failover and explain the difficulty of the failover process. We'll also discuss the various aspects of application design and Oracle network configuration you'll need to know about in order to implement application failover. Many of the techniques we'll describe here for OPS environments are equally applicable when you're using a standby database or a replicated database for application failover.

The discussion in this chapter assumes some knowledge on your part of Net8, Oracle's networking product. You also should be familiar with the *tnsnames.ora* file and with the Oracle Names product.

Maintaining a Failover Database

As we mentioned, application failover is the ability of client applications to automatically, without user intervention, connect to a backup database when the primary database fails. When the backup database is not maintained, any failure of the primary instance results in downtime because users have to wait until the primary database becomes available again. By maintaining a backup database, also referred to as a *failover database*, and implementing application failover, you can decrease or eliminate downtime from database failures.

There are three commonly used methods for maintaining a failover database:

- Using OPS to ensure that you have a backup instance available
- Using Oracle's replication features to maintain a replicated database
- Using Oracle's standby database features to maintain a standby database

In addition to the three methods discussed here, many sites have implemented proprietary ways to maintain a backup database. For the Windows NT environment, Oracle also offers a product called Fail-Safe, which is used to implement failover.

In an OPS environment, there is only one shared database. Consequently, failover occurs to a backup *instance*, not to a backup database. When replicated or standby databases are used, failover occurs to a backup *database*. In this chapter, we use the term *backup database* when we are talking about failover in general and not in reference to a specific method.

Using an OPS Database for Failover

In an OPS environment, multiple nodes access a shared database. When one database instance fails because of hardware or software failure, the client applications connected to the failed instance can reconnect to another OPS instance. This allows users to continue working. Figure 12-1 shows a two-node OPS database where a client begins by using the Oracle instance on node 1 to access the database. When node 1 fails, the client application fails over to the Oracle instance running on node 2. The mechanism for achieving this automatic application failover is discussed later in this chapter.

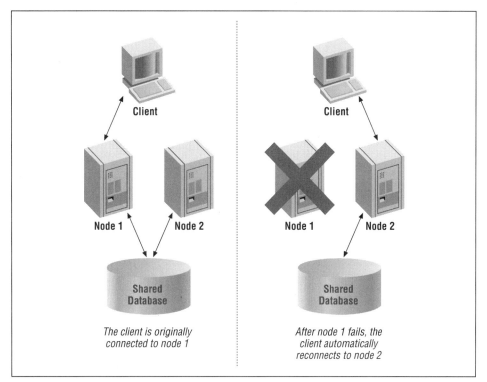

Client

Node 1   Node 2

Shared
Database

The client is originally
connected to node 1

Client

Node 1   Node 2

Shared
Database

After node 1 fails, the
client automatically
reconnects to node 2

Figure 12-1. Application failover

Advantages of OPS-based failover

The OPS-based approach to failover has some distinct advantages over the replication-based approach and the standby database-based approach:

- In an OPS configuration, all of the instances concurrently access the database. Under normal circumstances, these instances also are being used for processing other transactions. The result is an efficient use of hardware resources, because you don't need to have a dedicated (and unused) backup system that kicks in only when a failure occurs.

- When OPS is used to support failover, the failure of a node impacts only the subset of users who are connected to that node. Users connected to the remaining nodes are not affected and continue to access the database without interruption.

- A final advantage of OPS is the immediacy with which clients can switch to a backup instance. When one node fails, clients can *immediately* connect to another node, because a database instance is already up and running on that node. In contrast, using a standby database for failover requires that the standby database be recovered and opened before it can be used. (There are some factors that can add to the failover time in an OPS environment, and we'll discuss those issues later in this chapter.)

Disadvantages of OPS-based failover

Everything in life seems to be a tradeoff. While using of OPS to support failover has some distinct advantages, there are also disadvantages to consider:

- With OPS, the shared disk used to store the database files represents a single point of failure. This is because all OPS instances access the database. When a disk failure occurs, the hardware failure has to be rectified first. Then the database has to be restored and recovered. The OPS database is unavailable until the recovery is complete. This situation is illustrated in Figure 12-2. To guard against hardware failures like this, you can mirror your data on multiple disks.

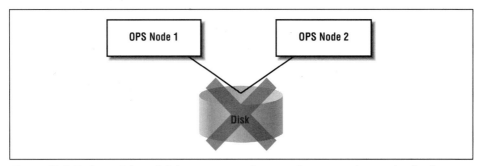

Figure 12-2. Failure of shared disk prevents any instance from operating on the database

- OPS systems require either cluster or MPP architectures. In both types of architectures, nodes must be located in close proximity to each other due to the performance requirements of the interconnect. In essence, all nodes must be in the same physical location. This means that an OPS system cannot provide protection from a site failure. If your building burns down, all your OPS nodes will go with it. For disaster recovery, you may consider other failover configurations, such as a standby database or a replicated database. Also, these configurations can be used in combination with OPS.

Using a Replicated Database for Failover

Oracle's advanced replication features can be used to maintain a failover database. With multi-master replication, changes made to one database are replicated to the other database. In contrast to the standby database setup described in the next section, a replicated database is always available for transactions. Replication can be done either synchronously or asynchronously. Figure 12-3 illustrates failover to a replicated database.

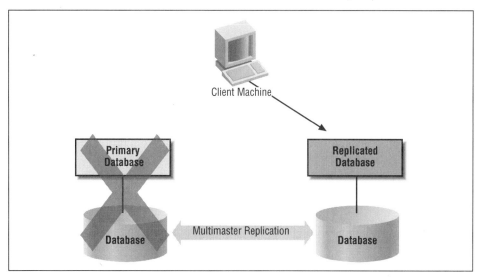

Figure 12-3. Failover to a replicated database

Advantages of replicated database-based failover

The use of a replicated database to support failover has two significant advantages:

- A replicated database can provide protection when there is a disaster at the primary site. Protection from a disaster comes from the fact that a replicated database does not need to be physically close to the master database. By placing your replicated database in a separate geographic location, you ensure that you will still have a database even in the event of a fire or other such disaster at the primary site.

- A replicated database can eliminate the shared disk system as a single point of failure. In contrast to an OPS configuration in which many instances share one database, when multi-master replication is used, each replicated instance has its own database. As each replicated database resides on its own disk system, the loss of one disk system will not bring down all your databases. With OPS, if the disk fails, none of the instances can run.

Disadvantages of replicated database-based failover

Along with the good comes the bad. Replication also has several disadvantages when it comes to supporting failover:

- Multi-master replication does not support the replication of tables with LONG RAW columns. Use of the LONG RAW datatype is diminishing in favor of Oracle's newer large object types, but if you are currently using LONG RAWs, having to write your own routines to replicate them could present a formidable challenge.

- Oracle's replication mechanism may not be able to handle very high transaction volumes; for example, those on the order of a hundred or more transactions per second. The actual scalability limit of replication depends on the hardware platform, network characteristics, and so on.

- Updates to the main database may conflict with data in the replicated database. You have to write conflict-resolution routines to resolve those conflicts, and developing these routines can be challenging and time consuming.

Using a Standby Database for Failover

A standby database is another approach to maintaining a copy of a primary database that can be used as a backup in case the primary database fails. Initially, you create the standby database as a copy of the primary database. You then continually apply archived redo log files from the primary database to the standby database. In essence, the standby database is in continual recovery mode. This mechanism allows the standby database to remain synchronized with the primary database. In the event of a primary database failure, you apply the last of the redo logs to the standby database and then open it for use. Figure 12-4 illustrates this scenario.

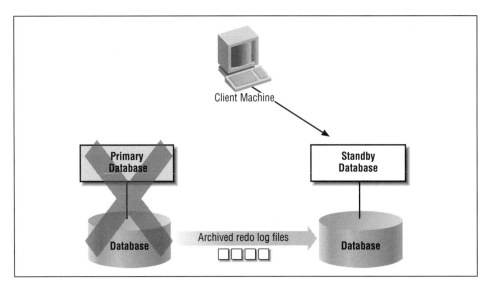

Figure 12-4. Failover to a standby database

Advantages of standby database-based failover

There is one main advantage to using standby databases for failover. The standby database can be maintained in a physical location separate from the primary database. Consequently, a standby database, like a replicated database, can provide protection from site-wide disasters. Standby databases do not suffer from the same scalability limitations as replicated databases, so they can be effectively maintained for a database with a very high transaction volume.

Disadvantages of standby database-based failover

There are also a few drawbacks to using standby databases for failover:

- In contrast to OPS instances, a standby database is not immediately available when the primary database fails. Before applications can failover to a standby database, all of the achived redo logs have to have been applied, and then the database needs to be opened.

- Use of a standby database for failover requires that you have two systems, each with its own disk storage. You also have the administrative overhead of maintaining two separate databases. And, in contrast to an OPS configuration, the additional system resources cannot be utilized during normal operations. The one exception is that in Oracle8*i*, it is possible to temporarily open a standby database in read-only mode.

Planning for Failover with OPS

When a failover occurs in an OPS environment, the workload of the node that failed is redirected to one or more designated backup OPS nodes. When you're planning for failover in such an environment, you have to consider the impact of failover on the performance of the designated backup nodes and also on application partitioning. A new Oracle8*i* OPS feature we describe in this section can be used to designate one of the nodes as a primary instance and the other as a secondary instance where OPS is exclusively used for failover purpose.

Capacity and Workload Issues

After a failover, the applications that were running on the failed instance will be running on one or more of the surviving instances. OPS instances must be able to accommodate this additional workload. You need to design your OPS environment so that any instances that you plan to use for failover purposes have enough extra memory and CPU resources to handle the additional workload that results when a failover occurs. Otherwise, a failover might result in a performance bottleneck. Another approach to this issue is to design your applications so that the workload on nodes designated as failover nodes is reduced when a failover occurs. You could, for example, stop nonessential reports from running in order to free up resources for mission-critical transaction systems.

Redistributing applications in an OPS environment during a failover has implications for application partitioning. After the workload has been redistributed, the data access patterns of the nodes will be different. If you don't properly plan for this situation, the surviving nodes may experience increased pinging as a result of contention for the same database objects. This will have an adverse impact on performance. This issue is not a factor in a two-node OPS setup, because in that setup, when one node fails, only one node remains to access the database. However, in an OPS environment with several nodes, your failover planning should take into consideration the application partitioning issues discussed in Chapter 11, *Partitioning for OPS*.

Exclusive Failover Instance in OPS

In a two-node OPS environment, you can use a new feature of Oracle8*i* to configure one OPS node as the primary instance and the other as the secondary instance. You activate this feature by adding the following initialization parameter to the parameter files for both of the instances:

```
ACTIVE_INSTANCE_COUNT = 1
```

The instance that first mounts the database becomes the primary instance, and it (and only it) registers with the Net8 listeners. During normal operation, only the primary instance will accept connection requests from clients. The instance that starts last becomes the secondary instance and does not register with the Net8 listeners. For this reason, no client connections can be directed to the secondary instance. The Integrated Distributed Lock Manager (IDLM) monitors both instances. If the IDLM detects the failure of the primary instance, it notifies the secondary instance to take over. The secondary instance then registers itself with the Net8 listeners and accepts client connections. With this setup, contention between nodes is never a problem, because at any one time only one node is accessing the shared database. Application partitioning is not required.

Failover Performance Under OPS

With application failover, server-side database recovery and reconnections to the backup instance are transparent to end users. However, these activities have a performance impact on the surviving OPS instances, and they may cause client applications to stop or be delayed during failover. Failover performance is affected by the following:

- The time required to detect that an instance failure has occurred
- The time required to reconfigure the IDLM and to remaster PCM locks
- The time required for instance recovery to take place
- The time required for clients to reconnect to one of the surviving instances

It's the cluster manager's job to detect node failure, and the SMON process of a surviving instance detects instance failure. The cluster manager detects node failure by monitoring a periodic heartbeat signal generated by each of the nodes. When a node fails, the heartbeat from that node is lost. The cluster manager will eventually detect this loss of heartbeat communication and recognize that a node failure has occurred. The time required for the detection of a failed node depends on the threshold value set for the heartbeat communication. It's usually on the order of a few seconds.

After a node failure has been detected, the IDLM needs to reconfigure itself to run on the surviving instances. IDLM redistributes lock information among the surviving nodes. This process is referred to as *lock remastering*. The time required for lock remastering depends on the number of PCM locks allocated to various datafiles. This is one of the tradeoffs involved in PCM lock allocation. On the one hand, a higher number of locks provides better protecton against false pings, but on the other hand, a high number of locks delays recovery from a node failure.

Instance recovery is another task that must take place after a node failure. One of the surviving instances will automatically start instance recovery for the failed instance, so that no data from committed transactions is lost. Instance recovery involves rolling forward through the redo logs and applying all the changes made by the failed instance. The time required for this phase depends on the amount of redo that needs to be applied. You can minimize the amount of redo, and consequently the time needed for recovery, by having checkpoints occur frequently.

Not only does instance recovery involve the application of committed changes, it also involves the rollback of all uncommitted transactions that were in process on the failed instance. The time required for rollback depends on both the number of uncommitted transactions and the amount of data that these transactions modified. A new Oracle8 feature called *deferred transaction recovery* reduces the impact of this rollback activity by allowing new transactions to take place during the rollback phase of instance recovery, as long as those new transactions do not need to access rows involved in the uncommitted transactions being rolled back. If this happens (i.e., a new transaction needs to access rows involved in the uncommitted transactions), then only new transactions have to wait for the rollback of the failed transaction. A further improvement in Oracle8*i*, referred to as *fast-start rollback*, allows a new transaction to roll back only the rows it needs (rather than roll back the full transaction) when those rows are involved in the uncommitted transaction. This Oracle8*i* feature reduces recovery time when a long-running transaction is involved with the new transaction.

Another factor that impacts failover performance is the number of database connections to the failed instance. If the number of failed connections is large, then you might experience a performance impact as a result of all those connections reconnecting to the surviving instance(s) at the same time. With dedicated server connections, it is necessary to spawn a shadow process for each connection request. This has a significant performance impact. In an MTS configuration, the impact is much less because dispatcher processes are used to connect new clients to preexisting shared server processes

In later sections, we'll explain that it's possible to preconnect to a backup instance before failure of the primary instance. In this case, failover is quicker because connections to the backup instance already have been established. However, preconnecting takes up computing resources in the backup node during normal operations. Response time after a failover, however, still depends upon the capacity of the backup node to process the redirected workload of the failed instance.

 Application failover should occur transparently, and it is best if users don't notice that a failover has occurred. However, because of all the factors that can affect the time needed for a failover to occur, the time required might be long enough to confuse your users. Rather than have them think that the application has gone down entirely, it may be better to provide some feedback. Letting users know what is happening reduces both their uncertainty and their frustration. Feedback is not automatic, however; you need to program it into your applications.

Failover Complexity

The complexity of the failover process depends on the status of the client applications when the primary database fails. Failover of database applications can be divided into two broad categories, based on the status of the database connection at the time of failure:

Connect-time failover

> This type of failover occurs when an application fails to connect to the primary database and subsequently attempts to connect to a secondary database.

Runtime failover

> This type of failover occurs when a client application has already connected to the primary database, and the database then fails. Clients may or may not have an active transaction at the time of the failure.

The following sections describe conceptually the actions that are needed in the backup database in order to re-create the *same state* for the clients as they had in the primary database at the time the failure occurred.

Failover does not take care of failure at all levels. If a client application terminates for any reason or if the client system crashes, database failover mechanisms do not help. Failover mechanisms are designed only to handle database failures. In the case of client failure, the client application must be restarted by some other means.

Connect-Time Failover

Connect-time failover occurs when the primary database fails either before or during the connection attempt. The only thing then required for a successful failover is for the client application to connect to the backup database instead of the primary database. The only information required for such a failover is the user's username and password. There is no need to preserve any transaction state, because the failure precedes any database connection—no transactions will be in progress. Connect-time failover is relatively simple to implement, and clients will not notice that a failover has occurred.

Runtime Failover

In the case of a runtime failover, the client application has already connected to the database server. The complexities of such a failover depend on whether there is an active transaction at the time the failover occurs.

Failover without an active transaction

The simplest runtime failover scenario is the case in which the client application has connected to the primary database but does not have an active transaction in progress. In this case, the application will have already established a user session. Some of the session parameters—for example, NLS_LANGUAGE and NLS_DATE_FORMAT—may have been set explicitly by the application using ALTER SESSION commands such as the following:

```
ALTER SESSION
    SET NLS_DATE_FORMAT = 'YYYY-MON-DD';
```

As the application has no open transaction, it will not notice the failure of the primary database until the next transaction begins. In this case, a successful failover requires that two things happen: the application must connect to the backup database, and it must reestablish the same session environment that it had on the primary database. To do this, the application must resubmit the specific statements that were used to establish that environment.

Failover with an active transaction

The more complicated runtime failover scenario is the case in which the client application has a transaction in progress when the failover occurs. In this case, when reconnecting to the backup database, the client will need to worry about the following items:

- The session environment established using ALTER SESSION commands

- Any SQL cursors that were open at the time of failure

- PL/SQL package states, which include settings for global variables

- Any DML statements that may have been issued before the failure occurred

In order for a successful failover to occur when a client has an open transaction, the following steps must be taken:

1. The client application must connect to the alternate database.

2. The client application then must set up the same session environment that was in place on the primary database.

3. The client application must re-create any package states that were in effect at the time of the failure.

4. The client application must restart processing from the point at which the failure occurred.

The most difficult item in this list is the restarting of the application that was in progress so that processing continues from the point at which the failure occurred. Failover complexity depends on the type of database transactions within the client application. Transactions involving only SELECT statements are simpler to deal with than those involving INSERT, UPDATE, and DELETE operations. If the application was executing DML statements, some of those may have been committed. For example, a stored procedure may execute two UPDATE statements, and one of those may have already been committed when the failure occurred. When the primary database fails, committed transactions remain in place, but any uncommitted transactions are rolled back. You may need to code restart logic into your applications so that they will know where to pick up working after a failover occurs.

Failover Methods

Three methods are commonly used to implement application failover:

- Connection-time failover using Net8

- Transparent Application Failover (TAF) using Net8 and OCI8

- Failover using a three-tier architecture

The failover methods discussed here are equally applicable to OPS environments, environments that use standby databases, and environments that use replicated databases as a basis for failover.

Connect-Time Failover with Net8

Connect-time failover refers to application failover when it occurs during new connection attempts to a database. Using Net8, you can configure a service so that if a connection to the primary database is not successful, the connection is automatically routed to an alternate database. Net8 configuration in support of connect-time failover involves making appropriate entries in each client's *tnsnames.ora* file or in your Oracle Names server. Because clients go through Net8 to connect to a database, connect-time failover can be completely transparent to your applications.

tnsnames.ora configuration

On client machines, Net8 uses a configuration file named *tnsnames.ora* to translate a database service name into a specific hostname, port number, and instance name. When you connect to a service, Net8 reads this file to find out where that service resides. For any given service, you can define alternate database instances in order to implement connect-time failover. When you do this, any new connections to a service are first attempted using the first database instance in the list. If that attempt fails, Net8 automatically tries again using the second connection in the list. This process continues until a connection is made or until Net8 runs out of instances to try.

The following example shows a database service name definition from a *tnsnames.ora* file. The service name HADB contains three DESCRIPTION entries in its definition. One points to the database instance named HADB1 on NODE1. The other two point to the instance HADB2 on NODE2 and to the instance HADB3 on NODE3. When a client connects to the HADB service, Net8 will attempt to connect to the three instances in the order in which they are listed. HADB1 will be tried first. If that connection cannot be made for any reason, Net8 will try HADB2. If the connection attempt to HADB2 also fails, Net8 will move on to HADB3:

```
HADB =
  (DESCRIPTION_LIST =
    (DESCRIPTION =
      (ADDRESS=
        (PROTOCOL=TCP)(HOST=NODE1)(PORT = 1521)
      )
      (CONNECT_DATA = (SID = HADB1))
    )
    (DESCRIPTION =
      (ADDRESS=
        (PROTOCOL=TCP)(HOST=NODE2)(PORT = 1521)
```

```
        )
        (CONNECT_DATA = (SID = HADB2))
      )
  (DESCRIPTION =
      (ADDRESS=
        (PROTOCOL=TCP)(HOST=NODE3)(PORT = 1521)
      )
      (CONNECT_DATA = (SID = HADB3))
    )


  )
```

Connect-time failover happens transparently without requiring any changes to the client application. Note that *tnsnames.ora* allows the failover configuration to be different for each client machine. Thus, it is possible to configure a different order for failover instances for different client machines. For example, in the *tnsnames.ora* file of some client machines, the order of failover configuration for service name HADB can be set as HADB1, HADB2, and HADB3. On some other client machines, the order could be set as HADB1, HADB3, and HADB2. This permits the failover load to be balanced between HADB2 and HADB3 when HADB1 fails.

Net8 release 8.1.5 uses the service name rather than the SID to identify a database. When using the service name, it is not necessary to specify connect data for every SID. Using service names, our sample *tnsnames.ora* configuration looks like this:

```
HADB =
  (DESCRIPTION =
    (ADDRESS=
      (PROTOCOL=TCP)(HOST=NODE1)(PORT = 1521)
    )
    (ADDRESS=
      (PROTOCOL=TCP)(HOST=NODE2)(PORT = 1521)
    )
    (ADDRESS=
      (PROTOCOL=TCP)(HOST=NODE3)(PORT = 1521)
    )
    (CONNECT_DATA= (SERVICE_NAME= HADB))
  )
```

Refer to Oracle Corporation's *Net8 Administrators Guide, Release 8.1* for detailed information on *tnsnames.ora* configuration, and for information about Net8 features that facilitate load balancing in an OPS environment.

Name server configuration

Sometimes, Oracle Names is used to resolve database service names. This is very helpful when you have a large number of clients that connect to a database. Oracle Names allows you to centralize the management of service name definitions, so that whenever there is a change to be made, you can do it in one central location instead of having to go out and edit each *tnsnames.ora* file on each individual client machine. For purposes of failover, alternate databases instances are registered in Oracle Names in a manner similar to that used for *tnsnames.ora*.

Transparent Application Failover with Net8 and OCI8

Transparent Application Failover (TAF) is a new feature in Oracle8. It provides connect-time failover as well as runtime failover. However, some restrictions apply when TAF is used for runtime failover. The use of TAF is possible for applications developed using either Net8 or the Oracle Call Interface 8 (OCI8). To support TAF, Net8 requires additional configuration information in your *tnsnames.ora* file. An additional requirement is that your applications must use the failover-related API calls in OCI8.

Currently, Oracle has implemented TAF in SQL*Plus using the new failover features of OCI8. Client sessions using SQL*Plus can automatically failover to a backup instance when the connection to the primary instance is lost. In the future, Oracle will build TAF capabilities into other tools and products such as Developer 2000, the Pro*C precompiler, and the JDBC-Thick driver, which uses OCI8.

Net8 provides two TAF parameters that you specify in the *tnsnames.ora* file. These parameters, TYPE and METHOD, control the failover operation and are described in the following two sections.

The TYPE parameter

The TYPE parameter is used in a *tnsnames.ora* connect string to specify the type of failover functionality that you want for the connection. There are three possible selections:

NONE
   No failover is to be attempted. This is the default setting.

SESSION
   A connection to a backup database is automatically established in the event that the primary database goes down. However, TAF does not apply any of the ALTER SESSION commands to re-create the session environment.

SELECT
   A connection to a backup database is automatically established in the event that the primary database goes down. SELECT statements that were in progress in the primary database are then automatically reexecuted in the backup database.

The METHOD parameter

The METHOD parameter is used in a *tnsnames.ora* connect string to determine when the connection to the backup database occurs. It has two possible values:

BASIC
    Connects to the backup database only when the connection to the primary database fails. This is the default value.

PRECONNECT
    Connects to the backup database at the same time that the connection to the primary database is made.

Using the PRECONNECT setting saves time when a failure occurs, because you will already be connected to the backup database. The tradeoff, however, is the overhead caused by the normally unused connections to the backup database.

TAF limitations

TAF has several restrictions. When a runtime failover occurs using TAF, the effects of any ALTER SESSION statements that were executed in the primary database are lost. They are not carried over to the backup database. The state of any PL/SQL package variables is also lost. TAF is helpful with query-only transactions when the value of the TYPE parameter is set to SELECT. In that case, the OCI8 library keeps track of the number of rows fetched by the SELECT statements being executed in an instance. When a failover occurs, OCI8 automatically reexecutes the queries in the backup database. The rows that were already fetched before are ignored, and the remaining rows are visible to the user. However, because the query has to be processed twice, the query response time will be slower than normal.

DML transactions represent the most difficult case to handle in a failover situation. Currently, failover-aware products such as SQL*Plus cannot failover transactions composed of DML statements such as INSERT, UPDATE, and DELETE. Remember that when a primary instance fails, one of the surviving instances will recover any lost transactions. All committed changes are reapplied, and all uncommitted changes are rolled back. To take care of any DML transactions interrupted by a failover, your application will need to have failover-specific code. This failover code will have to re-create the session environment and resubmit the failed transaction to the backup instance. Also, if the application is a batch application, the failover code needs to be sophisticated enough to skip over transactions that were already committed prior to the failover, allowing the application to resume processing from the point at which the failure occurred.

A TAF example

The following excerpt from a *tnsnames.ora* file shows an example of two net service names configured for TAF. The two services back each other up. HADB2

serves as the backup for HADB1 and vice versa. In this configuration, runtime
failover is indicated by the FAILOVER_MODE parameter:

```
HADB1 =
  (DESCRIPTION =
    (ADDRESS = (PROTOCOL = TCP)(HOST = NODE1)(PORT = 1521))
    (CONNECT_DATA =
      (SID = HADB1)
      (FAILOVER_MODE = (TYPE = SESSION)(METHOD = BASIC)
                       (BACKUP = HADB2))
    )
  )

HADB2 =
  (DESCRIPTION =
    (ADDRESS= (PROTOCOL = TCP)(HOST = NODE2)(PORT = 1521))
    (CONNECT_DATA =
      (SID = HADB2)
      (FAILOVER_MODE = (TYPE = SESSION)(METHOD = BASIC)
                       (BACKUP = HADB1))
    )
  )
```

Using SQL*Plus, you can easily test the TAF configuration illustrated in the sample
tnsnames.ora file. You can test failover by shutting down the primary database.
You also can use the ALTER SYSTEM DISCONNECT SESSION command to trigger
a failover even though the primary instance is alive. Note that failover does not
occur when the user process (the Oracle shadow process) is killed when the primary instance is alive. In other words, using a "kill –9" command to kill a SQL*Plus
session won't result in failover. For a user session, you can verify the TAF failover
configuration and check to see if the session has failed over, using the following
query against the V$SESSION view:

```
SELECT sid, username, failover_type,
              failover_method, failed_over
FROM V$SESSION
WHERE sid = sid;
```

The example in this chapter uses a simple *tnsnames.ora* configuration to explain
how the TAF mechanism works. TAF also may be used in conjunction with other
Net8 options such as the Oracle Names Server. For information on how to configure TAF in different Net8 environments, refer to Oracle Corporation's *Oracle8i
Net8 Administrator's Guide.*

Failover in a Three-Tier Architecture

Three-tier architectures often are used in OLTP environments with high transaction volumes. As the name suggests, there are three distinct logical layers that participate in the processing of a transaction:

- The frontend is responsible for presentation and interaction with the user.

- Often, the middle tier contains Transaction Processing (TP) monitors that are responsible for transaction routing. Application servers are also often on the middle tier and implement the business logic to process client requests.

- The backend database servers provide access to the data from the application servers.

You may have several different types of application servers in a three-tier environment, with each application server providing a specific type of service. TP monitors then distribute the workload among application servers. In an OPS environment, TP monitors can reduce synchronization overhead by helping to achieve application partitioning. TP monitors can route transactions to the appropriate application server and database server combination based on the data access requirements of those transactions.

Application servers register their service with the TP monitor when they are up and have successfully connected to the backend database. In the event that any service is unavailable because a database instance has failed (or for any other reason), the service is deregistered from the TP monitor. Thus, when the TP monitor routes a new client transaction, it routes to an application server that is available and is still connected to a database instance. This mechanism achieves connect-time failover indirectly.

Application servers can trap database errors to detect instance failures that occur once they begin working on a specific transaction assigned by the TP monitor. Instance failures that occur before a transaction starts usually are indicated by one of the following errors:

```
ORA-1033: ORACLE initialization or shutdown in progress
ORA-1034: ORACLE not available
ORA-1089: immediate shutdown in progress—no operations are permitted
```

If the database connection is lost during a transaction, then the application server will typically get one of the following errors:

```
ORA-3113: end-of-file on communication channel
ORA-3114: not connected to ORACLE
ORA-1092: ORACLE instance terminated—disconnection forced
```

Application servers can be programmed to check for these errors and to reconnect to a predetermined backup database when these errors occur. Application servers then can resubmit any failed transaction. The actual mechanisms used to implement application failover vary between different implementations of three-tier architecture. The specific mechanisms used depend on the capability and features of the TP monitor and of the application server. Figure 12-5 illustrates a failover situation in a three-tier architecture. One instance has failed, and the application servers have connected to the backup instance.

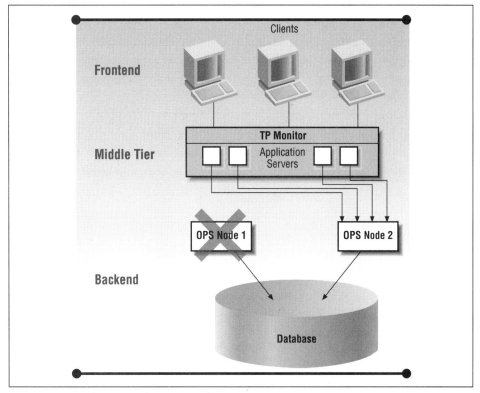

Figure 12-5. Failover in a three-tier architecture

The physical location of the different layers in a three-tier architecture may vary greatly. Sometimes, the middle tier and the database servers are all located on the same physical system. In other implementations, the TP monitors and application servers may be located on physically separate systems, in effect creating a four-tier environment. Often, the middle layer is deployed on more than one system in order to eliminate the TP monitor and application servers as a single point of failure. BEA's Tuxedo three-tier architecture is one of the widely used TP monitor architectures.

Failback

Failback refers to the process by which client applications that have failed over to a backup node are reconnected to the primary node after the database instance on that node has been successfully restarted. Failback involves disconnecting the client application from the backup instance at an appropriate time, so that ongoing transactions are not interrupted. The client application then is reconnected to the original instance.

In a two-tier architecture, failback is achieved when the application exits and restarts. When the application restarts, it is by default connected to the primary instance. In a three-tier architecture, the middle layer handles failback. Instead of restarting the middle-tier applications, which would disrupt a large number of users, a signal may be sent that causes the middle-tier applications to attempt a reconnect to the original database instance.

In this chapter:
• *How Parallel
  Execution Works
  with OPS*
• *Disk Affinity*
• *Instance Groups for
  Parallel Execution*

13

*Parallel Execution
in OPS*

Parallel execution (discussed in Chapter 3, *Parallel Execution Concepts*) works in both OPS and non-OPS environments. In OPS environments, you can exploit the processing power of all of the available nodes to parallelize SQL operations.

How Parallel Execution Works with OPS

In a parallel execution environment, Oracle breaks down a SQL statement into several smaller tasks and assigns these tasks to multiple parallel slave processes. The slave processes then execute their tasks concurrently. Oracle Parallel Server extends this feature by executing parallel slave processes on multiple nodes of the parallel server.

Let's look at an example of a four-node parallel server database, when a user issues the following query:

```
SELECT /*+ PARALLEL (orders, 2, 2) */
COUNT(*)
FROM orders;
```

This statement includes a PARALLEL hint specifying DEGREE 2 and INSTANCES 2. Oracle will divide the work of executing this query between two instances and will use two slave processes on each instance to do the work, as illustrated in Figure 13-1.

We mentioned in Chapter 3 that the degree of parallelism could be specified either through a hint or in the table/index definition. The degree of parallelism specification consists of two components: DEGREE and INSTANCES. The INSTANCES component controls the number of instances that will be used to execute the statement in parallel. The DEGREE component specifies the number of parallel slave processes working for the statement on each instance. When the INSTANCES is specified as 1, the parallel slave processes are limited to one instance only.

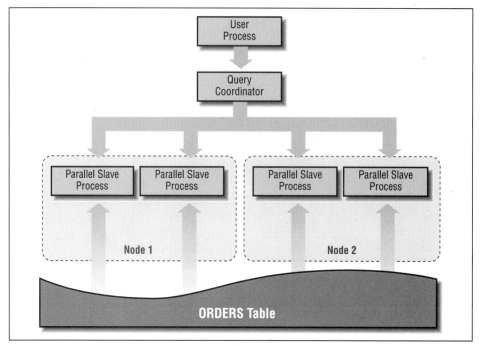

Figure 13-1. Parallel execution in an OPS environment

Disk Affinity

An OPS instance is said to have *affinity* for a device if the device is directly accessible from the node on which the instance is running. Figure 13-2 shows two instances on two different nodes: disk A is directly connected to node 1, and disk B is directly connected to node 2. A high-speed interconnect makes this configuration a shared disk architecture in which both disks are accessible from both nodes.

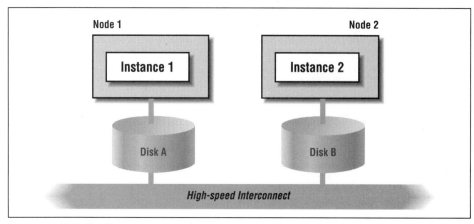

Figure 13-2. Disk affinity

Since disk A is local to node 1, the instance running on that node is said to have affinity for disk A. In this case, instance 1 has affinity for disk A. Similarly; instance 2 has affinity for disk B. I/O operations will be faster and more efficient when an instance is accessing disks for which it has affinity.

Extending the device-to-instance affinity concept to datafiles, an instance has affinity for a file if it has affinity for the disk on which that file is stored. In Figure 13-2, instance 1 has affinity for files stored on disk A, and instance 2 has affinity for files stored on disk B.

When allocating parallel execution tasks to parallel slave processes on multiple nodes, Oracle takes disk affinity into account. However, this affinity is transparent to the application or user invoking the task.

Disk Affinity is Platform-Specific

Not all platforms recognize disk affinity. Please refer to your platform-specific documentation, or contact Oracle Support to find out if disk affinity is recognized on your platform.

Not only is support for disk affinity platform-specific, but whether it is used by default also depends on the specific Oracle release that you are using. On IBM SP systems, for example, the following statements regarding disk affinity are true:

- In Oracle7, disk affinity is ON by default.
- In Oracle8, disk affinity is OFF by default. You can turn it on by setting the initialization parameter _AFFINITY_ON to TRUE.
- In Oracle8*i*, disk affinity is ON by default.

The initialization parameter _AFFINITY_ON is undocumented. We recommend that you contact Oracle Support before changing the default setting of this parameter.

When disk affinity is not used, Oracle balances the allocation of parallel slave processes evenly across all available instances. When disk affinity is used, Oracle attempts to allocate parallel slave processes to the instances that are "nearest" to the data required by those processes. Disk affinity can reduce inter-node communication and improve the performance of parallel operations.

Even when disk affinity is supported, it is not used for all parallel operations. Table 13-1 identifies operations in which Oracle will make use of disk affinity information and those in which it won't.

Table 13-1. Disk Affinity Support for Parallel SQL Operations

Operation	Recognizes Disk Affinity	Does Not Recognize Disk Affinity
Parallel table scan	✓	
Parallel temporary tablespace allocation	✓	
Parallel INSERT, UPDATE, or DELETE	✓	
Parallel index scan	✓	
Parallel table creation		✓
Parallel index creation		✓

Instance Groups for Parallel Execution

While parallelizing SQL statements in an OPS environment, Oracle doesn't have to use all of the OPS instances. You can use instance groups to specify which instances to use.

We introduced instance groups in Chapter 7, *Administering an OPS Database*. One of the major applications of instance groups is to specify the instances to use for parallel execution. Assuming that you have used the INSTANCE_GROUPS initialization parameter to group your OPS instances, you can then use the PARALLEL_INSTANCE_GROUP initialization parameter to identify the group that you want Oracle to use when it executes a SQL statement in parallel. This parameter can be specified in the initialization parameter file as shown in this example:

```
PARALLEL_INSTANCE_GROUP = groupB
```

All parallel operations initiated from this instance will spawn parallel slave processes on the instances belonging to the group named groupB.

The PARALLEL_INSTANCE_GROUP parameter can be changed while an instance is running using the ALTER SESSION or ALTER SYSTEM command, for example:

```
ALTER SESSION SET PARALLEL_INSTANCE_GROUP = 'groupB';
ALTER SYSTEM SET PARALLEL_INSTANCE_GROUP = 'groupB';
```

ALTER SESSION changes the parameter for the current session only, whereas ALTER SYSTEM changes the setting for the current instance. Any changes to the setting using ALTER SYSTEM take effect immediately for all existing sessions of the instance.

The default setting for the PARALLEL_INSTANCE_GROUP parameter is a group composed of all the running instances of the OPS database. If you don't set this parameter, all available instances will be used for parallel execution.

Let's expand on the example of a four-instance OPS configuration by showing the effects of different settings for the PARALLEL_INSTANCE_GROUP parameter. Table 13-2 shows the settings for our four instances.

Table 13-2. Instance Group Settings for This Chapter's Example

Instance	INSTANCE_GROUPS	PARALLEL_INSTANCE_GROUP
1	g12, g14, g123	g12
2	g12, g23, g123	g123
3	g23, g123	None
4	g14	g23

Here's how the groups and instances relate:

- When a user runs a parallel SQL statement from instance 1, the parallel slave processes will be spread over the instances in group g12. Group 12 includes instances 1 and 2.

- When a user runs a parallel SQL statement from instance 2, group g123 will be used. Group g123 comprises instances 1, 2, and 3.

- When a user runs a parallel SQL statement from instance 3, the default instance group consisting of all four instances will be used.

- When a user runs a parallel SQL statement from instance 4, instance group g23 will be used, and Oracle will execute the statement using parallel slave processes on instances 2 and 3.

You need to be aware of these characteristics of the PARALLEL_INSTANCE_GROUP setting:

- When the value of INSTANCES (whether from a hint or from a table or index definition) is 1, parallel operations always will be executed on the local instance. The PARALLEL_INSTANCE_GROUP setting, if there is one, will be ignored.

- When the value of INSTANCES is less than the number of instances in the instance group pointed to by the PARALLEL_INSTANCE_GROUP parameter, Oracle will determine which of those instances actually are used for the parallel operation.

- When the value of INSTANCES is more than the number of instances in the instance group pointed to by the PARALLEL_INSTANCE_GROUP parameter, Oracle will still use only the instances in the specified instance group to run the parallel operation.

- A parallel operation may be initiated from an instance, and yet that instance may not be one of the instances on which the parallel slave processes for the operation would run. However, the parallel coordinator runs on the initiating instance.

- When the parameter PARALLEL_INSTANCE_GROUP is not explicitly set or when the parameter is set to an empty string (" "), Oracle will select from all of the running instances to run the parallel operation.

Appendix:
Case Studies

Throughout this book we have discussed the concepts and architecture behind Oracle's parallel execution and parallel server features. We also discussed various aspects of administering, monitoring, and tuning these features. This appendix takes the discussion of Oracle's parallel support to its logical conclusion by talking about the types of applications that can benefit from parallelism.

The three case studies chosen for this appendix cover the three most common hardware architectures used for parallel systems: SMP, MPP, and cluster. The case studies also cover two common types of applications: online transaction processing (OLTP) systems and decision support system (DSS) applications. The case studies include:

- An OLTP application on a Sun SMP platform

- An OLTP application on an IBM RS/6000 HACMP cluster

- A DSS application on an IBM SP, which is an MPP platform

Although these case studies discuss only Sun and IBM platforms, they are equally applicable to all platforms that support Oracle's parallel processing features.

Application Suitability

When you consider an application's suitability for use with Oracle's parallel feature set, you really need to consider two things separately. First, you need to look at your application with respect to Oracle Parallel Server (OPS). Not all applications are well-suited for OPS, and in some cases switching to OPS could drastically hurt performance and throughput. Second, you need to consider whether your application can benefit from the use of parallel execution features, such as parallel query and parallel DML. As with the use of OPS, use of Oracle's parallel execution features does not always result in a performance increase.

Application Suitability for OPS

Oracle Parallel Server databases offer a variety of advantages, such as high availability, better scalability, improved performance, load balancing, and so forth. However, not every application is suitable for OPS. In many cases, taking an application not designed for OPS and switching it to use an OPS database can result in serious performance problems caused by inter-instance contention. Chapter 8, *Locking Mechanisms in OPS*, discusses the issue of contention between instances on an OPS system.

The types of applications that can benefit from OPS are those that can be designed and partitioned in a way that minimizes contention for the same data by more than one instance; for example:

- OLTP applications using disjoint data
- OLTP applications using random data access patterns
- High-availability applications
- Departmental applications
- Collaborative applications
- DSS applications

The following sections discuss the suitability of OPS for each of these types of applications.

OLTP applications using disjoint data

Online transaction processing applications that modify disjoint sets of data are suitable for OPS. A good example of this type of application is a banking application in which each bank branch accesses its own accounts information and very rarely needs to access information from a different branch. In such a situation, each branch can access an OPS instance that is specific to that branch. Each instance then accesses its own set of data, for the branch that it supports. Since each instance is accessing data for a different bank branch, conflicts between the instances will be almost nonexistent.

OLTP applications using random data access patterns

Some OLTP applications access very large databases, but in a relatively random pattern. Income tax applications are a good example of this type, in which individual records accessed by one instance are highly unlikely to be accessed by another instance at the same time. These applications can exploit the benefits of Oracle Parallel Server without incurring the overhead costs of lock conversion and pinging that result when multiple instances contend for the same data.

High-availability applications

In today's globally competitive business environment, there is a growing need for high availability. Companies can't afford extended downtime for databases supporting mission-critical applications. The cost of downtime in a stock brokerage application, for example, can be extremely high. Applications requiring high availability can benefit from the application failover capability built into Oracle Parallel Server. When a connection to the database through one instance fails, an application can reconnect to the database through another instance (as we described in Chapter 12, *Application Failover*).

Departmental applications

Departmental applications sometimes are suitable for use against an OPS database. If you have multiple departmental applications each modifying a different set of tables, you can set up an OPS database with one instance for each application. Common reference data can be accessed (in read-only mode) by all the applications. For example, an organization can put its Sales application on one node, its Human Resource application on another, its Project Accounting application on a third, and so forth. All of these applications modify different sets of tables but occasionally access some common data (such as employee data, for example) in read-only mode. Because the applications do not modify the same data, conflicts between the OPS instances are minimized.

Collaborative applications

Collaborative applications involve messaging services, directory services, workflow, and document management services in which multiple-user groups work together to share, exchange, and manage information. These applications often are suitable for OPS. Each user group can connect to one instance, and the chance that the same information will be updated by multiple instances is very low. Multiple instances can conveniently share the common directory information and documents in read-only mode without causing any locking conflicts.

DSS applications

DSS applications, such as those accessing a data warehouse or a data mart, execute large, complex queries but comparatively few updates, inserts, and deletes. In most DSS applications, data is queried throughout the day, and any insert, update, and delete activities take place during off-peak hours. Because they are primarily read-only, DSS applications are well suited to OPS. Multiple OPS instances can simultaneously read the same data without causing contention between those instances. DSS applications can employ the processors on multiple nodes to improve the performance of large and complex queries.

Scalability is a very important requirement of DSS applications. With growth in the database size and increase in user population, you can conveniently add another node to the system and run an additional OPS instance to support that growth.

Application Suitability for Parallel Execution

You can use Oracle's parallel execution features with many applications and thereby significantly improve performance. Parallel execution involves the use of intra-query parallelism, in which multiple processors share in the task of executing a SQL statement, to speed up query execution. The following types of applications can benefit from parallel execution:

- DSS applications
- Reporting applications
- OLTP applications with large batch jobs
- Applications using advanced replication

DSS applications

DSS applications involve large and complex queries against a very large database. The databases used by DSS applications require regular feeds from transactional systems, and these feeds can be quite large. Parallel execution features such as parallel query, parallel data loading, and parallel table and index creation can very effectively improve the performance of DSS applications.

Reporting applications

Many organizations have large reporting requirements and use copies of transactional databases as reporting databases. Some companies may need to generate reports that run to hundreds of pages or that crunch gigabytes of data. Other organizations may need hundreds of reports generated on a regular basis. In either of these cases, you can use separate reporting databases to eliminate the reporting load from the transactional database. Reporting applications involve large queries with aggregate, summary, and sorting requirements. Oracle's parallel execution features can help improve the performance for these types of queries.

OLTP applications with large batch jobs

Many OLTP applications require large batch jobs to be run at off-peak hours. Some of these batch jobs are used to upload and download data to and from other databases, maintain indexes, and purge old data. You can use parallel DML and parallel DDL very effectively to reduce the runtime of these batch jobs.

Applications using advanced replication

Many organizations use replicated databases for disaster recovery. Oracle's advanced replication can help maintain multiple copies of database objects at multiple sites. The replicated database is a real-time copy of the operational database. In case of a hardware failure, database failure, or other disaster, the replicated database becomes the operational database. Maintaining a replicated database involves constantly updating the replicated database as changes are made to the operational database. Oracle's parallel replication propagation can be used to improve replication performance.

Case Study 1: An OLTP Application on an SMP Platform

Diversified Electronics is engaged in e-commerce and sells electronics products over the Web. Their product line ranges from cameras to camcorders to audiovisual equipment and accessories. The company maintains detailed technical information on hundreds of products from hundreds of manufacturers. Customers log on to the web site, pick items to buy, choose a method of delivery, and make payment by providing a credit card number in a secured environment. The database is the backbone of the web-based ordering system. At peak times, between 200 and 400 users access the database. The ordering system processes about 10,000 orders in an average month. The current size of the database is 20 GB.

The customer base of Diversified Electronics is growing at a rapid rate. Because of its rapid growth, the company can't afford to thrash around and re-architect their existing database platform. Instead, Diversified Electronics wants to maintain its database application on a scalable environment that can grow to match the anticipated growth in load for the next few years.

Application Requirements

Diversified Electronics' database contains business-critical information. In turn, this information is used by several mission-critical applications. Two of the most important requirements for the database involve the following:

High scalability

The e-commerce business of Diversified Electronics is growing rapidly, and a fourfold increase in sales volume is expected within a year's time. This growth is being reflected in an increased database size, an increased number of hits at their web site, and an increased number of transactions. One of the primary goals of the information system is to support the business growth without sacrificing performance. The database and the hardware platform must be scalable so they can sustain the increased load associated with the expected business growth.

Quick response time

The success of Diversified Electronics depends upon not only providing its customers the best prices in a secured environment, but also giving them a pleasant experience that includes a quick response time. Customers have various alternatives available, and if they don't get a timely response to their queries and transactions, a competitor is just one mouseclick away. To enable a quick response time on the web site, the backend database must provide quick response for online transactions.

System Configuration

Diversified Electronics' database is hosted on an SMP system. The specific hardware used is a multiprocessor Sun E4500 machine with 2 CPUs and 512 MB of RAM. This hardware is upgradable to a maximum 14 CPUs and a maximum of 14 GB of RAM. The operating system is Sun Solaris 2.6. The database software is Oracle Server Enterprise Edition 8.0.4.

The SMP platform provides good scalability for this application. Any increased load in terms of database size, number of users, or number of transactions can be supported simply by adding processors and memory to the system. As processors and memory are added, these new system resources will improve the inter-query and intra-query parallel capabilities of the system. For this application, the SMP architecture is good enough to meet the scalability requirements, and there's no need for the additional complexity of clustered or MPP systems.

Parallel Processing Features Used

The applications run by Diversified Electronics use the following of Oracle's parallel processing features:

Parallel query

Customers frequently query the system to search for products based on category, price range, and features. To respond to these customer queries, the application executes queries against the database that involve table scans and joins. A customer may run several of these queries before deciding on a specific product to buy and expects quick response to these queries. Oracle's parallel query feature effectively leverages the processing power of the system's multiple CPUs, resulting in a satisfactory response time for the customer.

Parallel DML

To support the business of Diversified Electronics, the ordering database integrates with other databases and applications in the organization. One such application is the pricing system. The pricing system resides on a separate platform and determines pricing for items based on market research, competitor's prices, supply, demand, and the price and availability of competitive models. The ordering application runs nightly batch jobs to download data from the pricing system. The nightly batch jobs involve large amounts of insert and update activity on various tables in the ordering database and must finish within a specific time window. Several other batch jobs run on a regular basis to purge old transaction records, moving that data to an archival database. Oracle's parallel DML feature is used to run these batch jobs efficiently.

Case Study 2: An OLTP Application on a Cluster

Bull-Bull, a stock brokerage company, maintains its trading application on an Oracle database. The database and the application are critical for the business of the firm. They need to be highly efficient and highly available, at least during business hours. The database has two types of users: direct and indirect. The direct users are the brokers; the indirect users access the database over the Internet. At peak hours of operation, the number of direct users goes up to 200, and the number of indirect users goes up to 800. The size of the database is 80 GB.

Application Requirements

The trading application is a mission-critical application for Bull-Bull firm. The success of the firm relies heavily on the performance and availability of this application. The application has the following performance and availability requirements:

High availability
> The main reason for Bull-Bull firm's existence is to buy and sell stock. Consequently, the availability of their trading application is of prime importance. The cost of unavailability is extremely high—on the order of millions of dollars per hour. Therefore, the hardware and the database application need to be configured in a way that eliminates single points of failure and that provides high availability.

Fast response to online users
> Hundreds of online users use the application during trading hours, and hundreds of transactions are in process at any given time. The expected response time is on the order of a few seconds. The database must process online transactions and queries efficiently and in a way that meets the response time requirements.

Quick recovery
> Since the application handles business-critical information, the database must be made available very quickly in the event of a database crash. Bull-Bull's customers can't afford to wait for a long recovery process to complete.

System Configuration

Bull-Bull uses an IBM RS/6000 cluster running Oracle Parallel Server to provide a highly available environment for their trading application. The cluster consists of two RS/6000 machines and runs the AIX 4.2.2 operating system. Apart from the operating system, additional system software is required to join the two servers in a cluster. IBM's HACMP software manages the cluster and allows both nodes to access the shared database on disk. This, in turn, allows Oracle Parallel Server to be used, with one instance running on each node. The application uses the redundancy of the cluster environment and the application failover capability of Oracle Parallel Server to achieve high availability.

Several different cluster configurations are possible using IBM RS/6000 machines. Possible configurations are based on the number of nodes, the networking topology that is used, and the disk technologies being used. Figure A-1 shows the two-node configuration used by Bull-Bull firm for their database application. It is a concurrent access configuration, in which all nodes are able to access all disks.

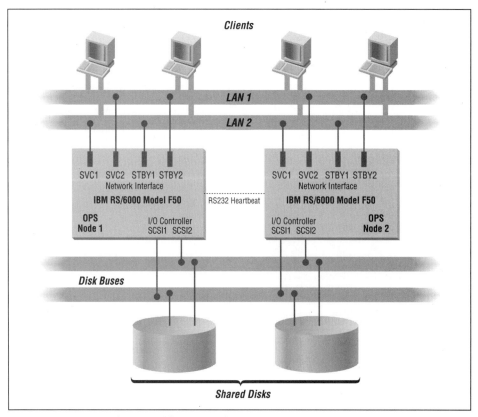

Figure A-1. A two-node IBM RS/6000 OPS cluster

Each node shown in Figure A-1 has two sets of network adapters for connection to the local area networks. There are two service adapters named SVC1 and SVC2 and two standby adapters named STBY1 and STBY2. The standby adapters act as backups for the service adapters. During normal operation, the service network adapters are used. The service adapters are configured with the IP addresses of their respective nodes. If a service adapter fails, then the HACMP software automatically switches the IP address from the service adapter to the standby adapter. The standby adapter then works as the new service adapter. Nodes in the cluster are connected to multiple networks, in this case LAN1 and LAN2, for protection against network failure. An RS-232 serial connection provides heartbeat communication between the nodes, so that the cluster manager on each node is aware of the status of the other node. If the heartbeat communication from a given node fails for a specified time-out period, then failure of that node is assumed.

The database resides in the external RAID disks. RAID level 0+1 is used. Disk mirroring is used to provide data redundancy. The RAID system is physically connected to both the nodes by two sets of SCSI adapters. As you can see from Figure A-1, there are backup components for network adapters, LANs, disks, disk adapters, and nodes. This redundant hardware setup, along with the HACMP software, provides high availability for the system by eliminating any single points of failure.

In addition to the shared RAID subsystem, each node of the cluster has its own disk system that is local to that node. The AIX operating system and Oracle8 RDBMS software are installed on these local disks and are not shared between nodes. Each node runs its own instance of the Oracle database software, which in turn accesses the shared database. Figure A-2 shows the different software layers present on each node.

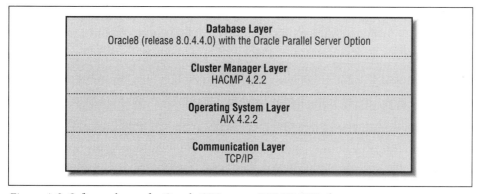

Figure A-2. Software layers for Oracle OPS on an IBM HACMP cluster

Failure of a node will cause the associated instance to fail. A node failure will be detected by the cluster manager software (HACMP). The cluster manager software on each node is always communicating with its counterpart on the other node. When a node failure occurs, the surviving node will detect the failure, and the Oracle instance on the surviving node will initiate instance recovery for the failed node. See Chapter 7, *Administering an OPS Database*, for more details of various failure types and recovery mechanisms.

Parallel Processing Features Used

To meet its performance and availability requirements, Bull-Bull uses the following parallel features of Oracle in its trading application:

Oracle Parallel Server

> The Parallel Server Option of the Oracle RDBMS is installed on both of the nodes, and a two-instance OPS database has been created. Users primarily connect to the Oracle instance on node 1, but when node 1 fails, the instance on node 2 is used to serve the users.
>
> Transparent application failover provides high availability to database connections. The application has been developed using the Oracle Call Interface (OCI) library, and the application has been designed and coded to be failover-aware. Clients connect to the database through Net8, and the *tnsnames.ora* file has been properly configured to specify the primary and backup instances. Also in the *tnsnames.ora* file, the failover type has been set to SESSION, and the failover method has been set to PRECONNECT. Refer to Chapter 12 for a detailed discussion of transparent application failover.

Parallel recovery

> In case of an instance failure, the surviving instance will perform instance recovery. Because the application is so critical, the recovery window is very short. To improve recovery performance and consequently minimize the time needed for recovery, Oracle's parallel recovery feature is being used. The initialization parameter RECOVERY_PARALLELISM is set to 4. This causes Oracle to use four parallel slave processes during the instance recovery process in order to more quickly apply changes recorded in the redo logs to the datafiles.

Availability Enhancements

The architecture shown in Figure A-1 provides for database availability when one node in the cluster fails. However, it can't provide availability during a site failure. To achieve high availability during a site failure, it's necessary to combine more than one high-availability solution. This can be accomplished by combining the OPS configuration with either a standby database or a replicated database. The Bull-Bull firm uses advanced multi-master replication to maintain a replicated database at a remote site. Figure A-3 illustrates Bull-Bull's environment.

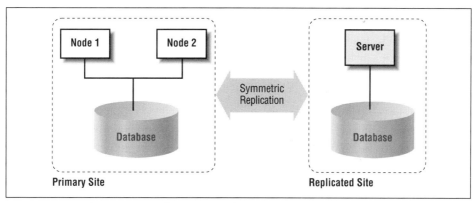

Figure A-3. Combining OPS with replication for disaster recovery

The primary site shown in Figure A-3 is a simplified representation of the OPS configuration shown earlier in Figure A-1. The replicated site is a single-instance database, and symmetric replication is used to keep both databases in sync. In case of a disaster at the primary site, users will connect to the database at the replicated site.

Case Study 3: A DSS Application on an MPP Platform

Framework Superstore is a large, nationwide department store dealing with items such as clothing, shoes, household goods, appliances, cosmetics, jewelry, and electronics. The company has a chain of stores spread throughout the country. The chain is organized into four regions: East, West, North, and South. The headquarters for these four regions are located in New York, San Francisco, Chicago, and Dallas, respectively.

An OLTP system holds the daily transactional data from all the stores. This transactional data then is loaded into a data warehouse for use in generating business intelligence for decision support. Store management uses the data warehouse to make decisions on pricing policies, discount policies, product promotions, inventory management, and so forth. This helps management to develop marketing programs targeted at various customer groups so as to enhance customer loyalty and produce tangible results that improve profitability.

The business managers run complex queries on the data warehouse to extract useful business intelligence such as price elasticity and product affinities by analyzing the raw transactional data. For example, a sales manager would be interested to know the impact of certain changes—for example, a 10 percent price increase on a certain brand of leather jacket and a 10 percent price reduction on another brand of overcoat—on the total sales volume and profitability of these two items. Another sales manager would like to know how many customers buy jewelry and cosmetics items together. To obtain proper answers to these questions, the warehouse must execute complex queries involving multiple tables. The queries may need to be run multiple times with varied inputs.

The source of data for the warehouse is the transactional system. Every night, batch jobs are run on the transactional system to extract data for the data warehouse. The extracted data then is transferred to the data warehouse server and loaded into appropriate tables. About 200 users, approximately 50 per region, access the warehouse data in various summarized forms. The size of the database used for the data warehouse is close to 600 GB.

Application Requirements

The data warehouse application handles large amounts of data and caters to a large group of users. To meet its business objectives, the data warehouse application has the following performance and availability requirements:

Efficient data loading

Every night, batch jobs run on the transaction system, generating datafiles to be loaded into the data warehouse. These files are transferred to the data warehouse server in the early hours of the morning. The data then needs to be loaded into various tables in the data warehouse database. All of this needs to happen overnight, and the data must be in place by 7:00 each morning. On average, about 200 MB of data needs to be loaded each day.

Fast query processing

To generate business intelligence from the warehouse data, complex queries are executed on large tables. Most of these queries involve multiple table joins, large sorts, and the use of aggregate functions. In addition, queries often need to be run multiple times in order to provide executives with the analysis necessary to arrive at proper decisions. It's essential, therefore, that the database be able to execute many complex queries in a very short time frame.

Efficient creation of summary tables

To support the decision-making process, monthly summary tables are created from the transactional data that is loaded into the data warehouse. Complex queries must run against gigabytes of data in order to create these summary tables. The summary tables hold data for one month. At the beginning of each new month, the tables are re-created and populated with summarized data for the previous month. The creation and population of these summary tables need to be done efficiently.

Maximum availability during working hours

Approximately 200 users use the data warehouse application. This number is made up of about 50 users from each of the four regions. As much as possible, these users need uninterrupted access to the database. In the event that a problem occurs, the goals are to minimize the number of users affected by that problem and to minimize the time during which those users are affected.

High scalability

The data warehouse is expected to grow to many times its current size. Over the next few months, for example, the size will almost double. New functionality also is planned, which will result in more users and a higher workload. The hardware and the database application both need to be configured to handle this growth without sacrificing performance.

System Configuration

An IBM SP system is used as the database server for the data warehouse. The SP system consists of four nodes connected together by a high-performance switch. Each node has two processors, 512 MB of memory, and local disks containing the operating system software and the Oracle software. Oracle Parallel Server is used, and an Oracle database resides on a shared disk subsystem. Oracle Parallel Server instances run on all the nodes, and access this shared database. IBM's Parallel System Support Program (PSSP) Version 2.4 cluster manager software ties these four nodes together into a cluster. Figure A-4 illustrates the system configuration.

Another IBM-provided software package used in this system is Recoverable Virtual Shared Disk (RVSD) Version 2.1. RVSD enables multiple nodes to share disks; in this case, the shared disks are the ones holding the database. Together, PSSP and RVSD make the IBM SP a shared disk architecture on which you can run Oracle Parallel Server. Inter-node synchronization of the shared database is achieved through the Integrated Distributed Lock Manager (IDLM), which is a set of background processes running on each node.

Figure A-5 shows the different software layers on each of the nodes.

You might be wondering why an MPP machine was used instead of an SMP cluster. The answer lies in the need for scalability—one of the prime requirements of the data warehouse application. As the data warehouse grows in terms of users and size, the workload will increase. To maintain an acceptable performance level with this increasing workload, the hardware needs to be highly scalable. MPP systems provide better scalability than SMP clusters, which is why an MPP machine was chosen for this data warehouse.

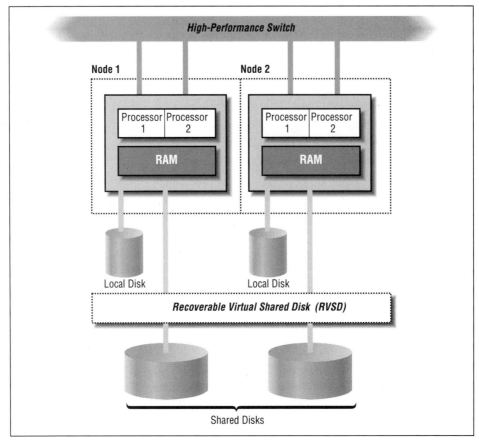

Figure A-4. An Oracle Parallel Server database on an IBM SP system

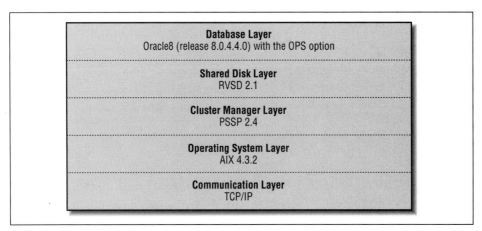

Figure A-5. Software layers for Oracle OPS on IBM SP

Parallel Processing Features Used

The following parallel features of Oracle are used in Framework Superstore's data warehouse system:

Oracle Parallel Server

A parallel server database, accessed by four instances, was created to implement the data warehouse. Each instance runs on one node, and all instances share the database, which resides on the shared disk array. The instances are region-specific. All users from a region connect to an instance specifically assigned to that region. The name of the database is DWHS, and the four instances are named as DWHSE, DWHSW, DWHSN, and DWHSS. These instances support users of the East, West, North, and South regions, respectively.

OPS helps to improve database availability. If one node goes down, only one region is affected. The users of other regions continue working without disruption. In addition, the connections to the failed instance can automatically failover to one of the surviving instances, allowing those users to continue working.

In addition to improving availability, OPS helps achieve better performance by allowing queries to be executed in parallel on multiple nodes.

Parallel data loading

Several tables are loaded daily from the transactional system into the data warehouse. To perform the load efficiently, Oracle's parallel data loading feature is used. To load each table, multiple input datafiles are created. These files then are loaded into the table using multiple SQL*Loader sessions running in parallel. This improves load performance significantly and helps ensure that all loads are completed in the specified time frame.

Parallel query

The objective of the data warehouse is to process the queries the users make to generate business intelligence. As we discussed earlier, efficient query processing is one of the primary requirements of the application. Oracle's parallel query feature enables large table scans, sorts, distinct operations, and group operations to be performed in parallel. The application can take advantage of the multiple processors on the node to which it is connected and can take advantage of the processors on the other nodes as well. All these processors can be used to parallelize queries, resulting in significant performance gains.

Parallel object creation

To generate business intelligence, the data warehouse application needs to summarize the raw transaction data and create summary tables on a regular basis. Summary table creation involves the join of multiple tables and the application of aggregate functions. Parallel CREATE TABLE . . . AS SELECT . . . FROM statements are used to create these summary tables. Also, the data warehouse has some large indexes that need to be rebuilt from time to time to maintain their efficiency. Oracle's parallel index rebuild feature is used to rebuild these large indexes quickly and efficiently.

Index

About the Authors

Tushar Mahapatra has been working as a software developer and consultant since 1987 and has worked on a variety of OLTP and DSS projects using the Oracle database. Presently, as a database architect for a Fortune 500 company, he is responsible for the design, implementation, and deployment of applications in an Oracle Parallel Server environment. He also runs a consulting company that provides database design, application development, and database administration services for Oracle databases. Tushar has a Bachelor of Science degree in Electrical Engineering, a Master of Technology degree in Industrial Management, and a Master of Science degree in Computer Science and Management. He lives in New Jersey with his wife Sasmita and their two children. He can be reached by email at *tushar@mitrasystems.com*.

Sanjay Mishra is a certified Oracle database administrator with more than nine years of IT experience. For the past six years, he has been involved in the design, architecture, and implementation of many mission-critical and decision support databases. He has worked extensively in the areas of database architecture, database management, backup/recovery, disaster planning, performance tuning, Oracle Parallel Server, and parallel execution. He has a Bachelor of Science degree in Electrical Engineering and a Master of Engineering degree in Systems Science and Automation. He can be reached at *sanjay_mishra@i2.com*.

Colophon

Our look is the result of reader comments, our own experimentation, and feedback from distribution channels. Distinctive covers complement our distinctive approach to technical topics, breathing personality and life into potentially dry subjects.

The illustration on the cover of *Oracle Parallel Processing* is a wasp and a wasp nest. The paper wasp (*Polistes fuscatus aurifer* and *Polistes apachus*) is the most common of the social wasps. As their name implies, paper wasps make their nests out of paper, or rather, chewed wood and plant particles combined with saliva to make a paper-like paste. Wasp nests are usually the size of a person's outstretched palm and are shaped like an umbrella. They hang under building eaves, roofs, and tree branches and are constructed with multiple tiers of vertical cells. A single nest houses anywhere from 15–200 wasps.

Paper wasps are social insects, indicated both by their caste system (made up of one or more queens, a few drones, and many workers) and by their food sharing. Drinking only liquids (either flower nectar or other insects' blood), adult wasps share their food with the young by regurgitating it. The young then produce a saliva that is 50 times more nutritious than the original nectar. Adults complete the cycle by receiving that saliva from the young.

Female wasps are capable of inflicting a painful sting on humans, causing swelling and redness for a few hours. However, 3% of people may go into anaphylaxis from a sting. This life-threatening allergic reaction causes hives, severe swelling, blocked airways, circulatory failure, and possibly death. Approximately 50 people die in the U.S. each year from anaphylactic shock caused by a sting. Wasps, unlike honeybees, can sting multiple times. Honeybees can sting only once since their stingers have barbs, causing the stinger to remain in the skin and detach from the bee, effectively killing it.

Paper wasps are one of the less aggressive wasps. They rarely attack people and only do so to defend their nests (which happens if nests are in highly-trafficked areas such as windows, doors, or even fruit trees in orchards). All social wasps are beneficial to humans in that they prey on many harmful, plant-feeding, and nuisance insects. For this reason, social wasp colonies should be protected, though preferably in areas uninhabited by humans.

Jeffrey Holcomb was production editor for *Oracle Parallel Processing*. Norma Emory was the copyeditor. Maureen Dempsey proofread the book. Emily Quill and Madeleine Newell provided quality control. Matt Hutchinson provided production support. Bruce Tracy wrote the index.

Edie Freedman designed the cover of this book. The cover image is a 19th-century engraving from the Dover Pictorial Archive. Emma Colby produced the cover layout with QuarkXPress 4.1 using Adobe's ITC Garamond font.

Alicia Cech and David Futato designed the interior layout based on a series design by Nancy Priest. Mike Sierra implemented the design in FrameMaker 5.5.6. The text and heading fonts are ITC Garamond Light and Garamond Book. The illustrations that appear in the book were produced by Robert Romano and Rhon Porter using Macromedia FreeHand 8 and Adobe Photoshop 5. This colophon was written by Jeffrey Holcomb.

Whenever possible, our books use a durable and flexible lay-flat binding. If the page count exceeds this binding's limit, perfect binding is used.